M. NIGHT S[…]

# THE LAST AIRBENDER

Story by Dave Roman & Alison Wilgus

Art by Joon Choi

Based on the series *Avatar: The Last Airbender* created by Michael Dante DiMartino and Bryan Konietzko. Based on the screenplay written by M. Night Shyamalan.

DEL REY

Ballantine Books * New York

*The Last Airbender* is a work of fiction. Names, characters, places, and incidents are the products of the authors' imaginations or are used fictitiously. Any resemblance to actual events, locales, or persons, living or dead, is entirely coincidental.

A Del Rey Manga Trade Paperback Original



Published in the United States by Del Rey, an imprint of The Random House Publishing Group, a division of Random House, Inc., New York.

DEL REY is a registered trademark and the Del Rey colophon is a trademark of Random House, Inc.

ISBN 978-0-345-51855-2

Printed in the United States of America

www.delreymanga.com

9 8 7 6 5 4 3 2 1

# CONTENTS

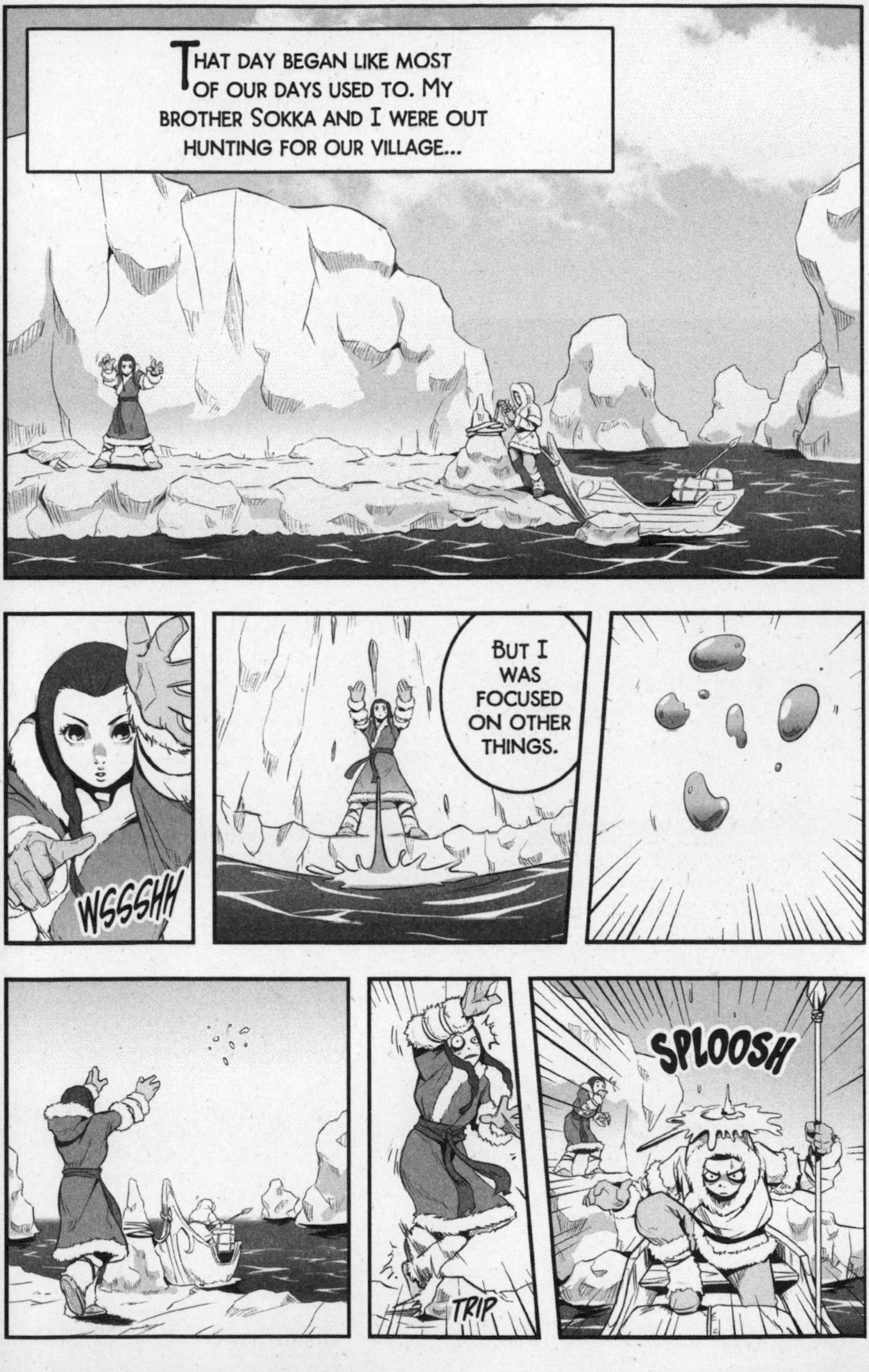
THAT DAY BEGAN LIKE MOST OF OUR DAYS USED TO. MY BROTHER SOKKA AND I WERE OUT HUNTING FOR OUR VILLAGE...
WSSSHH
BUT I WAS FOCUSED ON OTHER THINGS.
TRIP
SPLOOSH

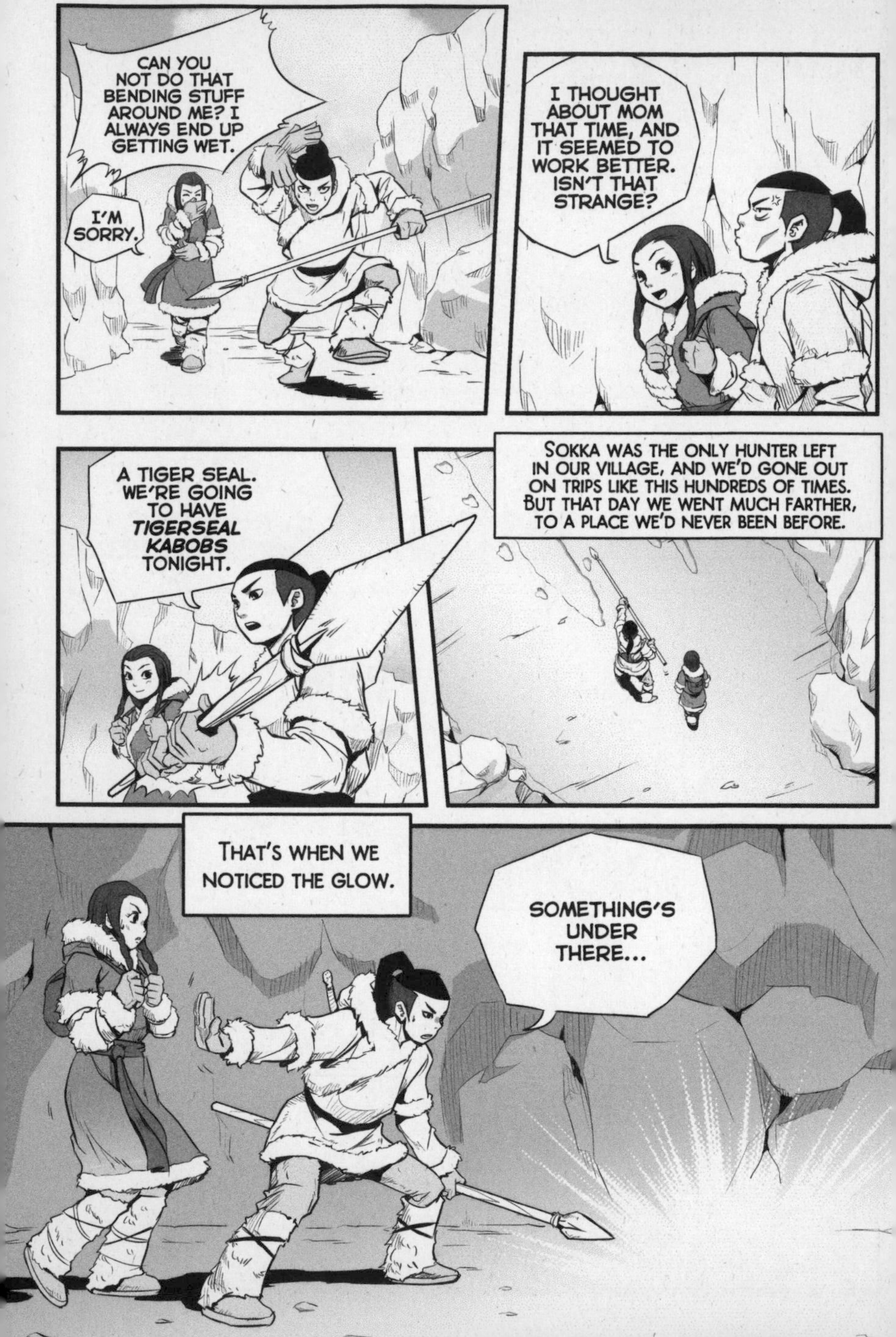
CAN YOU NOT DO THAT BENDING STUFF AROUND ME? I ALWAYS END UP GETTING WET.
I'M SORRY.
I THOUGHT ABOUT MOM THAT TIME, AND IT SEEMED TO WORK BETTER. ISN'T THAT STRANGE?
A TIGER SEAL. WE'RE GOING TO HAVE *TIGERSEAL KABOBS* TONIGHT.
SOKKA WAS THE ONLY HUNTER LEFT IN OUR VILLAGE, AND WE'D GONE OUT ON TRIPS LIKE THIS HUNDREDS OF TIMES. BUT THAT DAY WE WENT MUCH FARTHER, TO A PLACE WE'D NEVER BEEN BEFORE.
THAT'S WHEN WE NOTICED THE GLOW.
SOMETHING'S UNDER THERE...

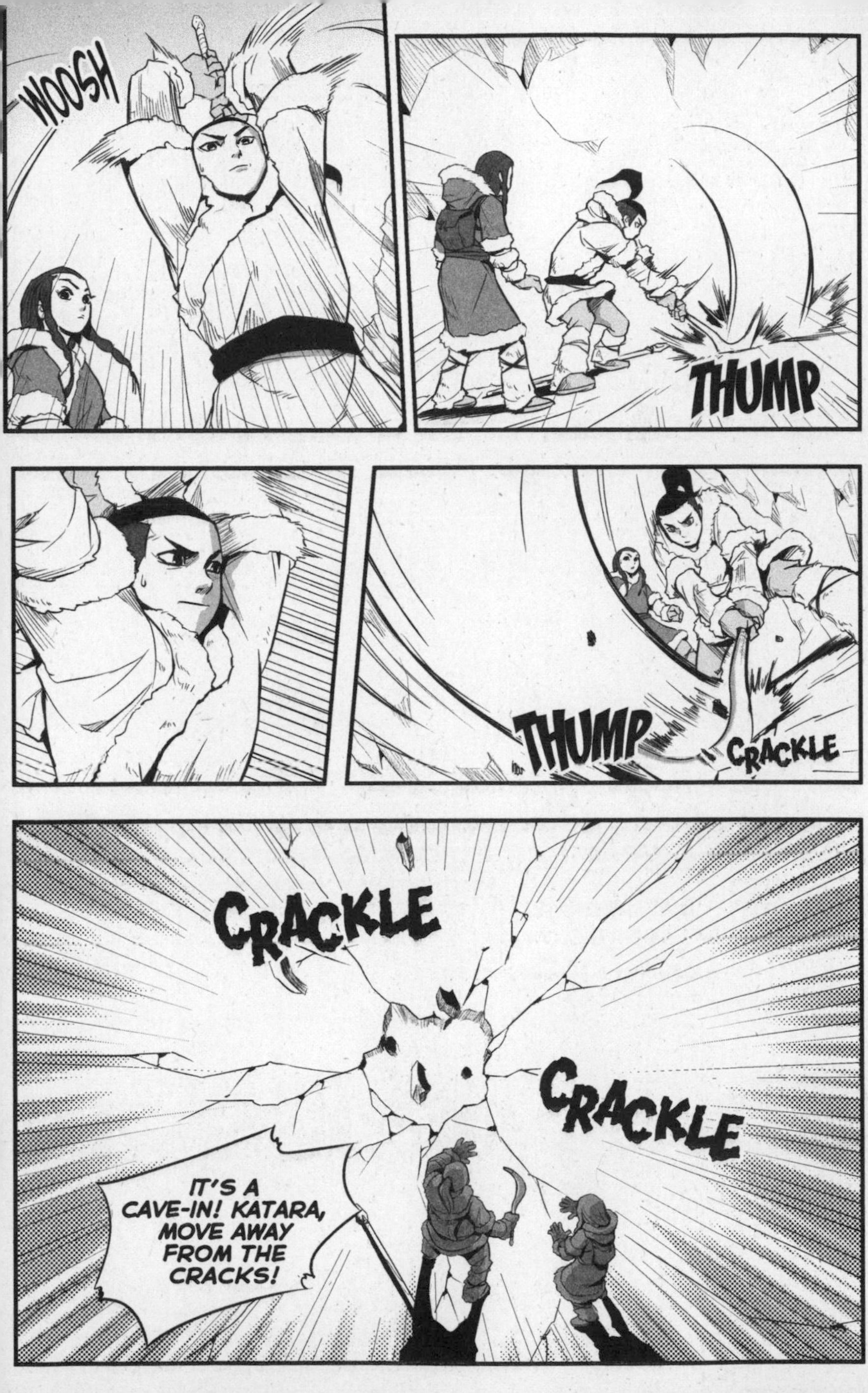
WOOSH
THUMP
THUMP
CRACKLE
CRACKLE
CRACKLE
IT'S A CAVE-IN! KATARA, MOVE AWAY FROM THE CRACKS!

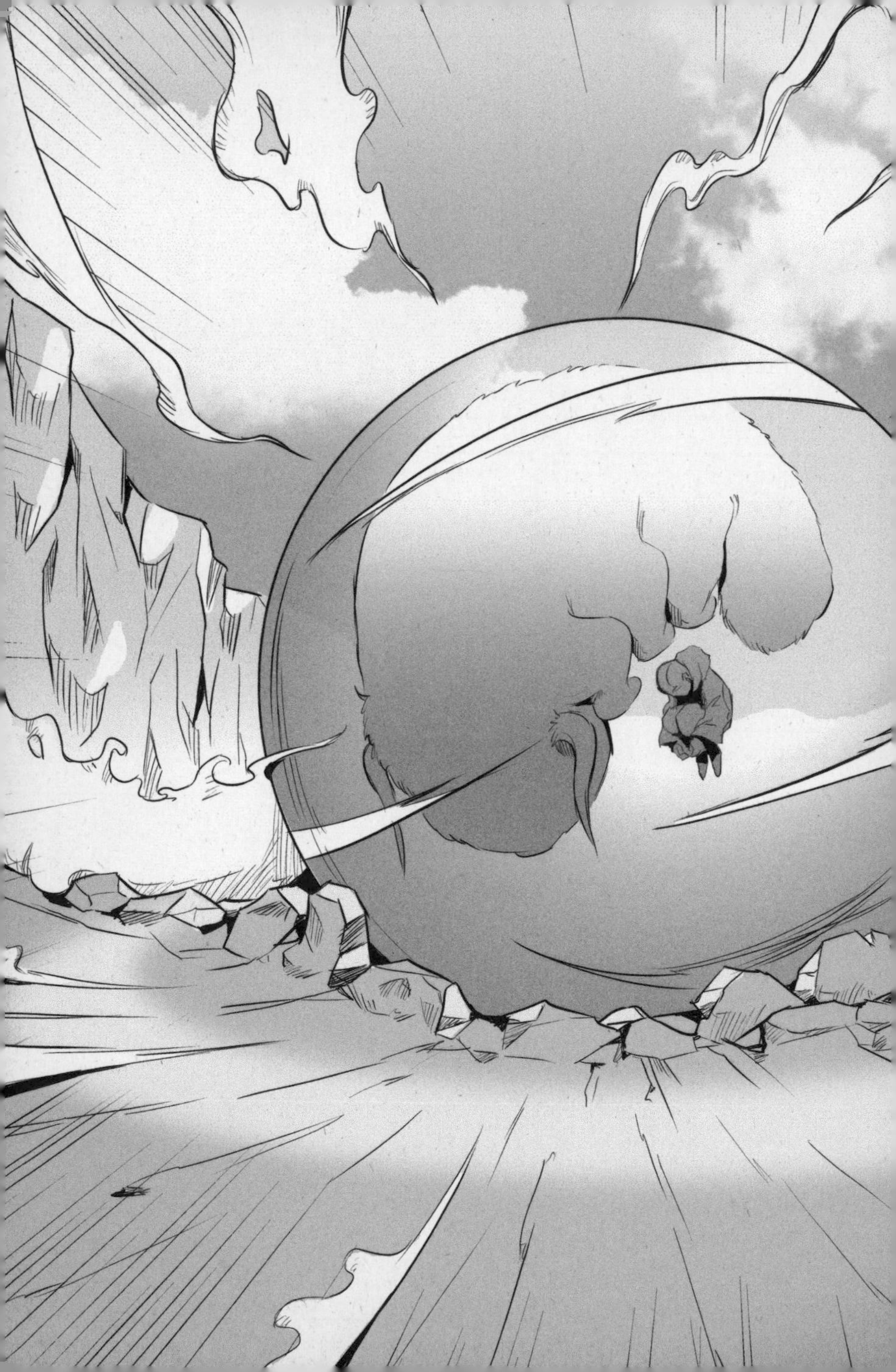

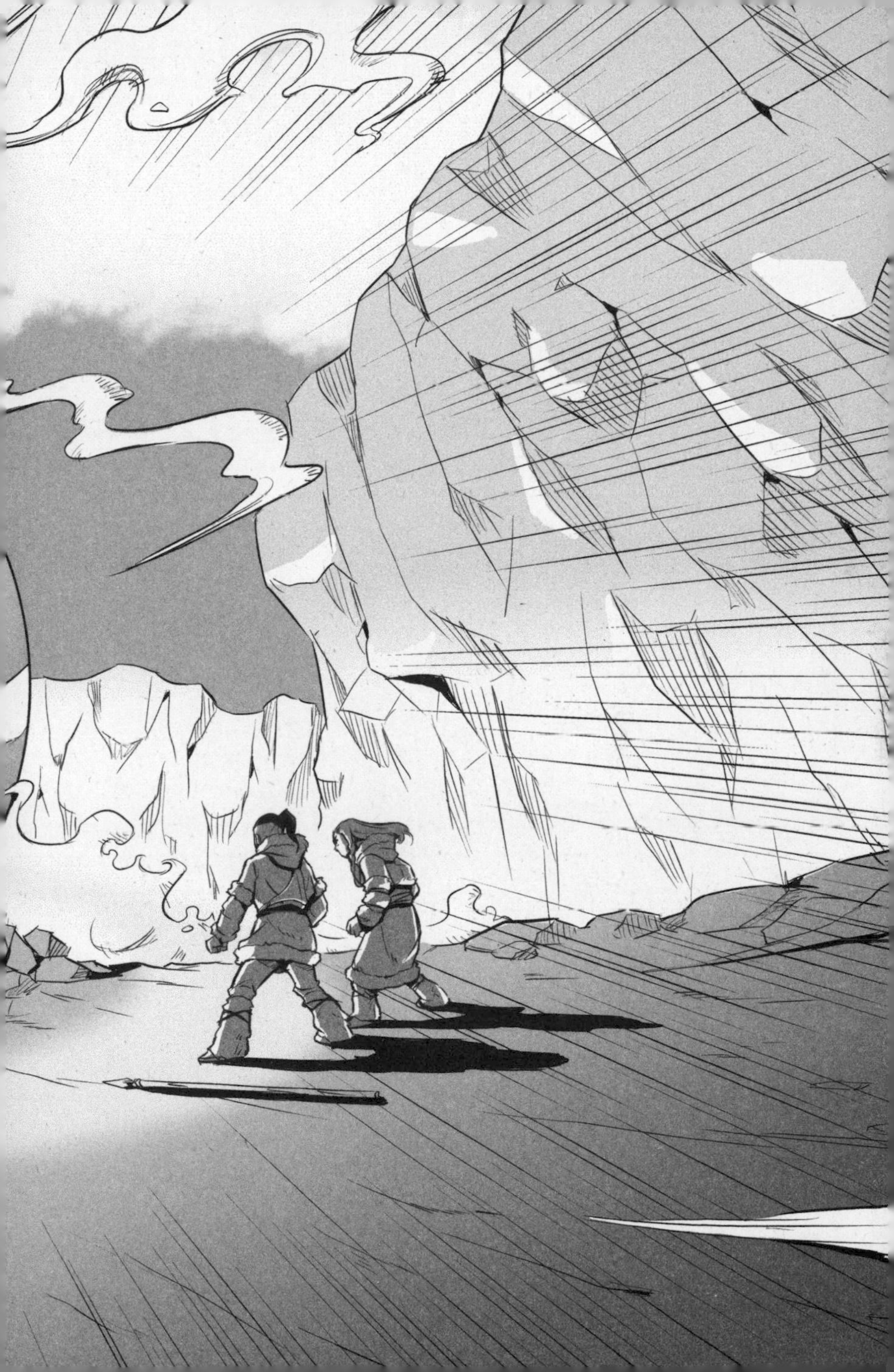

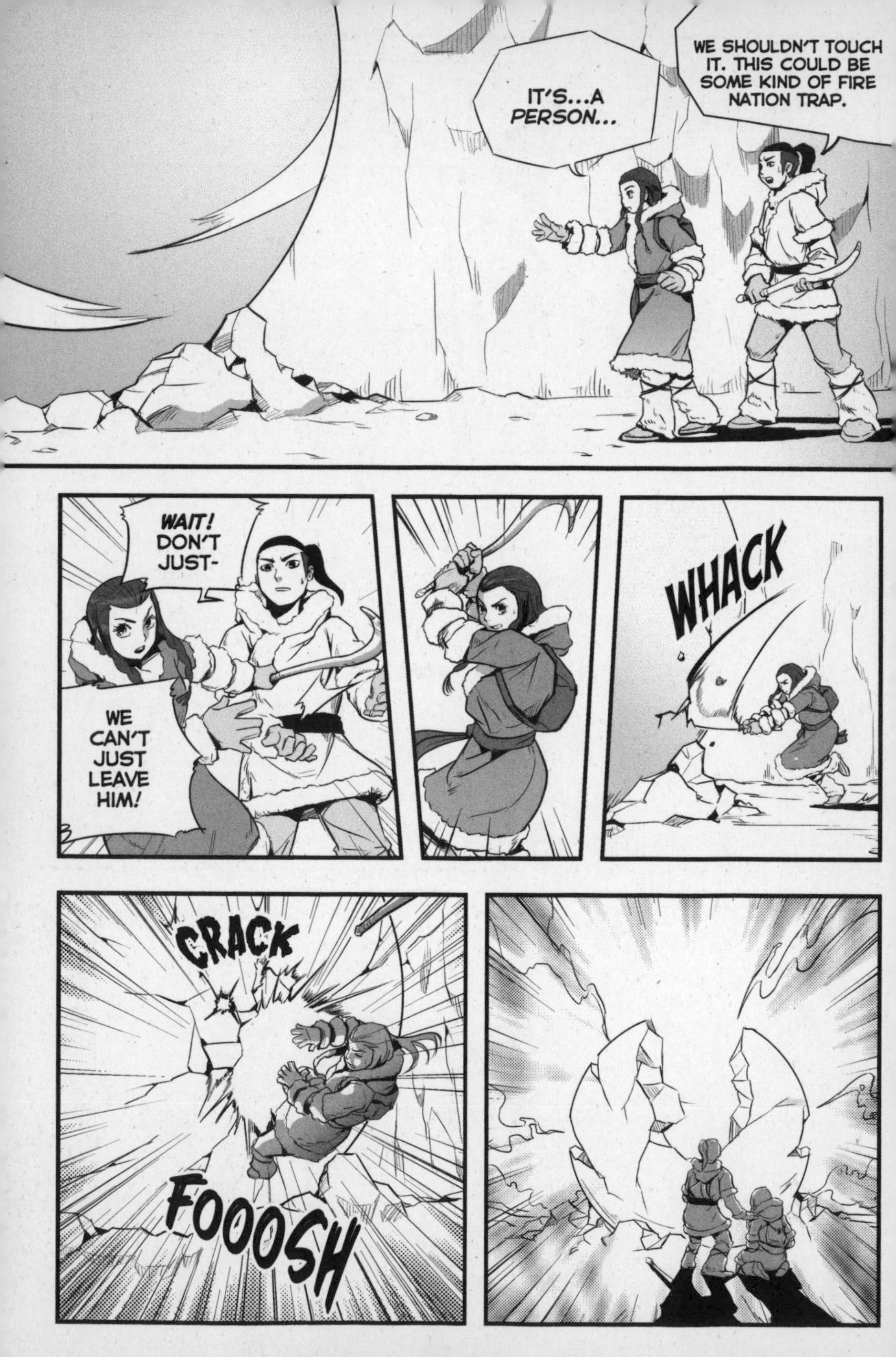
IT'S...A PERSON...
WE SHOULDN'T TOUCH IT. THIS COULD BE SOME KIND OF FIRE NATION TRAP.
WAIT! DON'T JUST-
WE CAN'T JUST LEAVE HIM!
WHACK
CRACK
FOOOSH

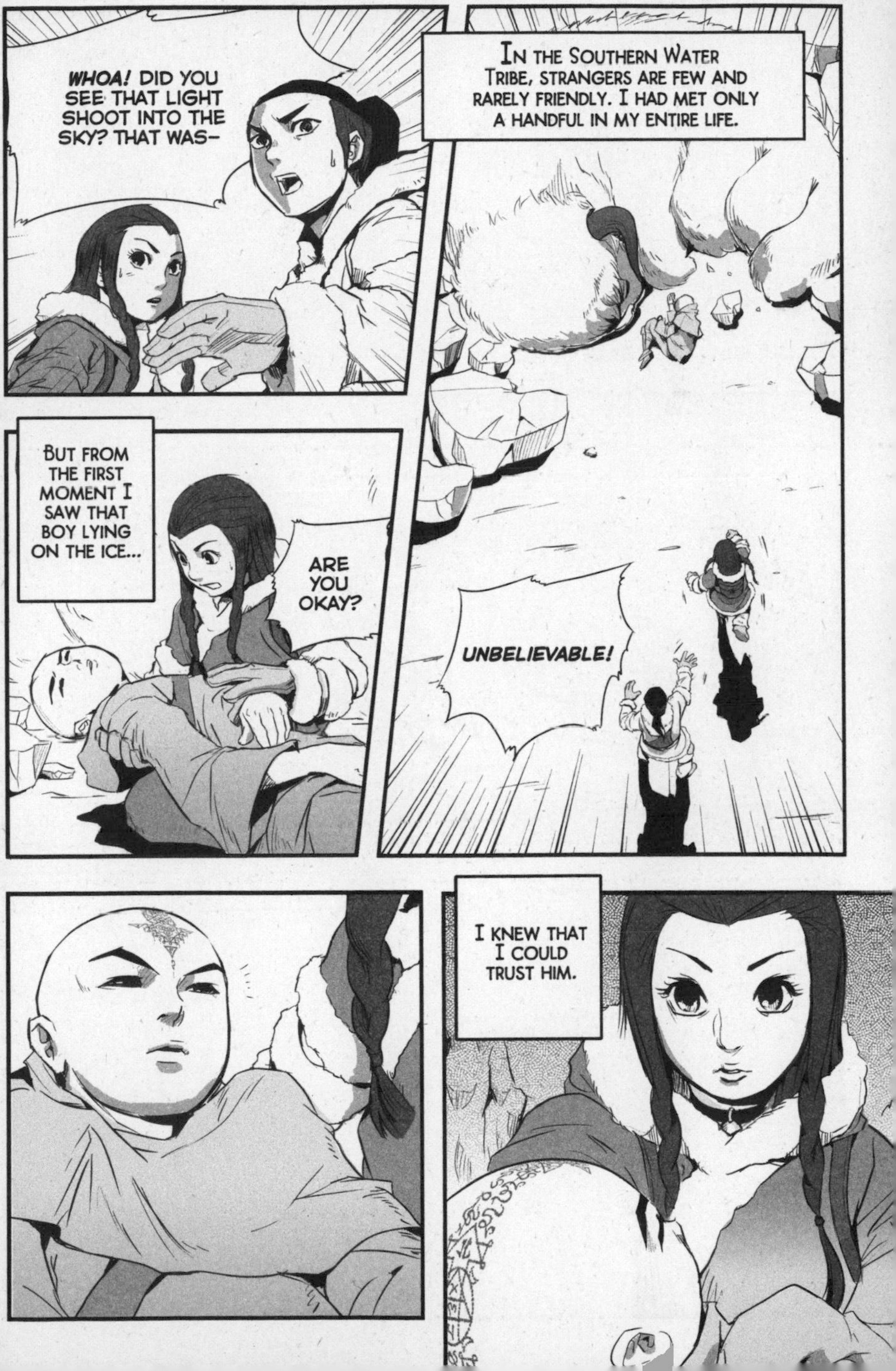
WHOA! DID YOU SEE THAT LIGHT SHOOT INTO THE SKY? THAT WAS-
IN THE SOUTHERN WATER TRIBE, STRANGERS ARE FEW AND RARELY FRIENDLY. I HAD MET ONLY A HANDFUL IN MY ENTIRE LIFE.
BUT FROM THE FIRST MOMENT I SAW THAT BOY LYING ON THE ICE...
ARE YOU OKAY?
UNBELIEVABLE!
I KNEW THAT I COULD TRUST HIM.

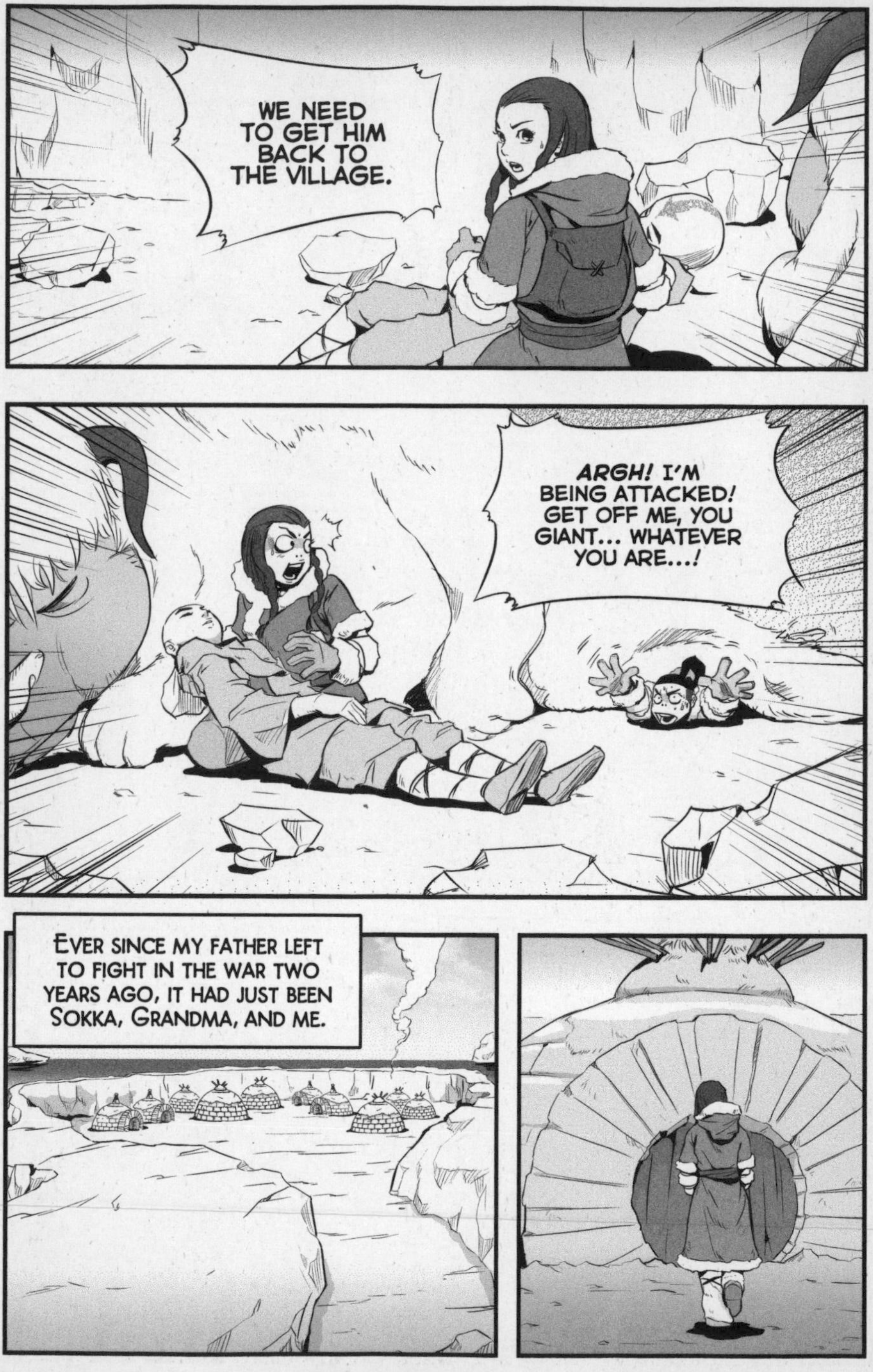
WE NEED TO GET HIM BACK TO THE VILLAGE.
ARGH! I'M BEING ATTACKED! GET OFF ME, YOU GIANT... WHATEVER YOU ARE...!
EVER SINCE MY FATHER LEFT TO FIGHT IN THE WAR TWO YEARS AGO, IT HAD JUST BEEN SOKKA, GRANDMA, AND ME.

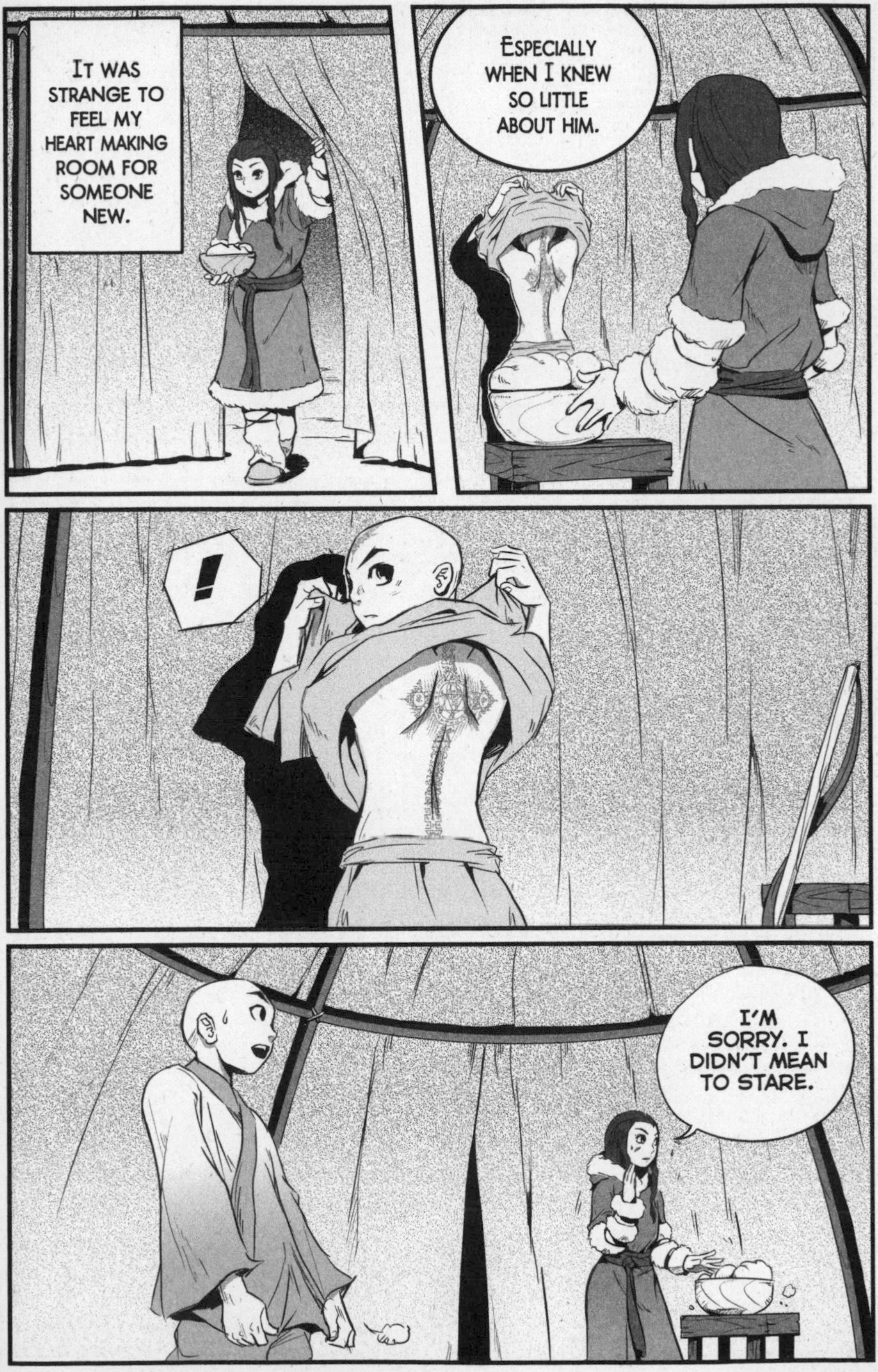
IT WAS STRANGE TO FEEL MY HEART MAKING ROOM FOR SOMEONE NEW.
ESPECIALLY WHEN I KNEW SO LITTLE ABOUT HIM.
!
I'M SORRY. I DIDN'T MEAN TO STARE.

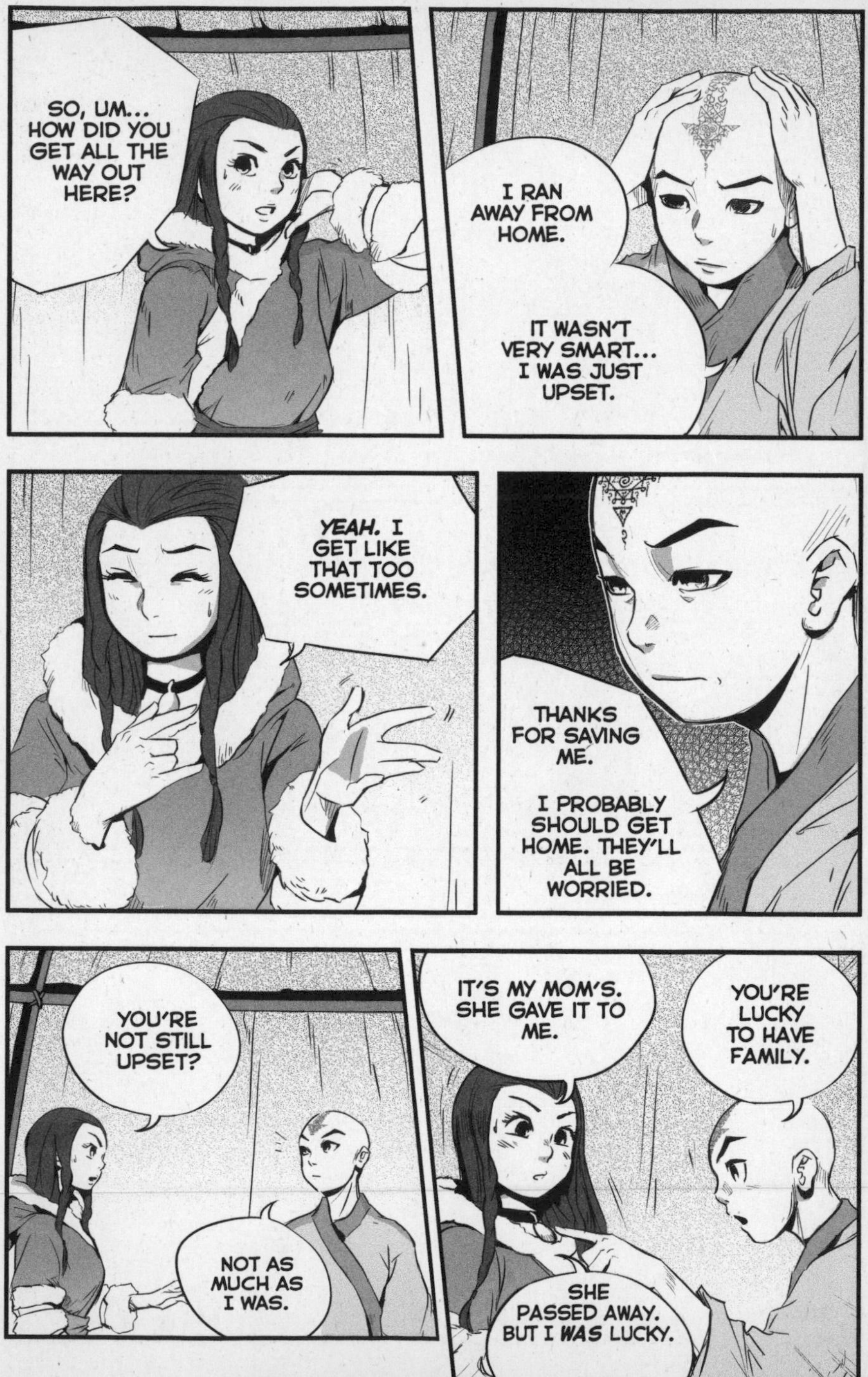
SO, UM... HOW DID YOU GET ALL THE WAY OUT HERE?
I RAN AWAY FROM HOME.
IT WASN'T VERY SMART... I WAS JUST UPSET.
*YEAH.* I GET LIKE THAT TOO SOMETIMES.
THANKS FOR SAVING ME.
I PROBABLY SHOULD GET HOME. THEY'LL ALL BE WORRIED.
YOU'RE NOT STILL UPSET?
NOT AS MUCH AS I WAS.
IT'S MY MOM'S. SHE GAVE IT TO ME.
YOU'RE LUCKY TO HAVE FAMILY.
SHE PASSED AWAY. BUT I *WAS* LUCKY.

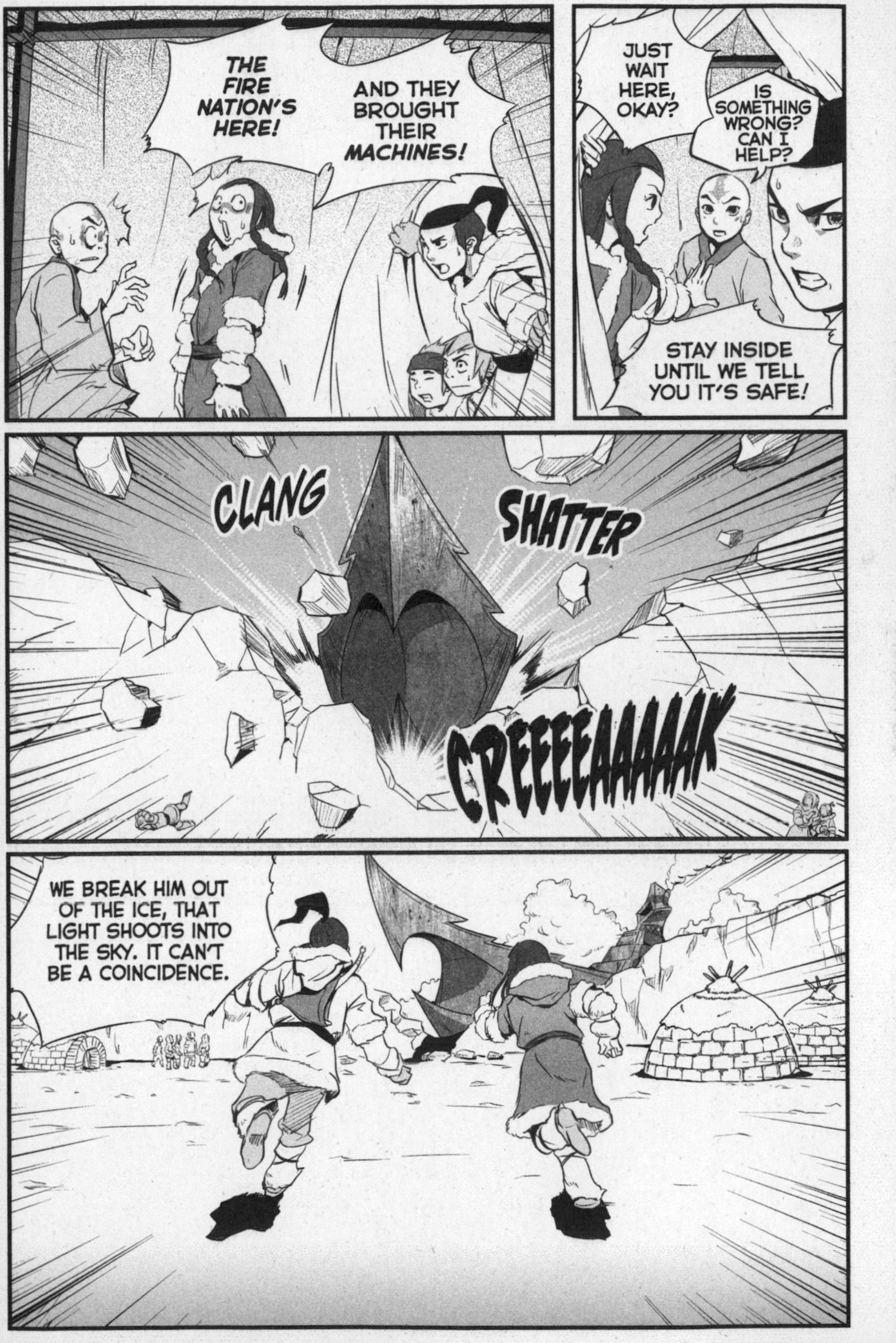
THE FIRE NATION'S HERE!
AND THEY BROUGHT THEIR MACHINES!
JUST WAIT HERE, OKAY?
IS SOMETHING WRONG? CAN I HELP?
STAY INSIDE UNTIL WE TELL YOU IT'S SAFE!
CLANG
SHATTER
CREEEEAAAAAK
WE BREAK HIM OUT OF THE ICE, THAT LIGHT SHOOTS INTO THE SKY. IT CAN'T BE A COINCIDENCE.

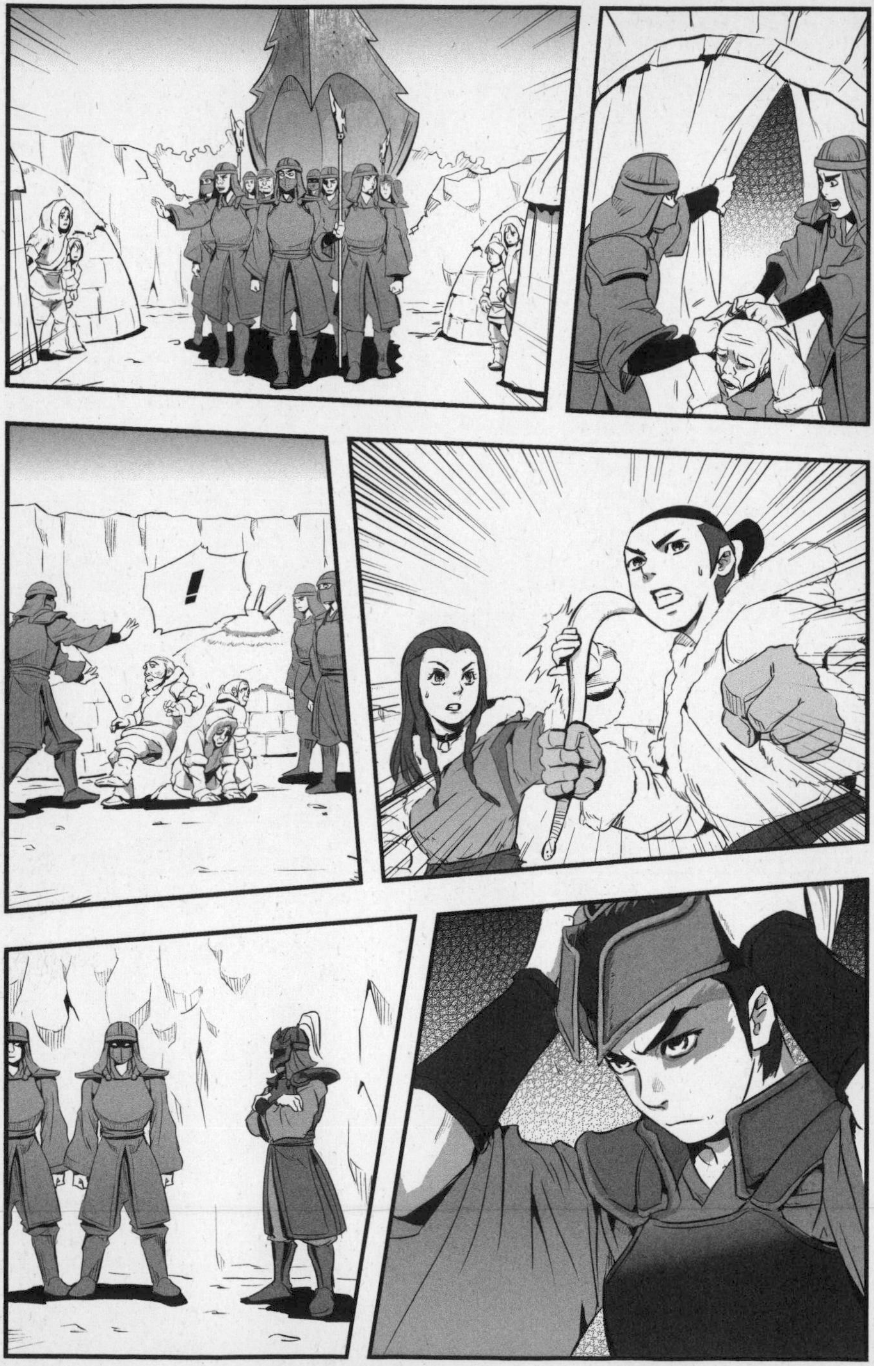
!

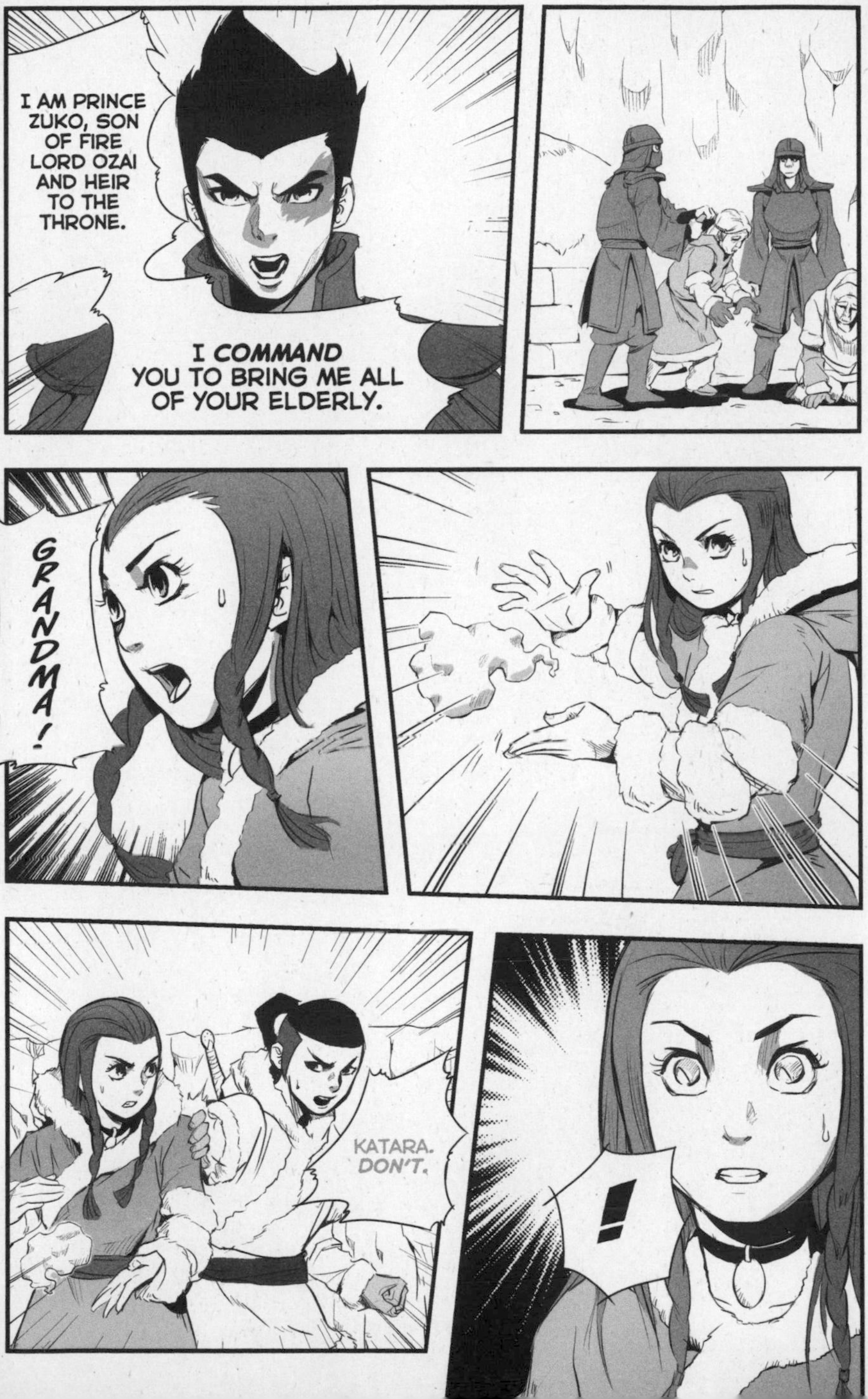
I AM PRINCE ZUKO, SON OF FIRE LORD OZAI AND HEIR TO THE THRONE.
I *COMMAND* YOU TO BRING ME ALL OF YOUR ELDERLY.
GRANDMA!
KATARA. *DON'T.*
!

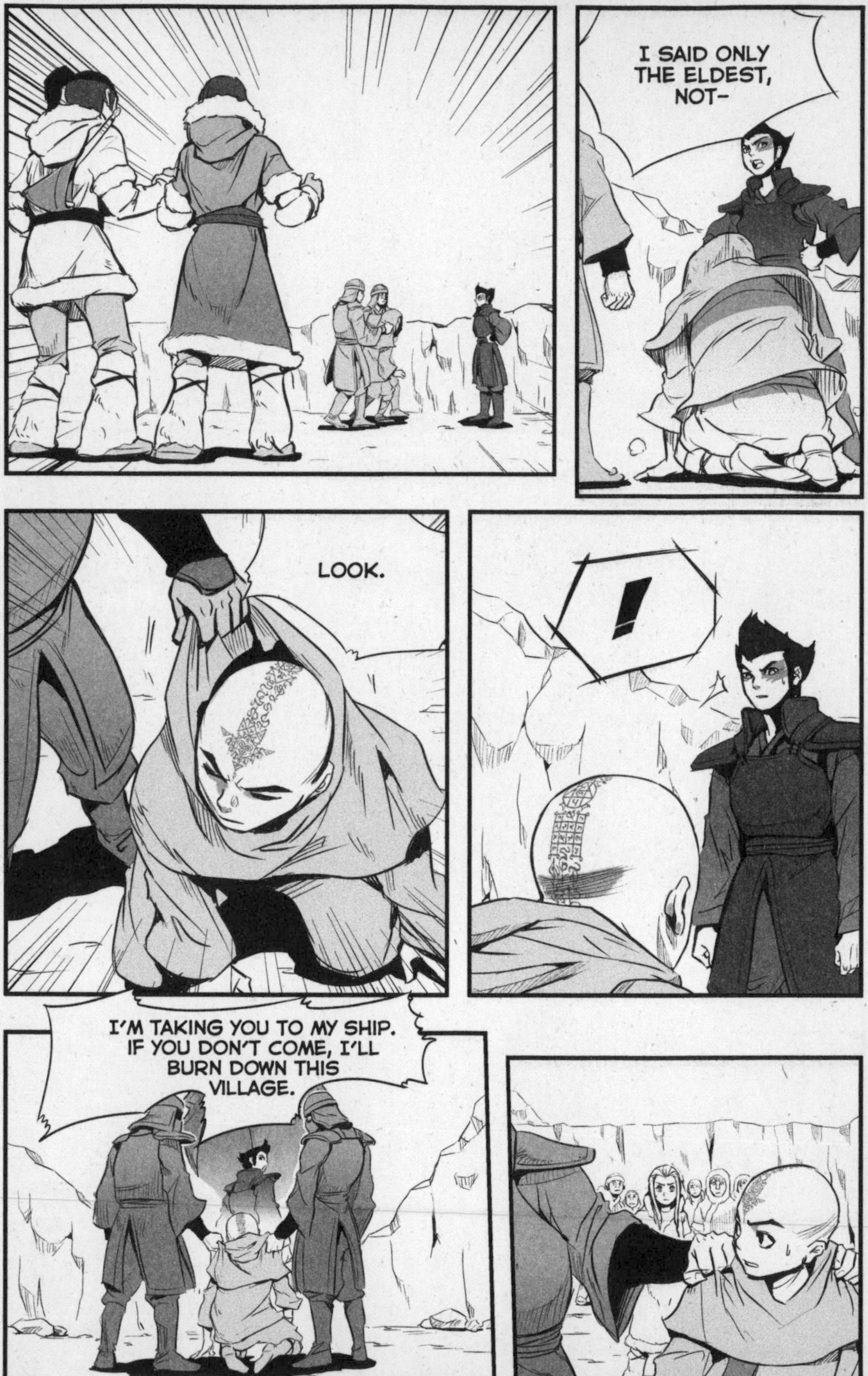
I SAID ONLY THE ELDEST, NOT-
LOOK.
!
I'M TAKING YOU TO MY SHIP. IF YOU DON'T COME, I'LL BURN DOWN THIS VILLAGE.

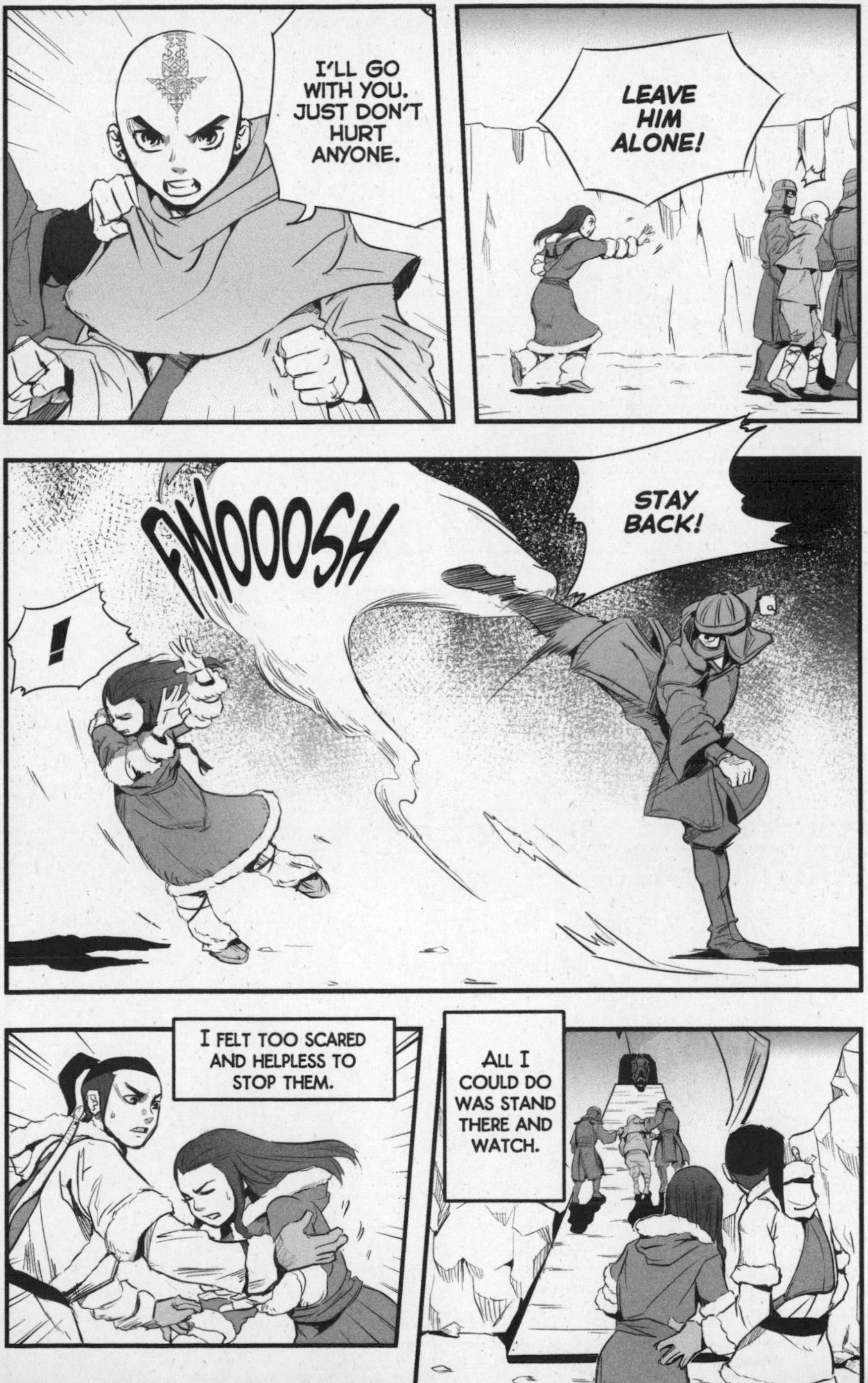
I'LL GO WITH YOU. JUST DON'T HURT ANYONE.
LEAVE HIM ALONE!
SWOOOSH
STAY BACK!
!
I FELT TOO SCARED AND HELPLESS TO STOP THEM.
ALL I COULD DO WAS STAND THERE AND WATCH.

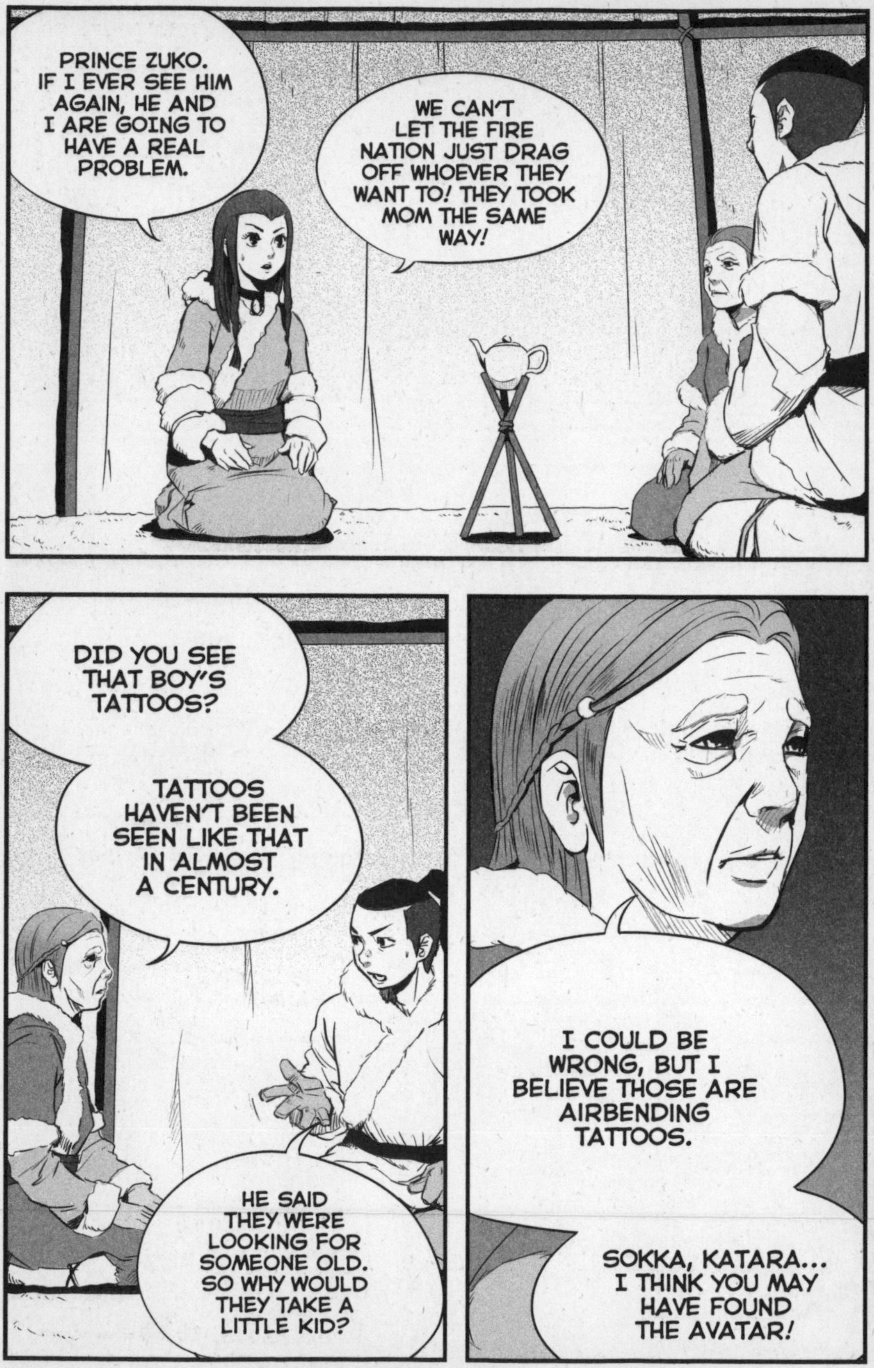
PRINCE ZUKO. IF I EVER SEE HIM AGAIN, HE AND I ARE GOING TO HAVE A REAL PROBLEM.
WE CAN'T LET THE FIRE NATION JUST DRAG OFF WHOEVER THEY WANT TO! THEY TOOK MOM THE SAME WAY!
DID YOU SEE THAT BOY'S TATTOOS?
TATTOOS HAVEN'T BEEN SEEN LIKE THAT IN ALMOST A CENTURY.
HE SAID THEY WERE LOOKING FOR SOMEONE OLD. SO WHY WOULD THEY TAKE A LITTLE KID?
I COULD BE WRONG, BUT I BELIEVE THOSE ARE AIRBENDING TATTOOS.
SOKKA, KATARA... I THINK YOU MAY HAVE FOUND THE AVATAR!

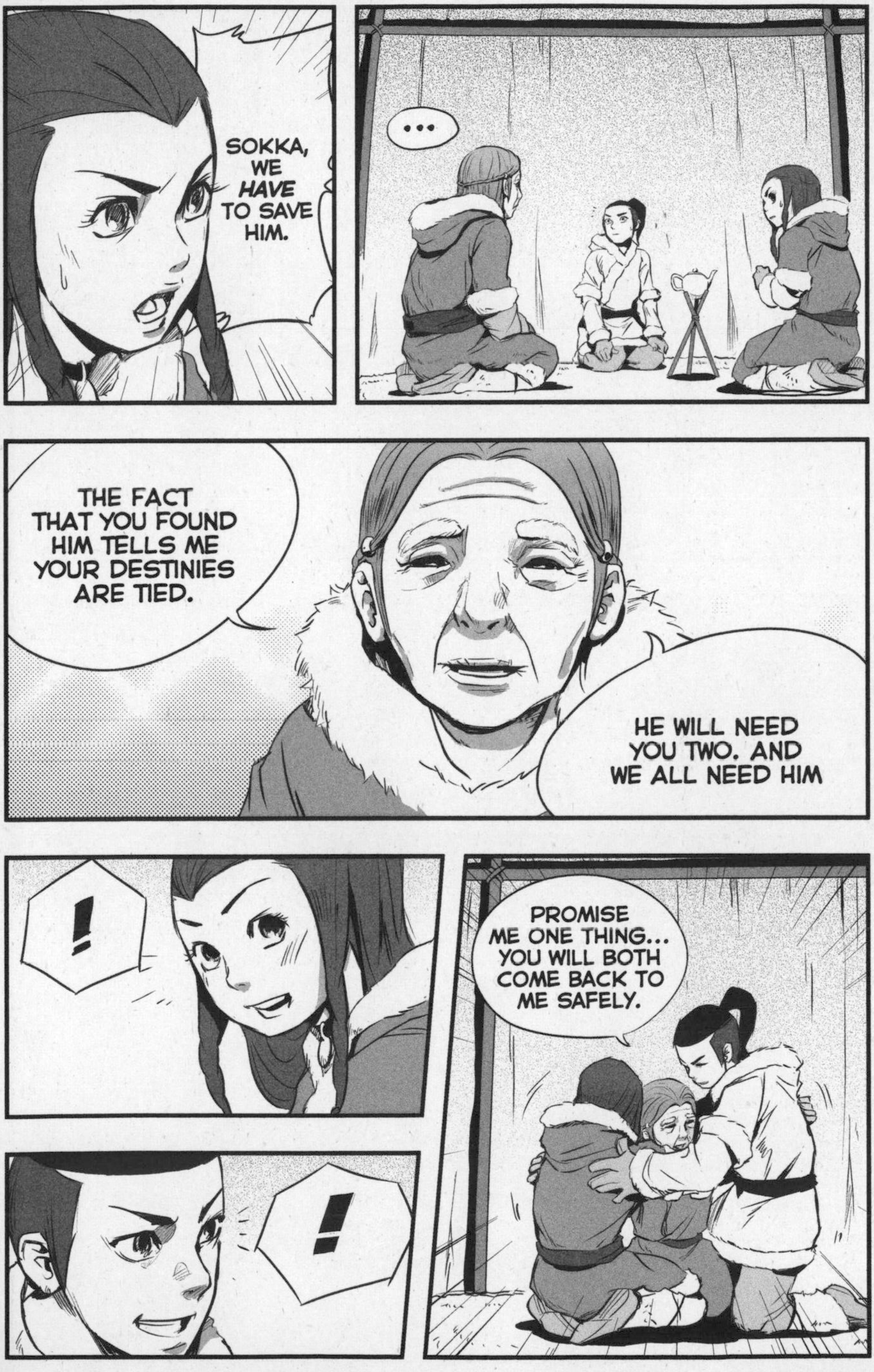
SOKKA, WE *HAVE* TO SAVE HIM.
...
THE FACT THAT YOU FOUND HIM TELLS ME YOUR DESTINIES ARE TIED.
HE WILL NEED YOU TWO. AND WE ALL NEED HIM
!
!
PROMISE ME ONE THING... YOU WILL BOTH COME BACK TO ME SAFELY.

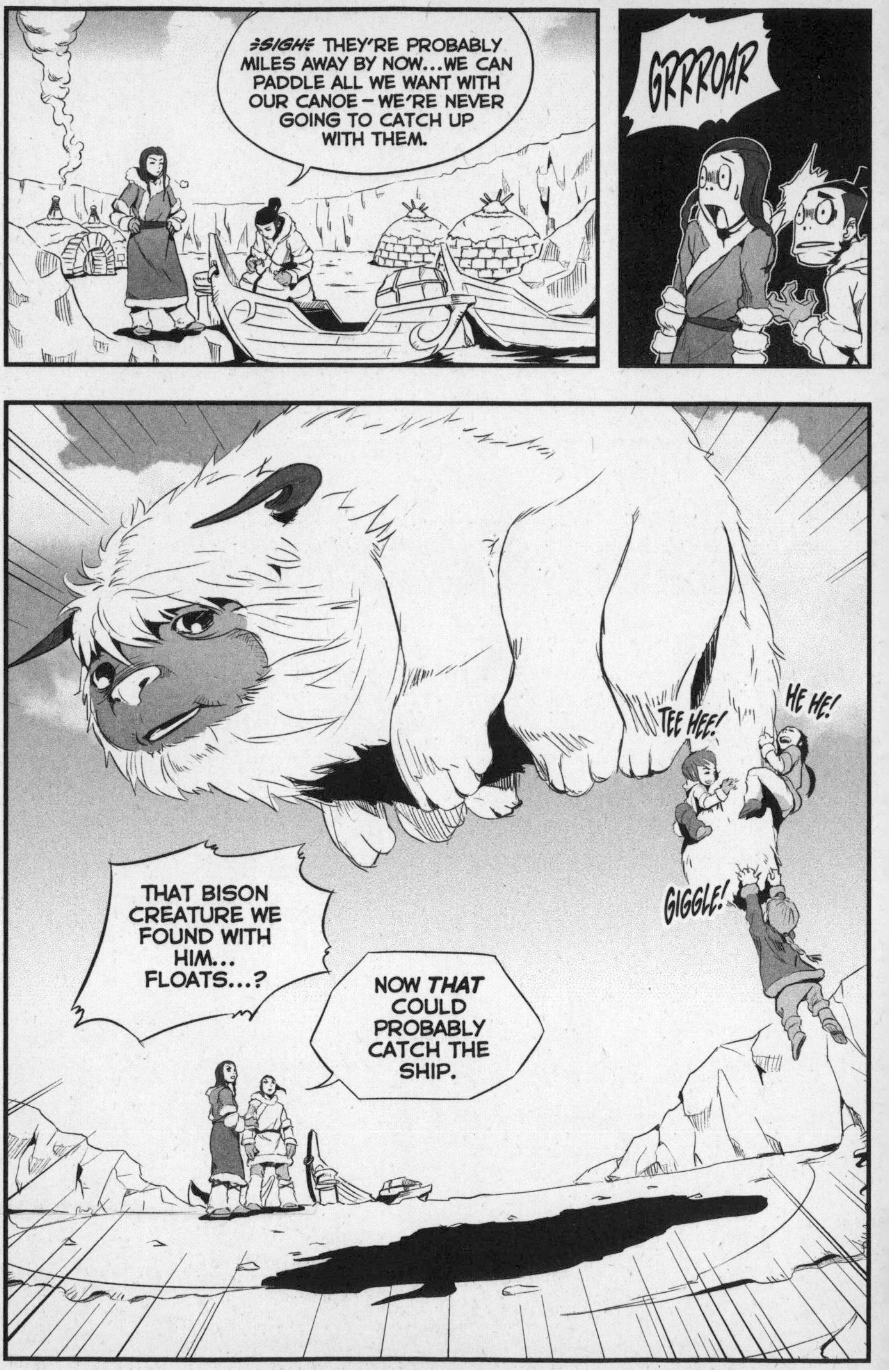
*SIGH* THEY'RE PROBABLY MILES AWAY BY NOW...WE CAN PADDLE ALL WE WANT WITH OUR CANOE – WE'RE NEVER GOING TO CATCH UP WITH THEM.
GRRROAR
TEE HEE!
HE HE!
GIGGLE!
THAT BISON CREATURE WE FOUND WITH HIM... FLOATS...?
NOW *THAT* COULD PROBABLY CATCH THE SHIP.

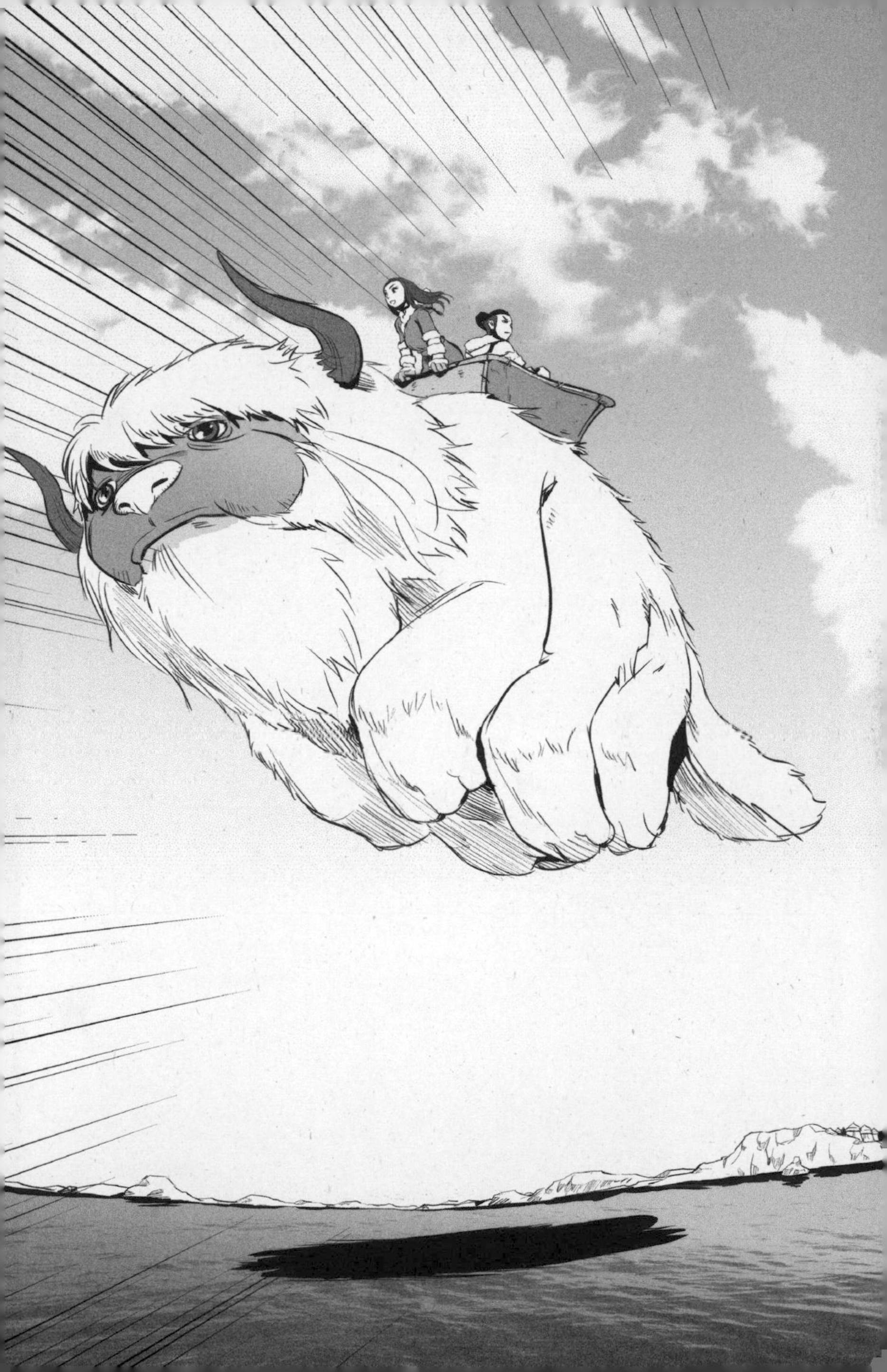

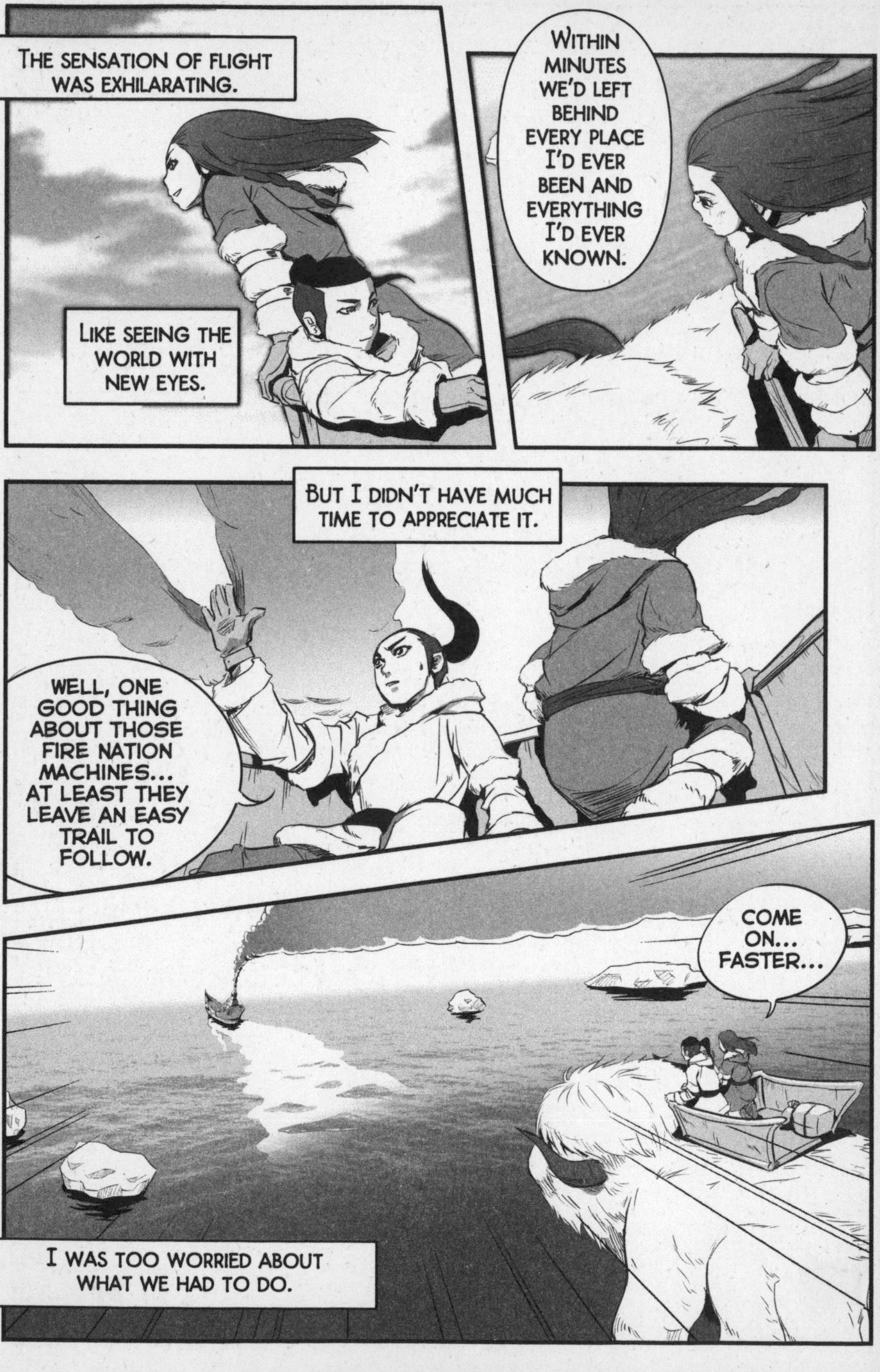
THE SENSATION OF FLIGHT WAS EXHILARATING.
LIKE SEEING THE WORLD WITH NEW EYES.
WITHIN MINUTES WE'D LEFT BEHIND EVERY PLACE I'D EVER BEEN AND EVERYTHING I'D EVER KNOWN.
BUT I DIDN'T HAVE MUCH TIME TO APPRECIATE IT.
WELL, ONE GOOD THING ABOUT THOSE FIRE NATION MACHINES... AT LEAST THEY LEAVE AN EASY TRAIL TO FOLLOW.
COME ON... FASTER...
I WAS TOO WORRIED ABOUT WHAT WE HAD TO DO.

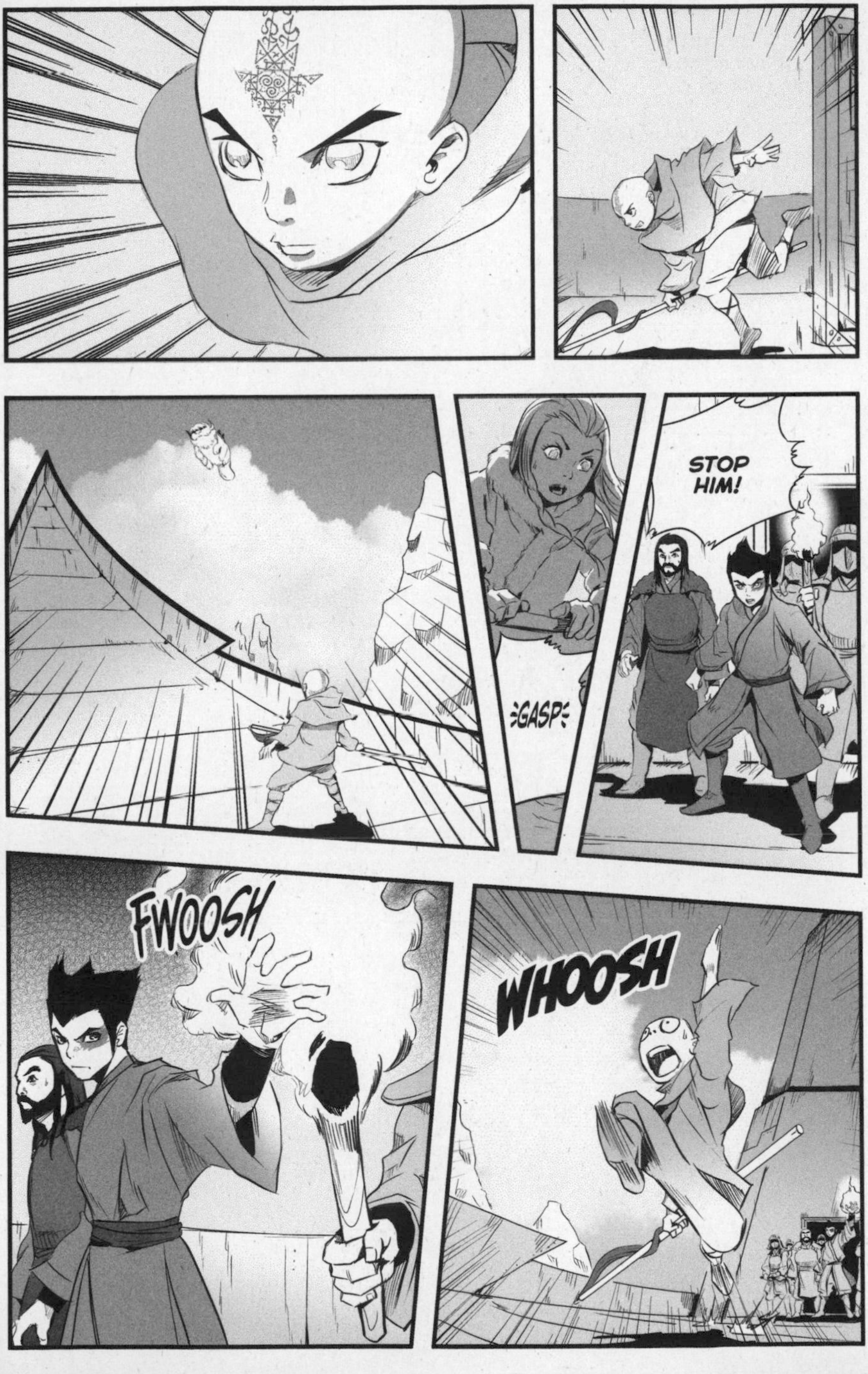

STOP HIM!
GASP
FWOOSH
WHOOSH

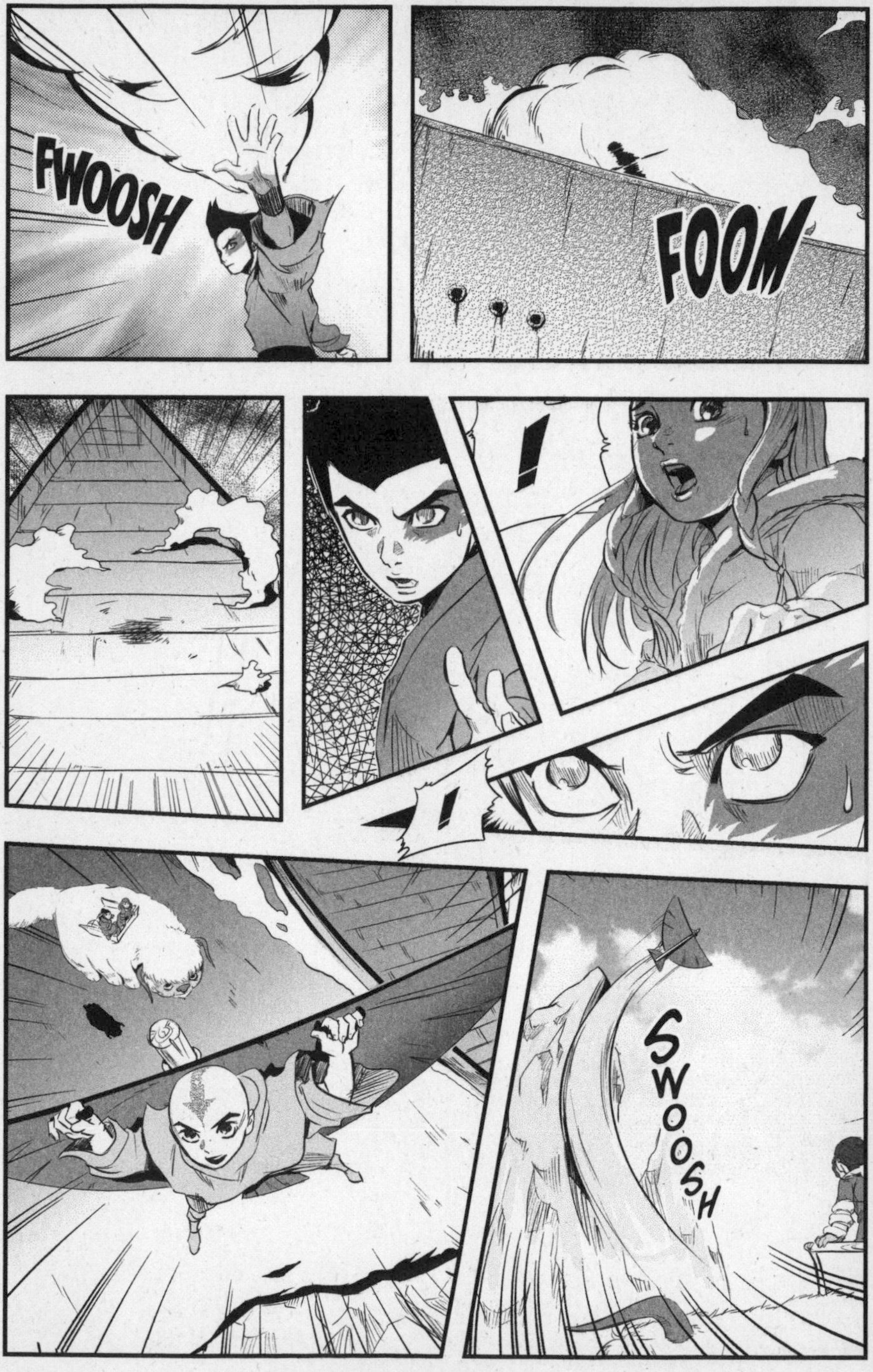
FWOOSH
FOOM
!
!
SWOOSH

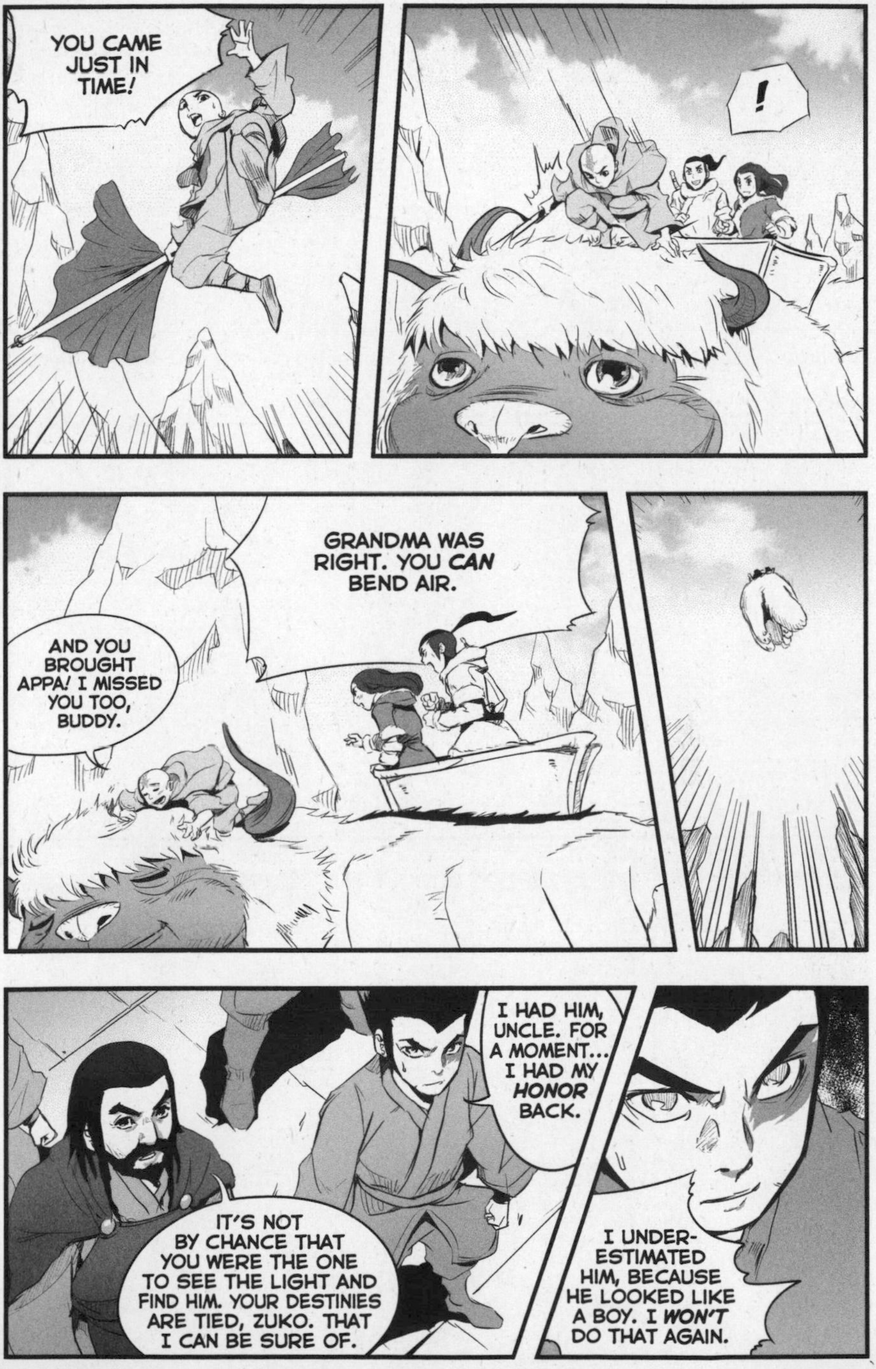
YOU CAME JUST IN TIME!
!
GRANDMA WAS RIGHT. YOU *CAN* BEND AIR.
AND YOU BROUGHT APPA! I MISSED YOU TOO, BUDDY.
I HAD HIM, UNCLE. FOR A MOMENT... I HAD MY *HONOR* BACK.
IT'S NOT BY CHANCE THAT YOU WERE THE ONE TO SEE THE LIGHT AND FIND HIM. YOUR DESTINIES ARE TIED, ZUKO. THAT I CAN BE SURE OF.
I UNDER-ESTIMATED HIM, BECAUSE HE LOOKED LIKE A BOY. I *WON'T* DO THAT AGAIN.

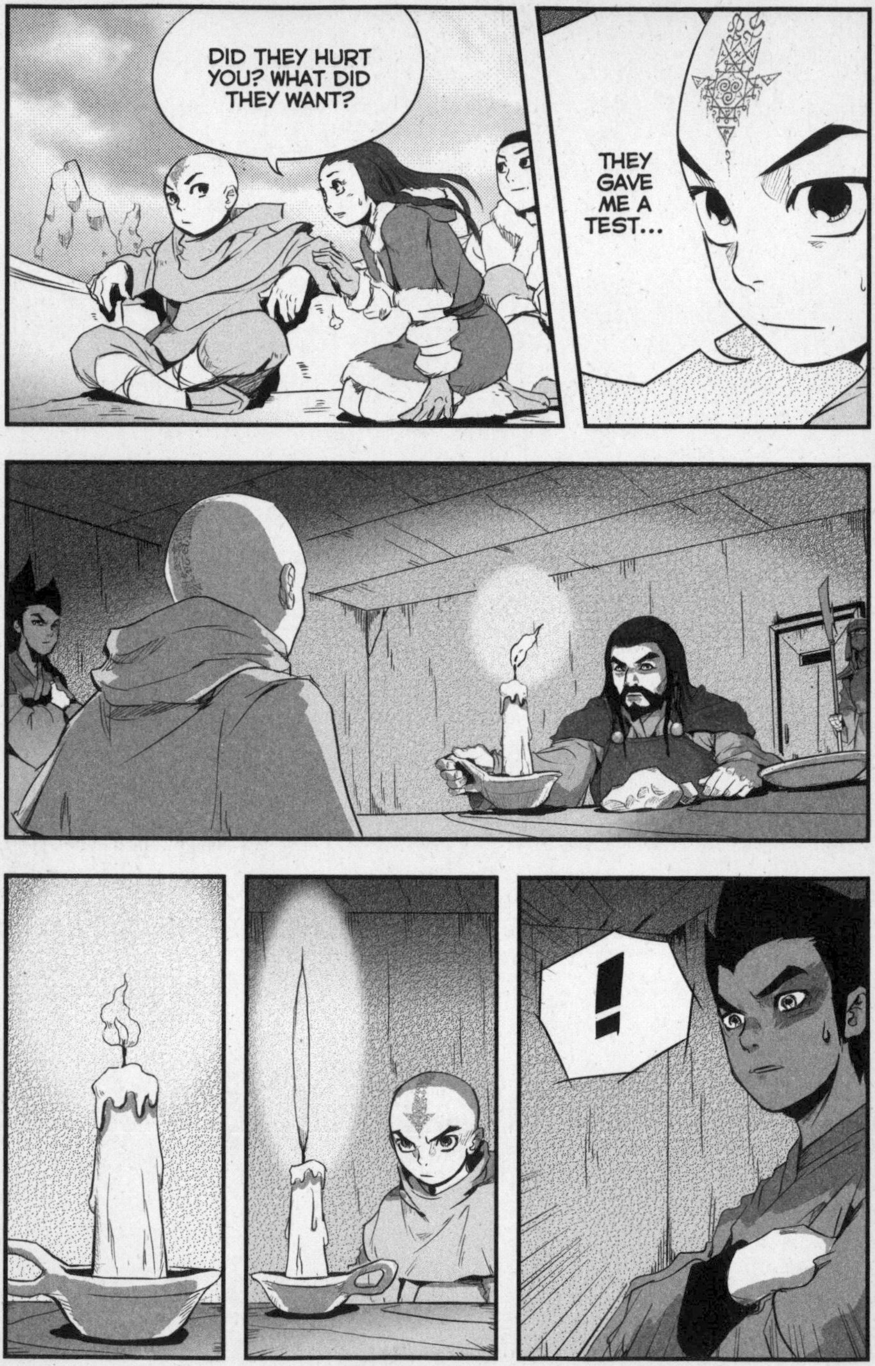
DID THEY HURT YOU? WHAT DID THEY WANT?
THEY GAVE ME A TEST...
!

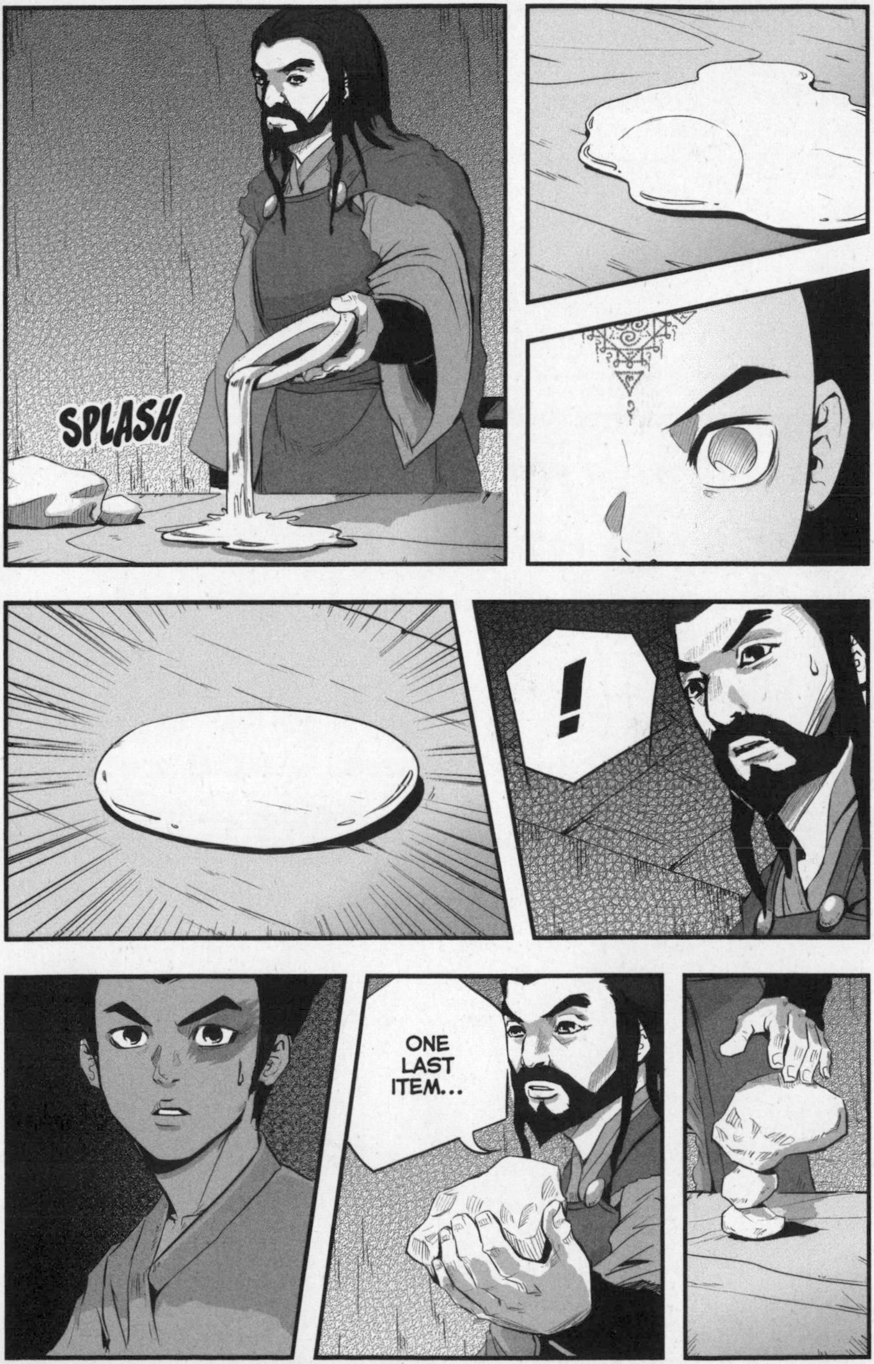
SPLASH
!
ONE LAST ITEM...

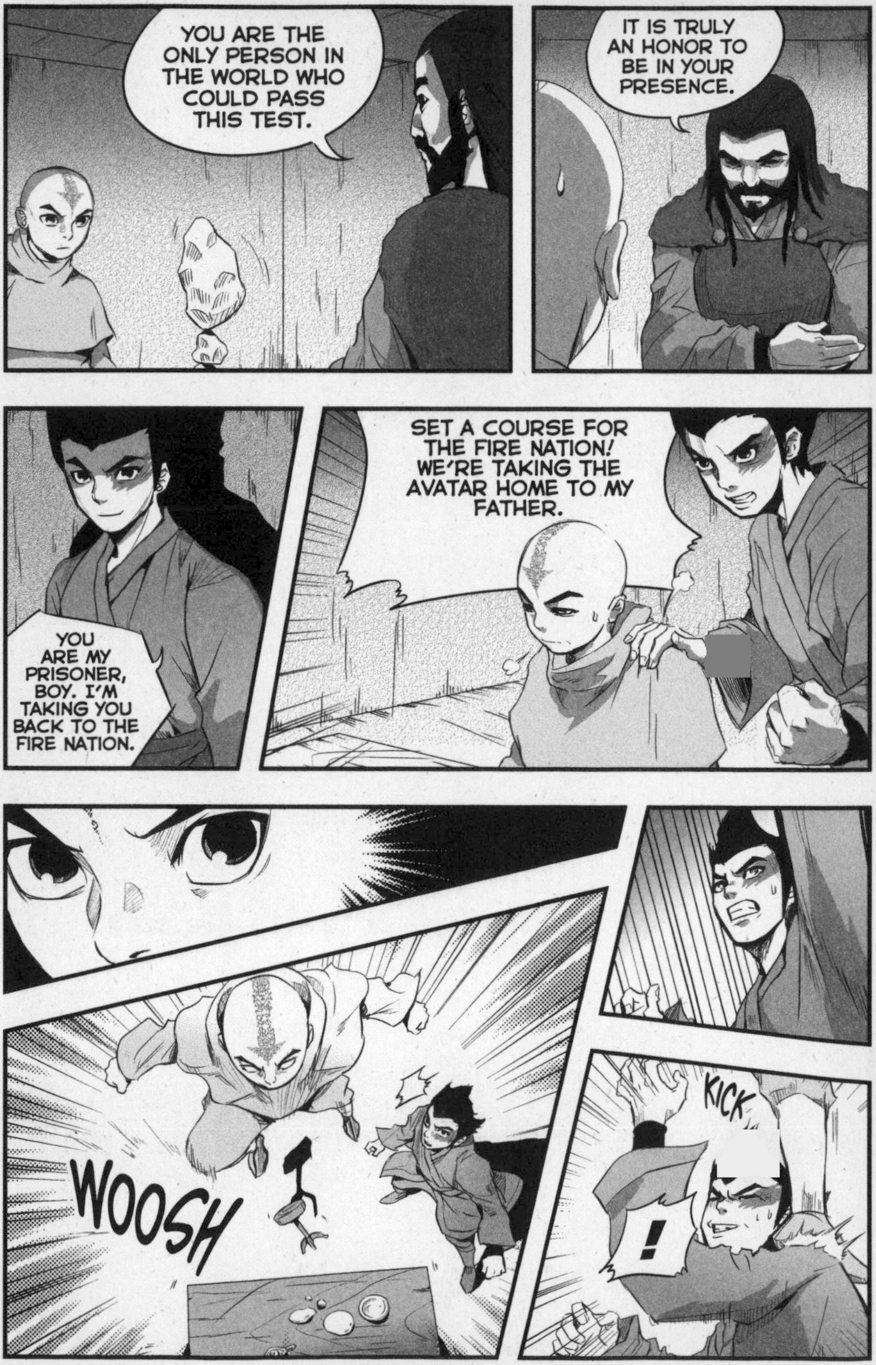
YOU ARE THE ONLY PERSON IN THE WORLD WHO COULD PASS THIS TEST.
IT IS TRULY AN HONOR TO BE IN YOUR PRESENCE.
YOU ARE MY PRISONER, BOY. I'M TAKING YOU BACK TO THE FIRE NATION.
SET A COURSE FOR THE FIRE NATION! WE'RE TAKING THE AVATAR HOME TO MY FATHER.
WOOSH
KICK
!

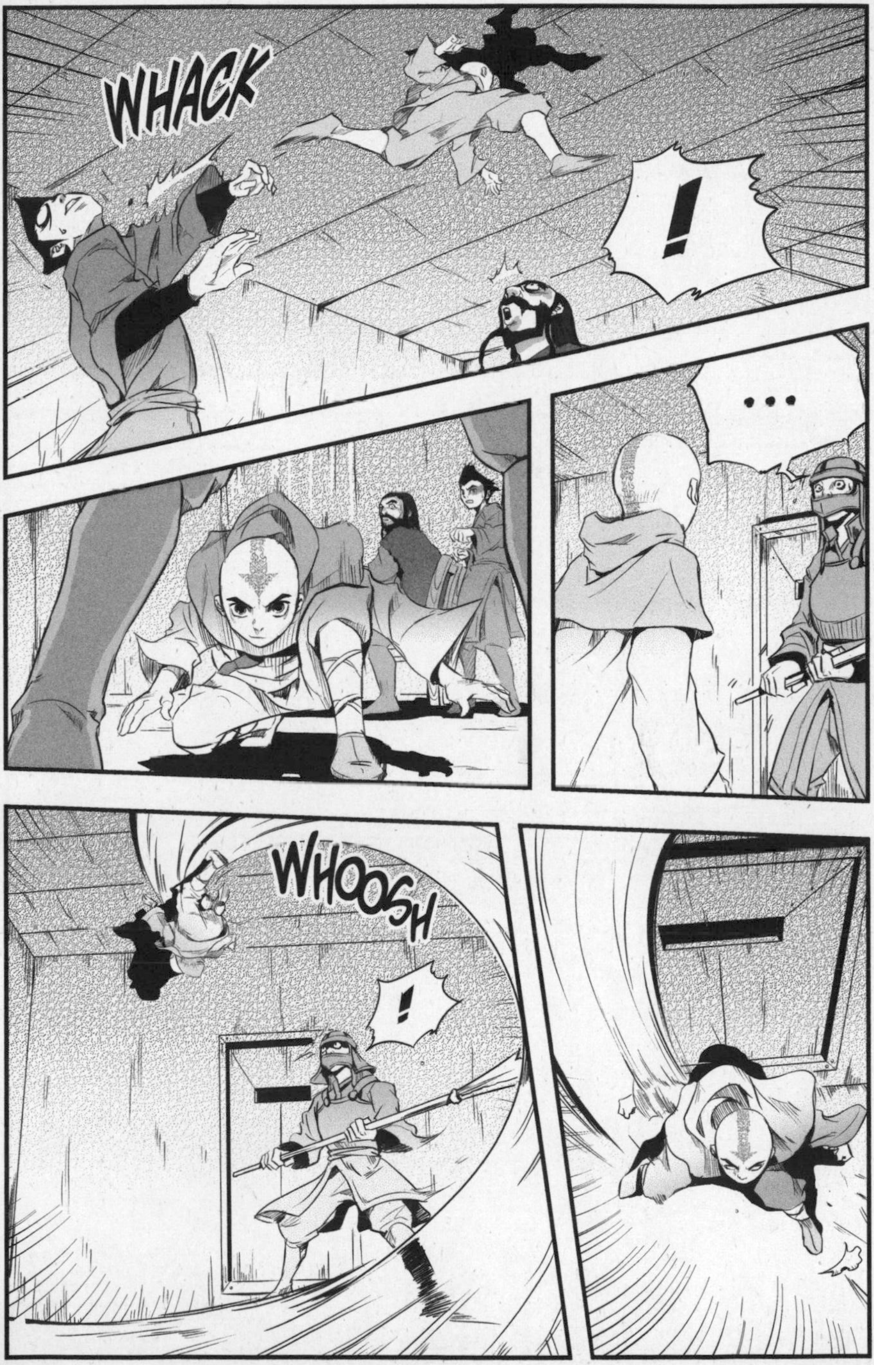

WHACK
!
...
WHOOSH
!

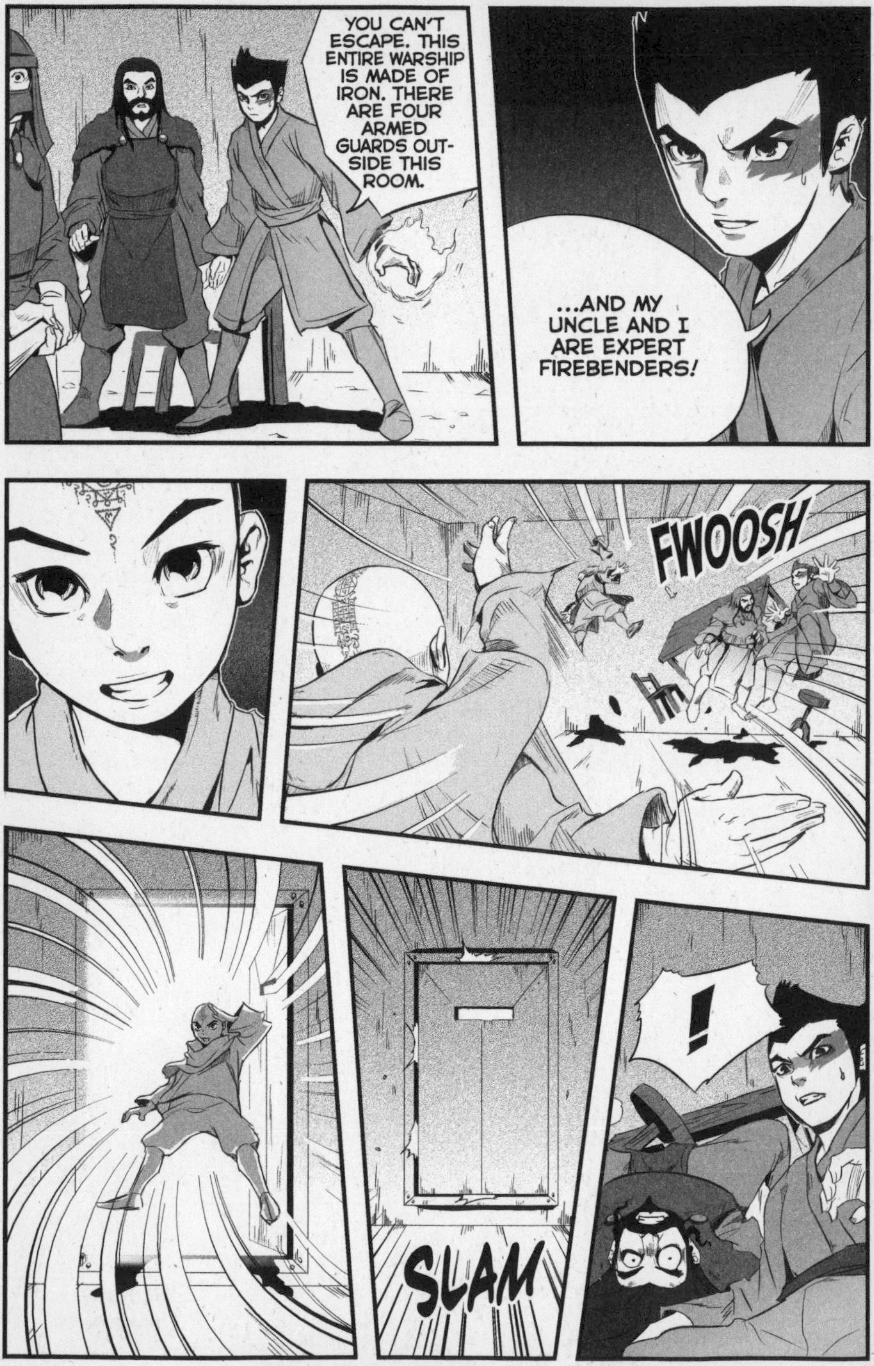
YOU CAN'T ESCAPE. THIS ENTIRE WARSHIP IS MADE OF IRON. THERE ARE FOUR ARMED GUARDS OUT-SIDE THIS ROOM.
...AND MY UNCLE AND I ARE EXPERT FIREBENDERS!
FWOOSH
SLAM
!

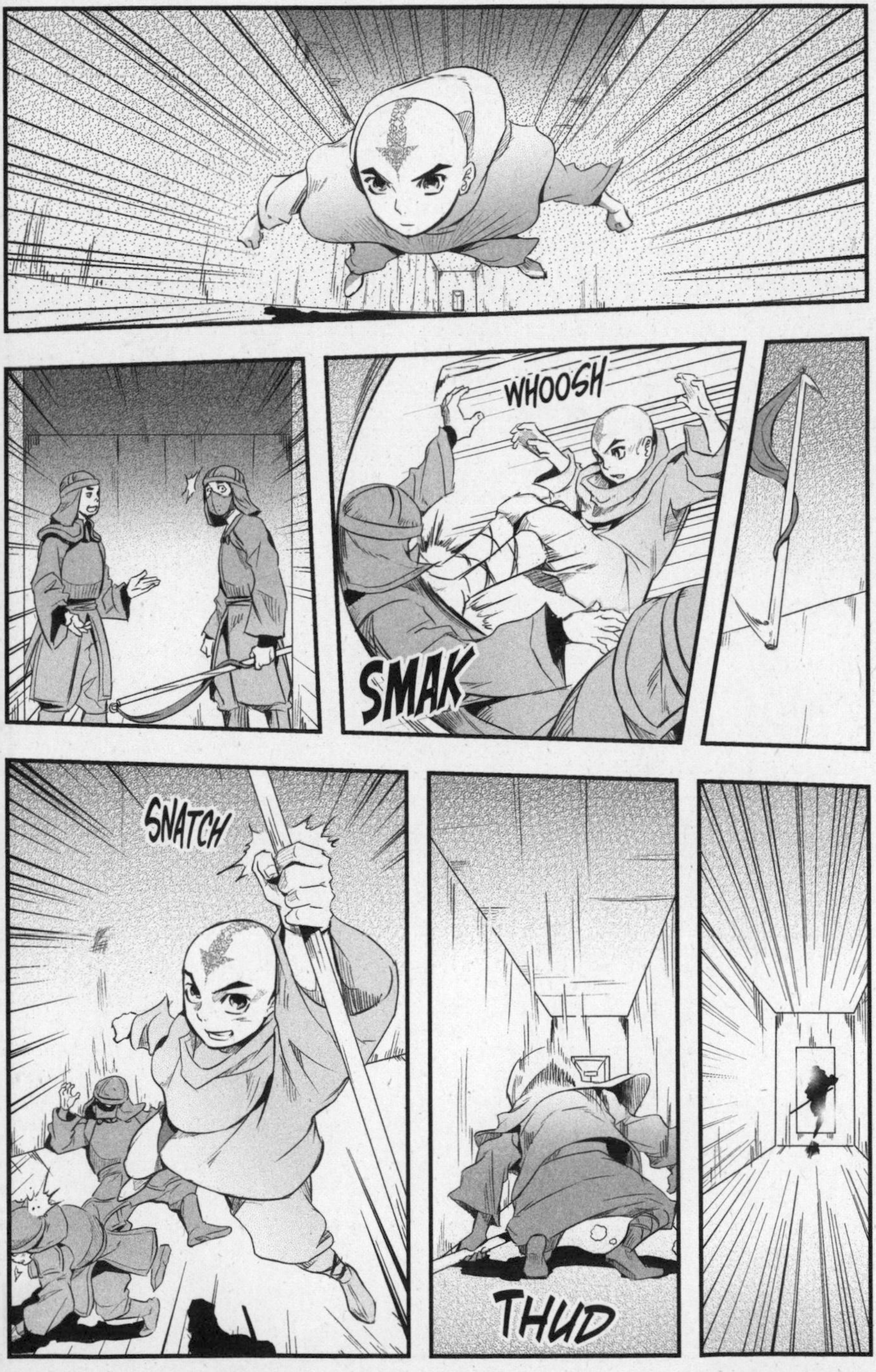
WHOOSH
SMAK
SNATCH
THUD

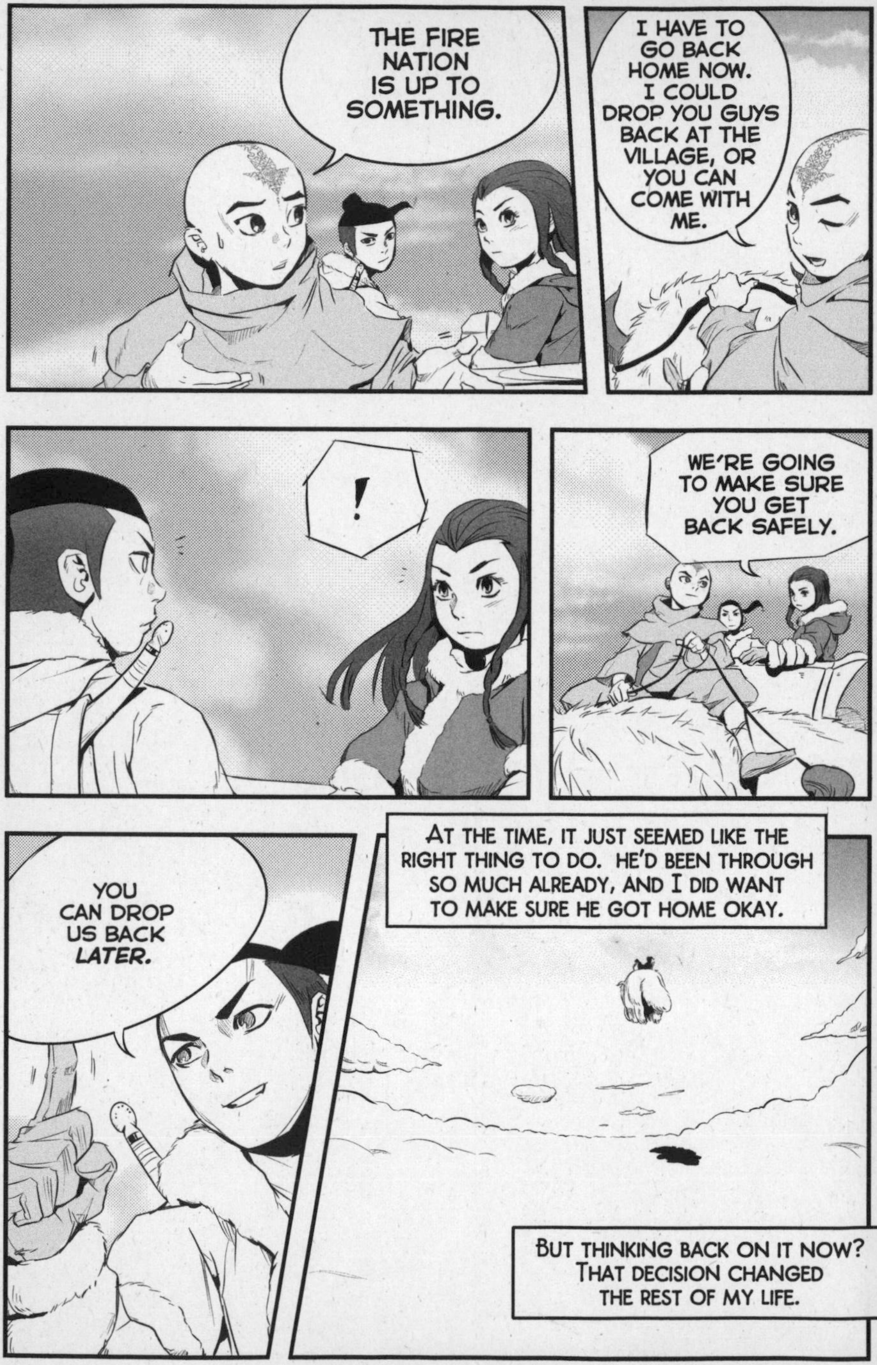
THE FIRE NATION IS UP TO SOMETHING.
I HAVE TO GO BACK HOME NOW. I COULD DROP YOU GUYS BACK AT THE VILLAGE, OR YOU CAN COME WITH ME.
!
WE'RE GOING TO MAKE SURE YOU GET BACK SAFELY.
YOU CAN DROP US BACK *LATER.*
AT THE TIME, IT JUST SEEMED LIKE THE RIGHT THING TO DO. HE'D BEEN THROUGH SO MUCH ALREADY, AND I DID WANT TO MAKE SURE HE GOT HOME OKAY.
BUT THINKING BACK ON IT NOW? THAT DECISION CHANGED THE REST OF MY LIFE.

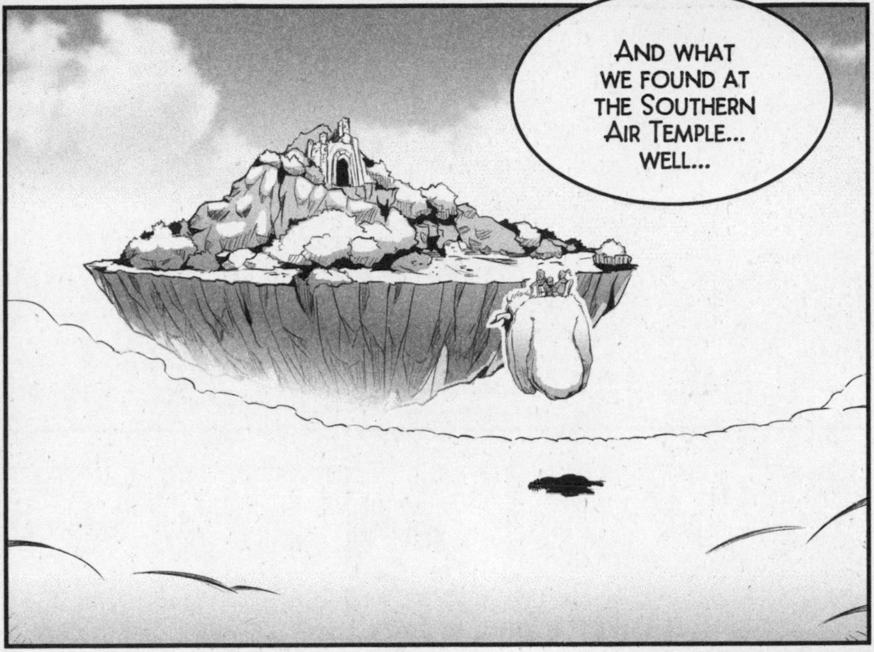
AND WHAT WE FOUND AT THE SOUTHERN AIR TEMPLE... WELL...
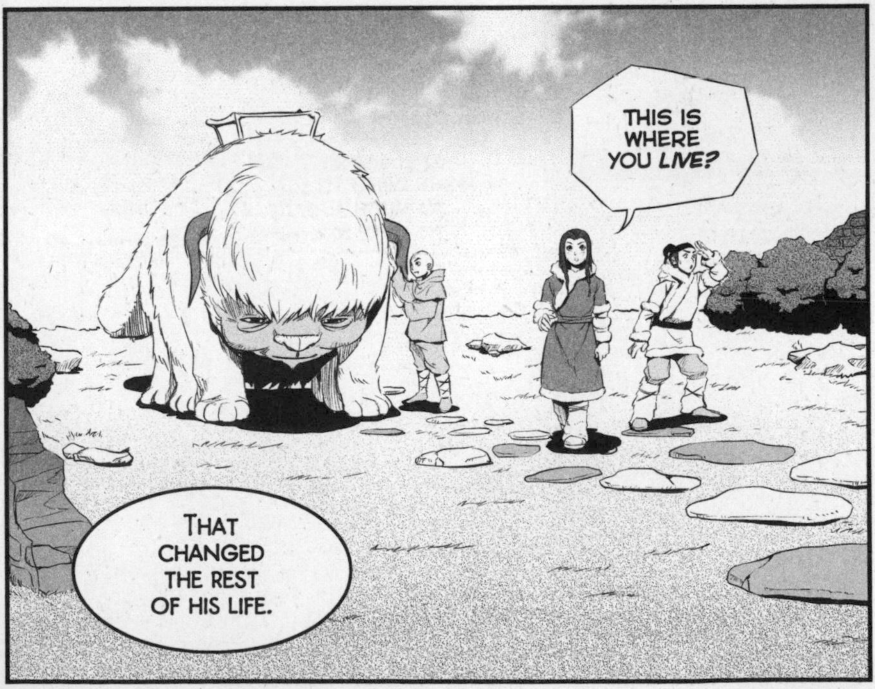
THIS IS WHERE YOU *LIVE?*
THAT CHANGED THE REST OF HIS LIFE.

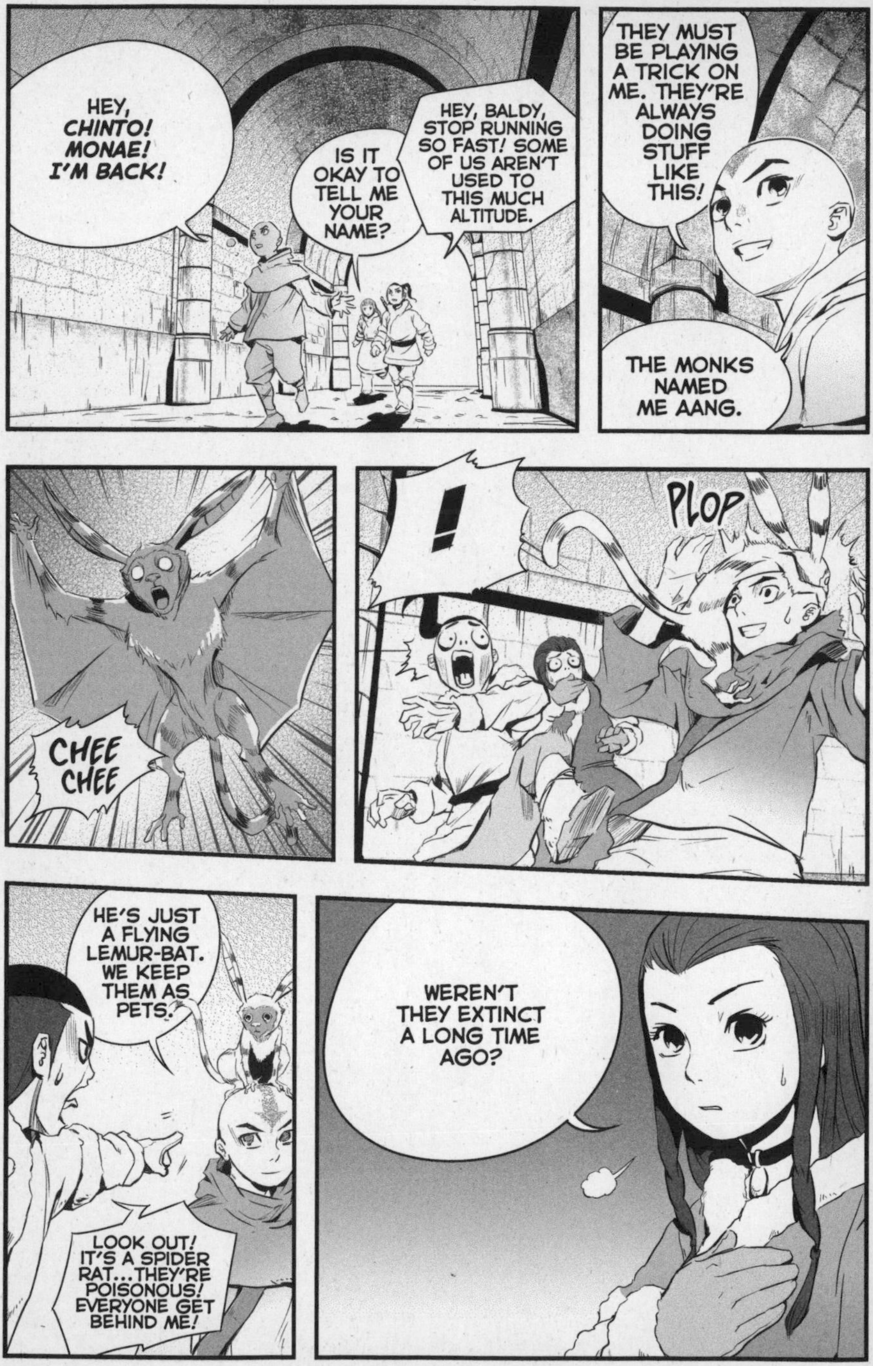
HEY, CHINTO! MONAE! I'M BACK!
IS IT OKAY TO TELL ME YOUR NAME?
HEY, BALDY, STOP RUNNING SO FAST! SOME OF US AREN'T USED TO THIS MUCH ALTITUDE.
THEY MUST BE PLAYING A TRICK ON ME. THEY'RE ALWAYS DOING STUFF LIKE THIS!
THE MONKS NAMED ME AANG.
CHEE CHEE
!
PLOP
HE'S JUST A FLYING LEMUR-BAT. WE KEEP THEM AS PETS.
LOOK OUT! IT'S A SPIDER RAT...THEY'RE POISONOUS! EVERYONE GET BEHIND ME!
WEREN'T THEY EXTINCT A LONG TIME AGO?

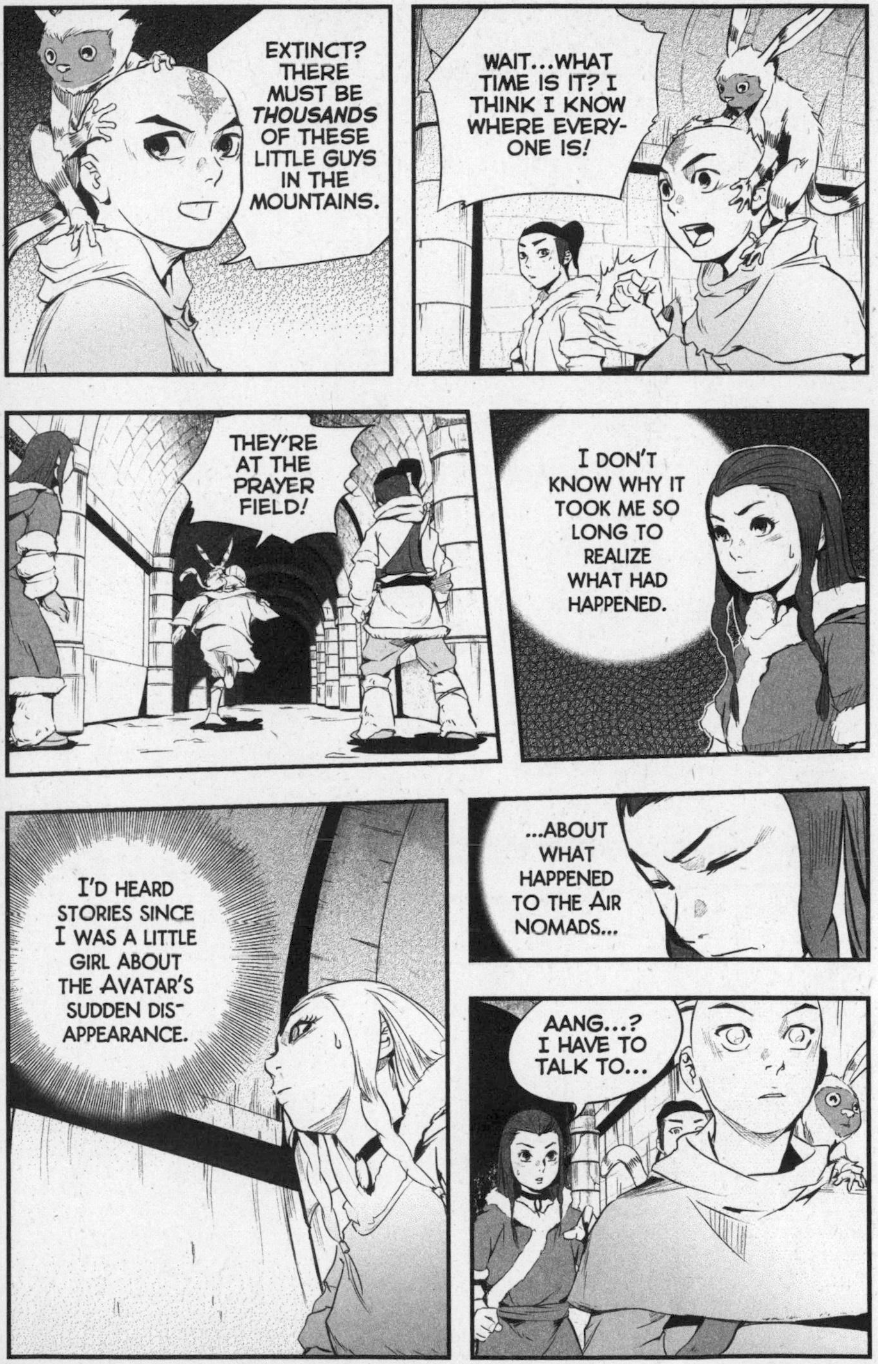
EXTINCT? THERE MUST BE *THOUSANDS* OF THESE LITTLE GUYS IN THE MOUNTAINS.
WAIT...WHAT TIME IS IT? I THINK I KNOW WHERE EVERY-ONE IS!
THEY'RE AT THE PRAYER FIELD!
I DON'T KNOW WHY IT TOOK ME SO LONG TO REALIZE WHAT HAD HAPPENED.
I'D HEARD STORIES SINCE I WAS A LITTLE GIRL ABOUT THE AVATAR'S SUDDEN DIS-APPEARANCE.
...ABOUT WHAT HAPPENED TO THE AIR NOMADS...
AANG...? I HAVE TO TALK TO...

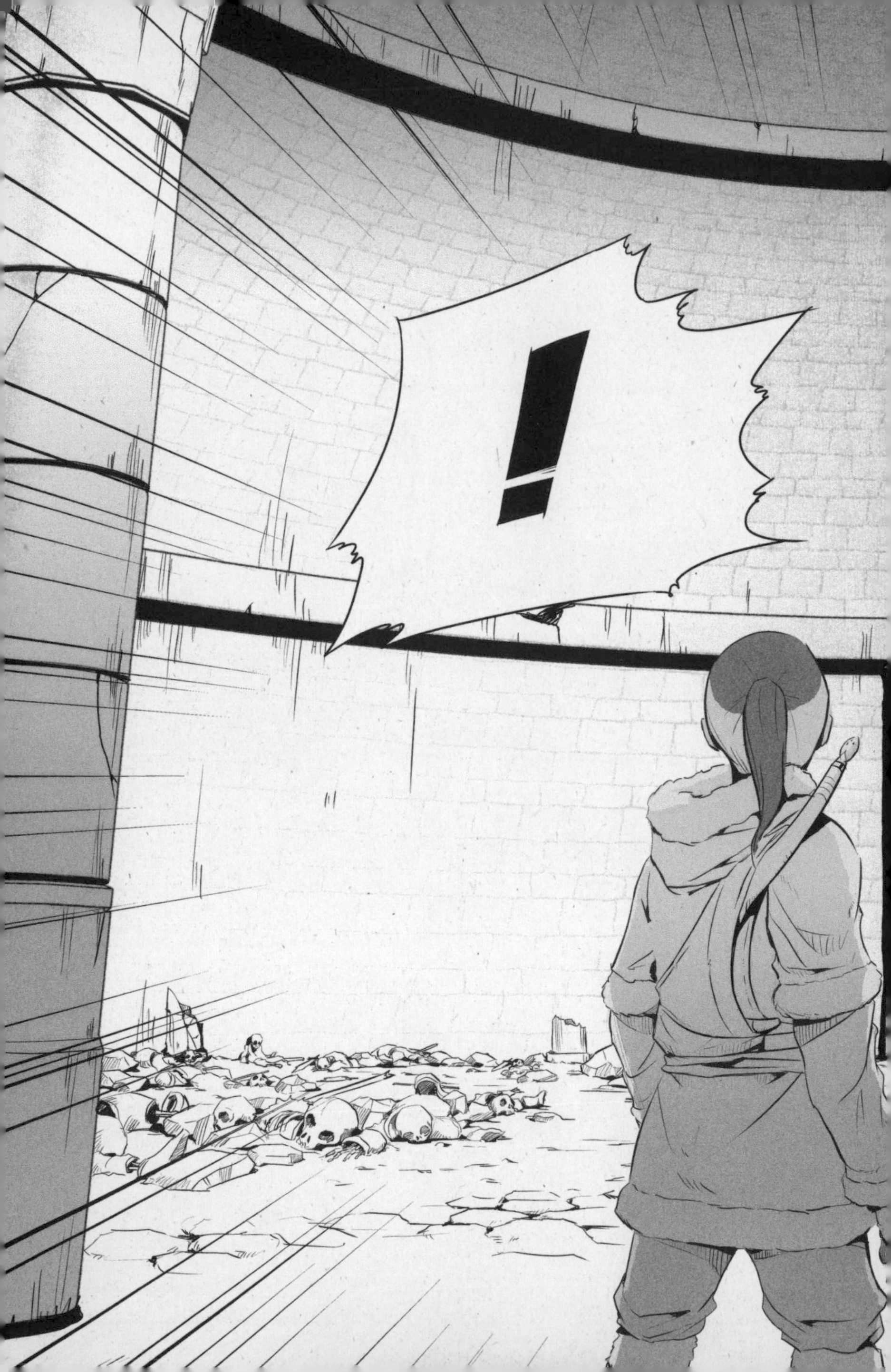
!

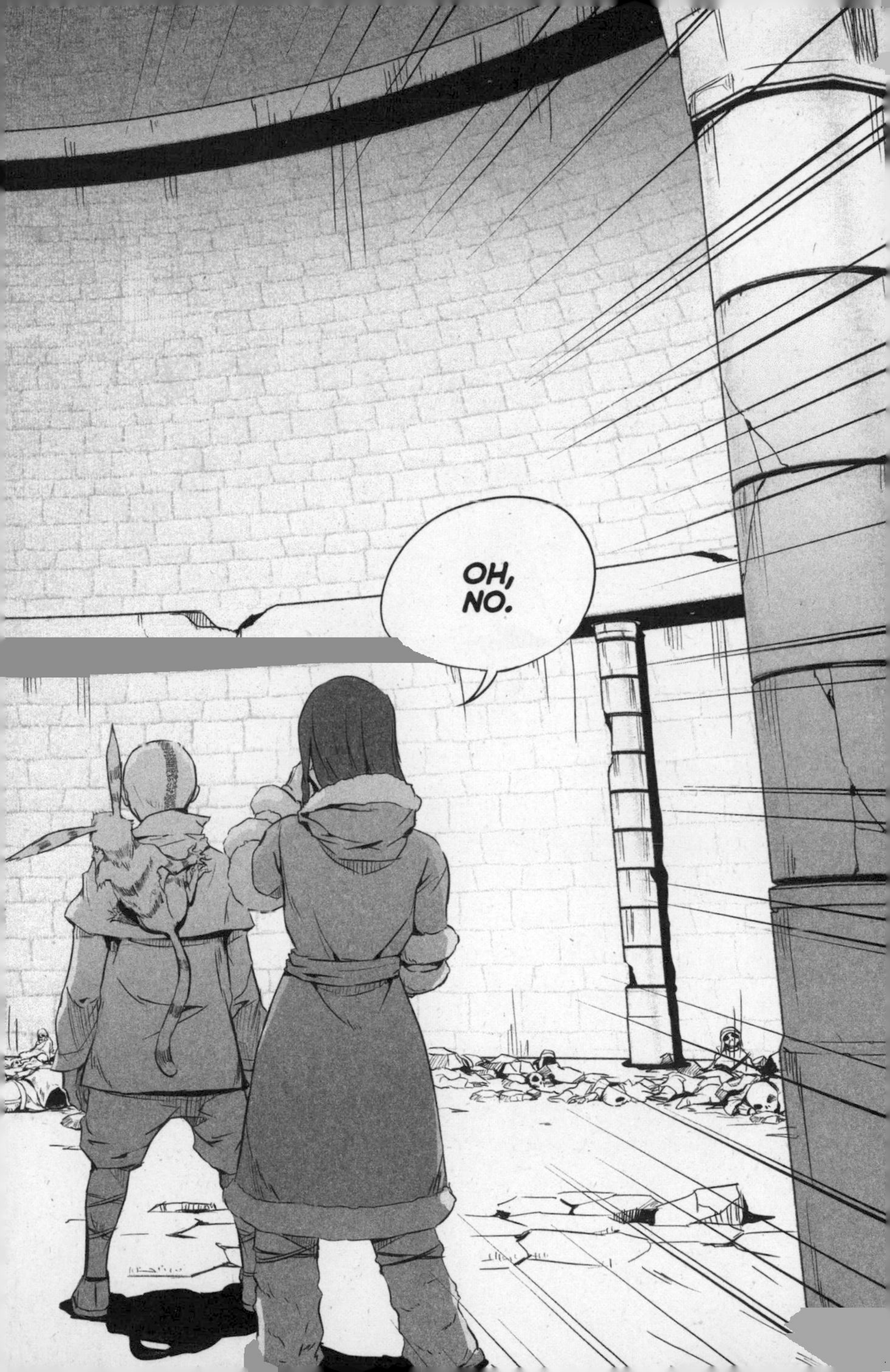
OH, NO.

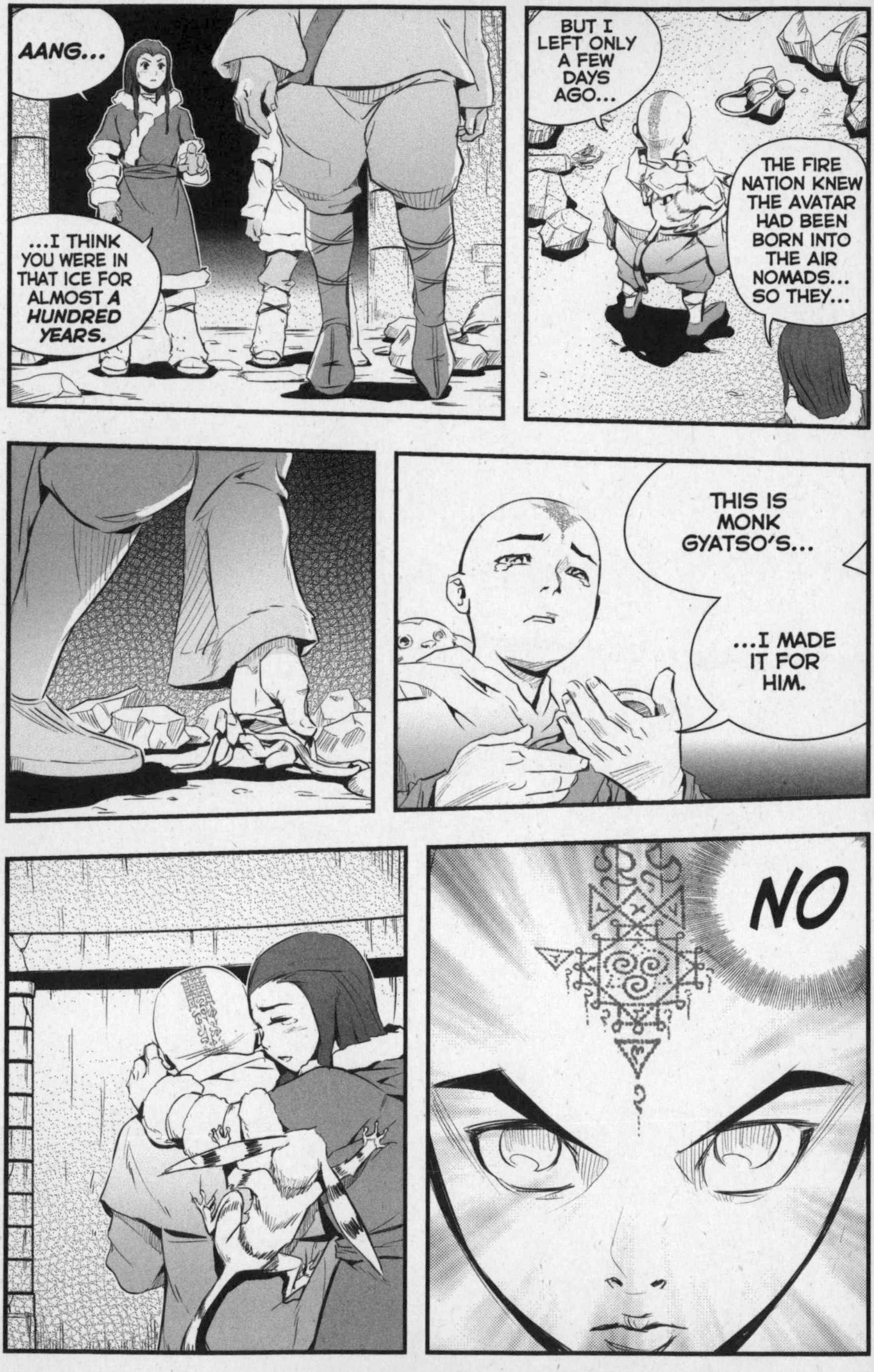
AANG...
...I THINK YOU WERE IN THAT ICE FOR ALMOST A HUNDRED YEARS.
BUT I LEFT ONLY A FEW DAYS AGO...
THE FIRE NATION KNEW THE AVATAR HAD BEEN BORN INTO THE AIR NOMADS... SO THEY...
THIS IS MONK GYATSO'S...
...I MADE IT FOR HIM.
NO

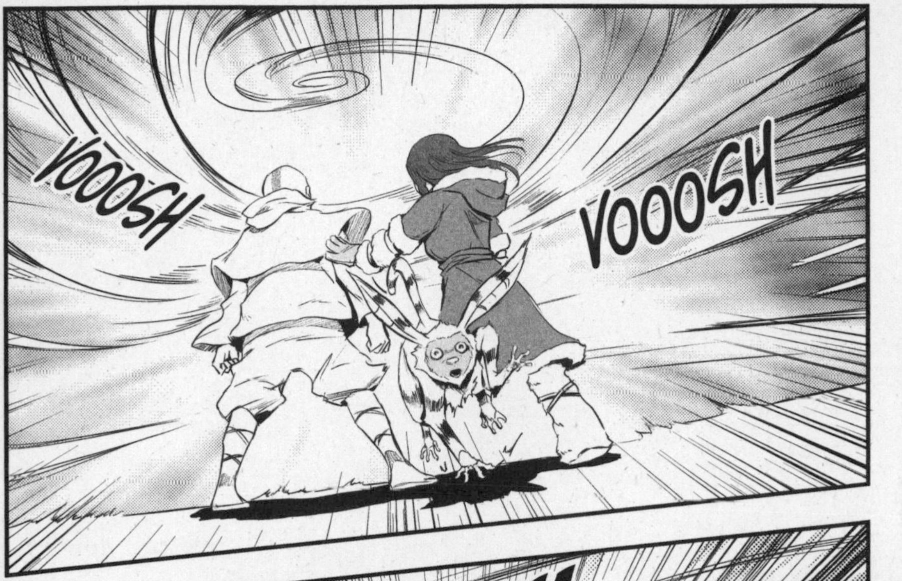
VOOOSH
VOOOSH
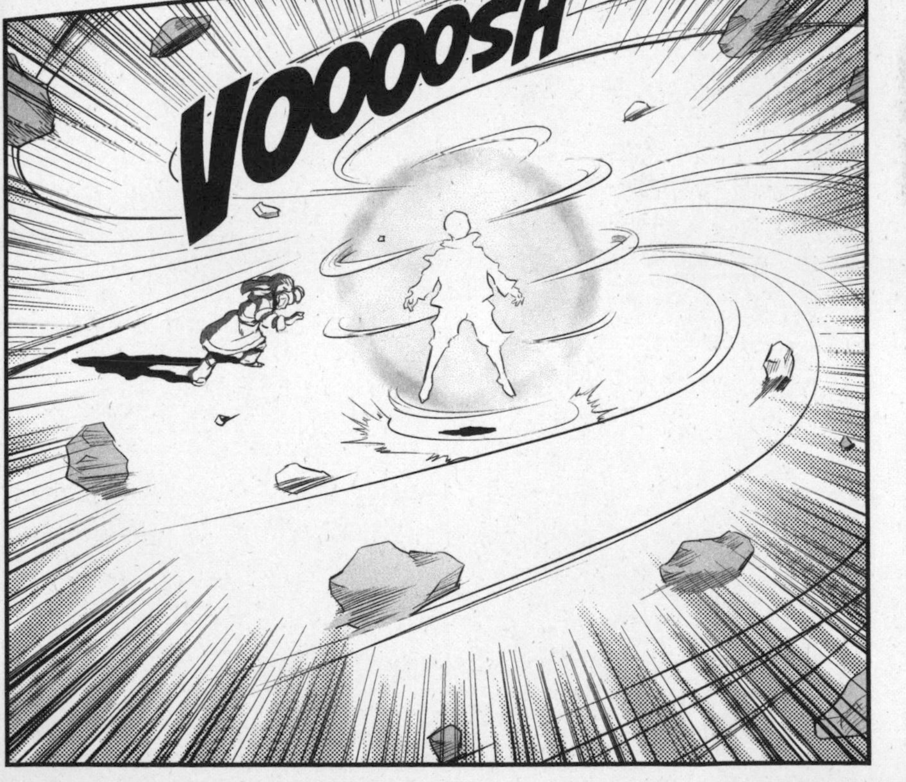
VOOOOSH

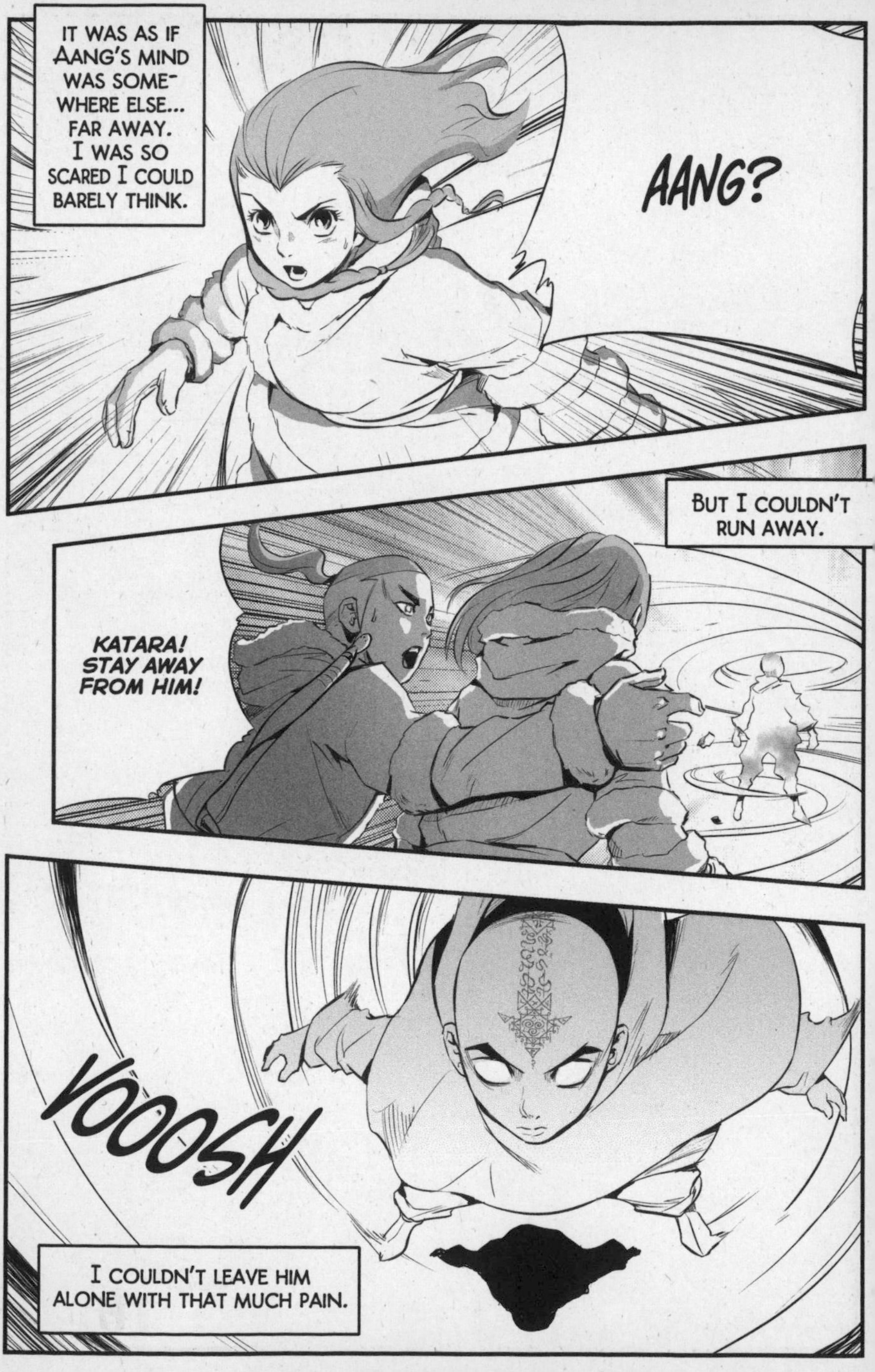
IT WAS AS IF AANG'S MIND WAS SOME-WHERE ELSE... FAR AWAY. I WAS SO SCARED I COULD BARELY THINK.
AANG?
BUT I COULDN'T RUN AWAY.
KATARA! STAY AWAY FROM HIM!
YOOOSH
I COULDN'T LEAVE HIM ALONE WITH THAT MUCH PAIN.

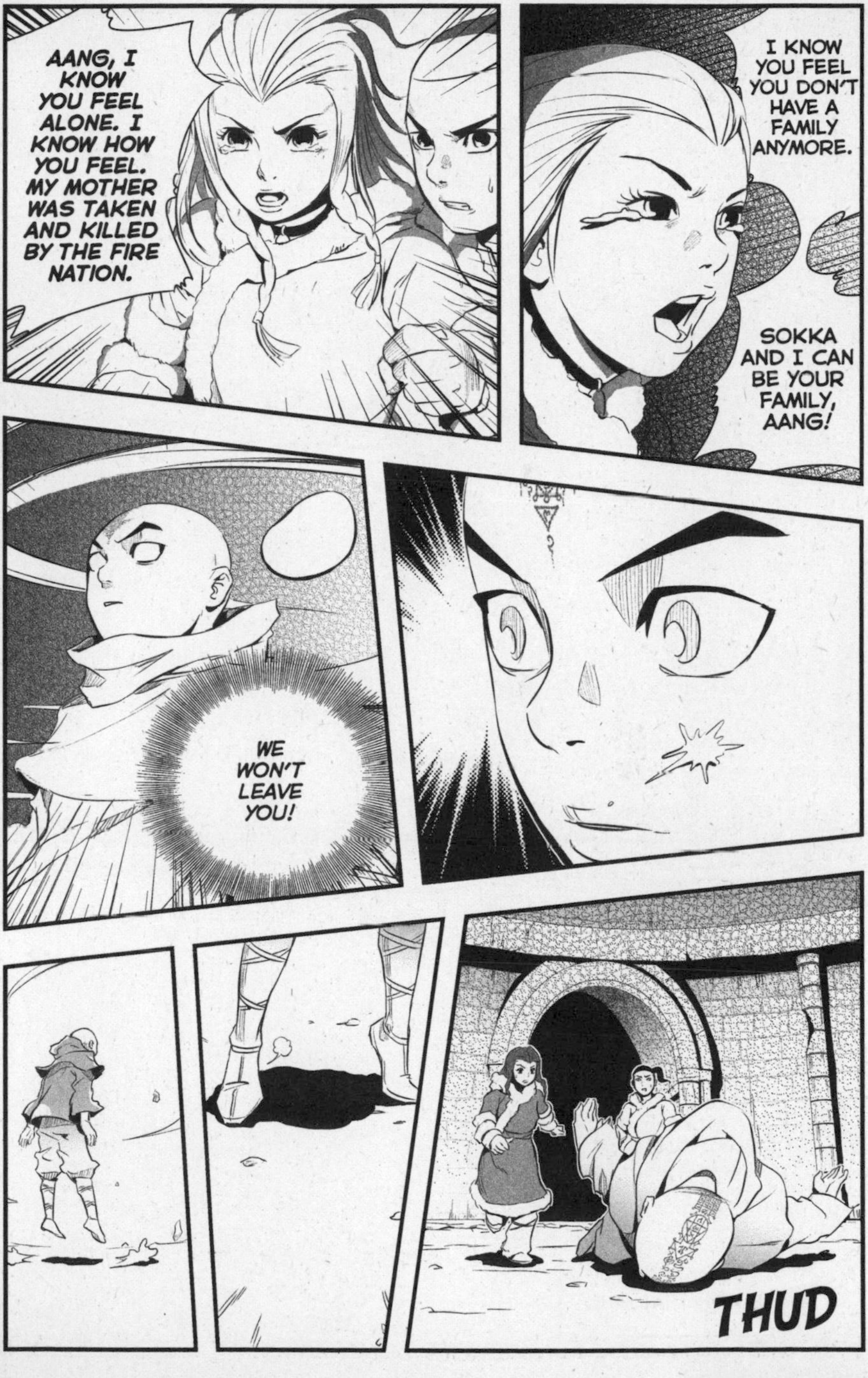
AANG, I KNOW YOU FEEL ALONE. I KNOW HOW YOU FEEL. MY MOTHER WAS TAKEN AND KILLED BY THE FIRE NATION.
I KNOW YOU FEEL YOU DON'T HAVE A FAMILY ANYMORE.
SOKKA AND I CAN BE YOUR FAMILY, AANG!
WE WON'T LEAVE YOU!
THUD

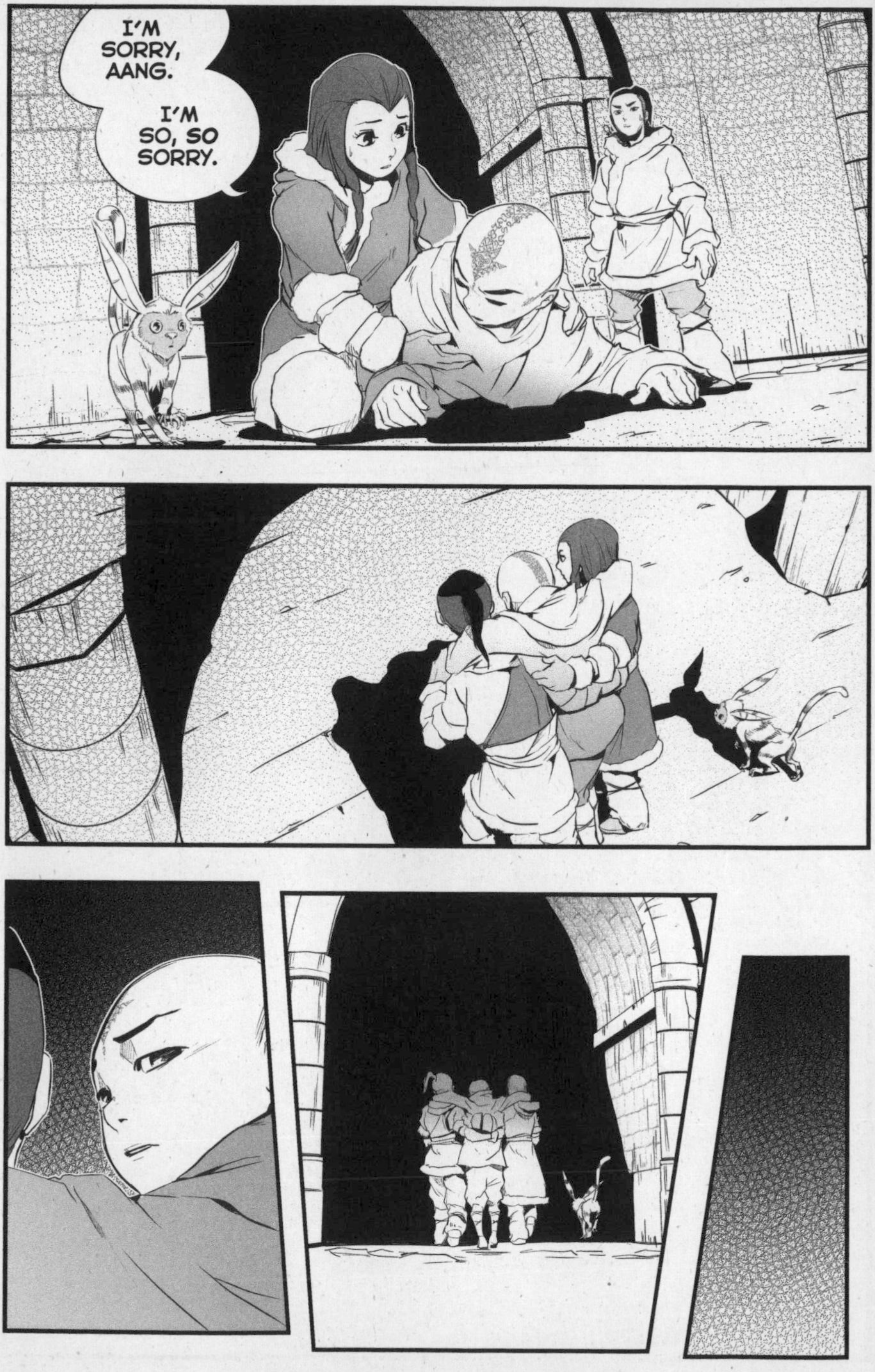
I'M SORRY, AANG.
I'M SO, SO SORRY.

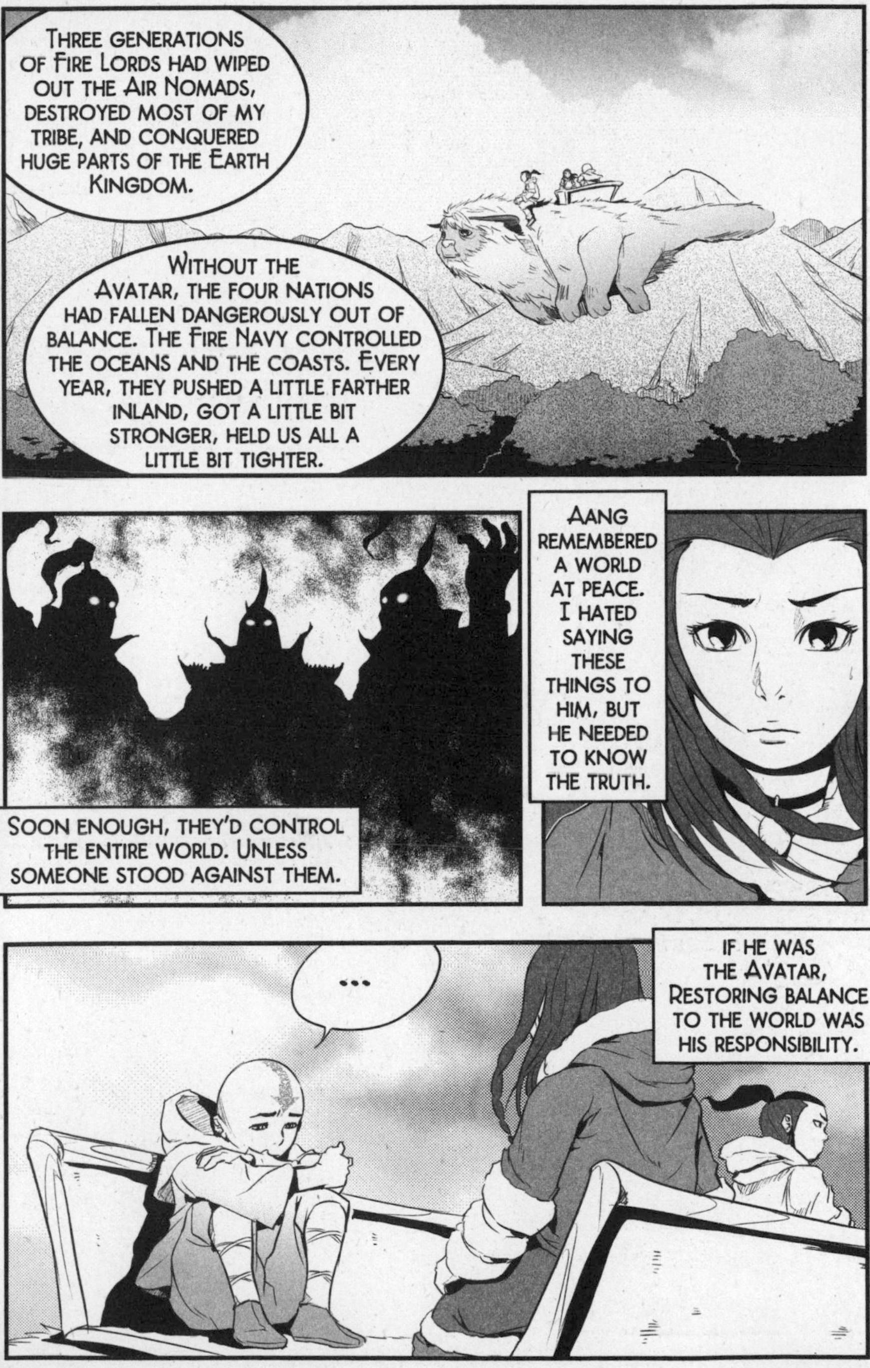
THREE GENERATIONS OF FIRE LORDS HAD WIPED OUT THE AIR NOMADS, DESTROYED MOST OF MY TRIBE, AND CONQUERED HUGE PARTS OF THE EARTH KINGDOM.
WITHOUT THE AVATAR, THE FOUR NATIONS HAD FALLEN DANGEROUSLY OUT OF BALANCE. THE FIRE NAVY CONTROLLED THE OCEANS AND THE COASTS. EVERY YEAR, THEY PUSHED A LITTLE FARTHER INLAND, GOT A LITTLE BIT STRONGER, HELD US ALL A LITTLE BIT TIGHTER.
SOON ENOUGH, THEY'D CONTROL THE ENTIRE WORLD. UNLESS SOMEONE STOOD AGAINST THEM.
AANG REMEMBERED A WORLD AT PEACE. I HATED SAYING THESE THINGS TO HIM, BUT HE NEEDED TO KNOW THE TRUTH.
...
IF HE WAS THE AVATAR, RESTORING BALANCE TO THE WORLD WAS HIS RESPONSIBILITY.

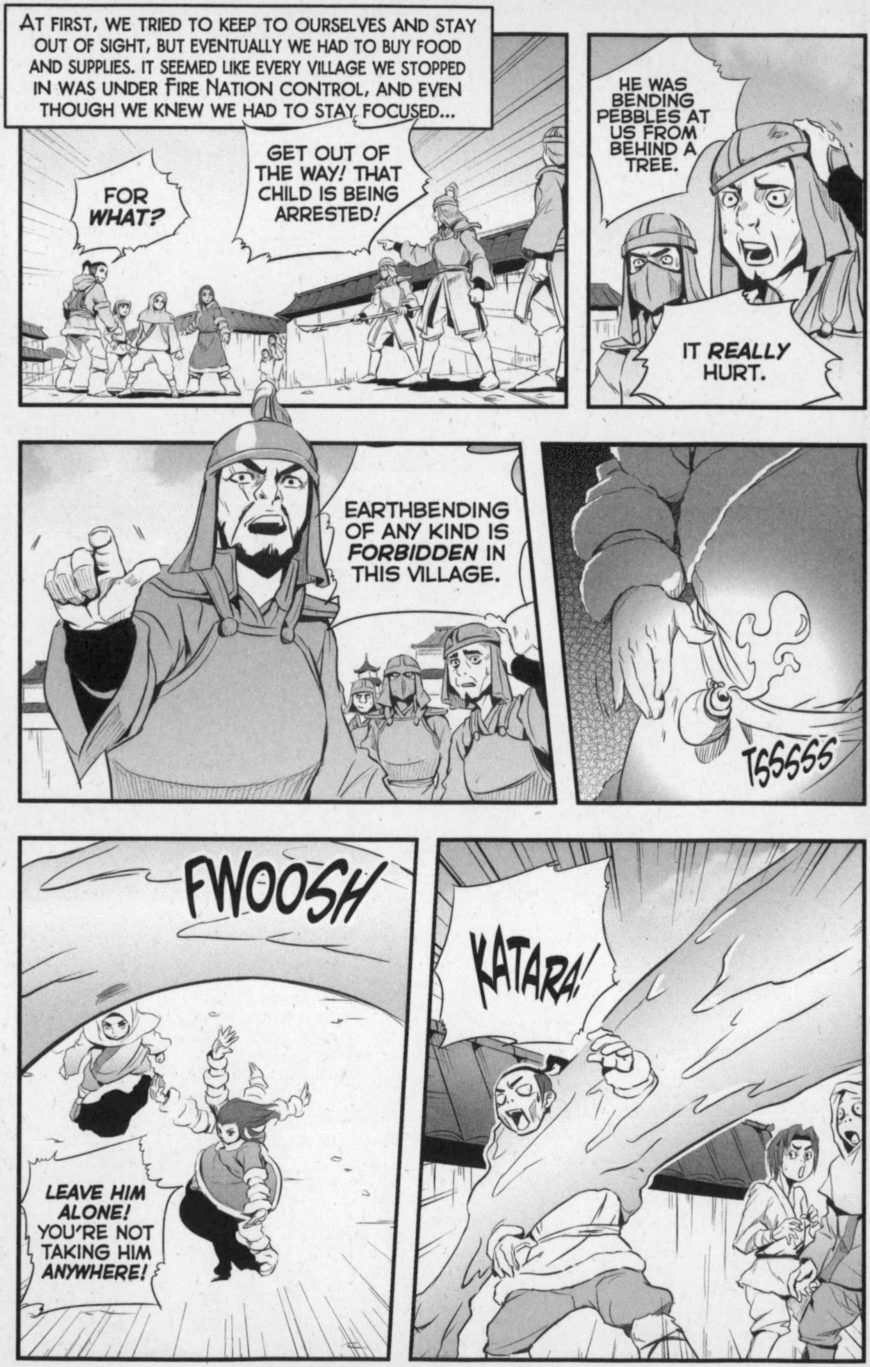

AT FIRST, WE TRIED TO KEEP TO OURSELVES AND STAY OUT OF SIGHT, BUT EVENTUALLY WE HAD TO BUY FOOD AND SUPPLIES. IT SEEMED LIKE EVERY VILLAGE WE STOPPED IN WAS UNDER FIRE NATION CONTROL, AND EVEN THOUGH WE KNEW WE HAD TO STAY FOCUSED...
GET OUT OF THE WAY! THAT CHILD IS BEING ARRESTED!
FOR WHAT?
HE WAS BENDING PEBBLES AT US FROM BEHIND A TREE.
IT REALLY HURT.
EARTHBENDING OF ANY KIND IS FORBIDDEN IN THIS VILLAGE.
TSSSSS
FWOOSH
LEAVE HIM ALONE! YOU'RE NOT TAKING HIM ANYWHERE!
KATARA!

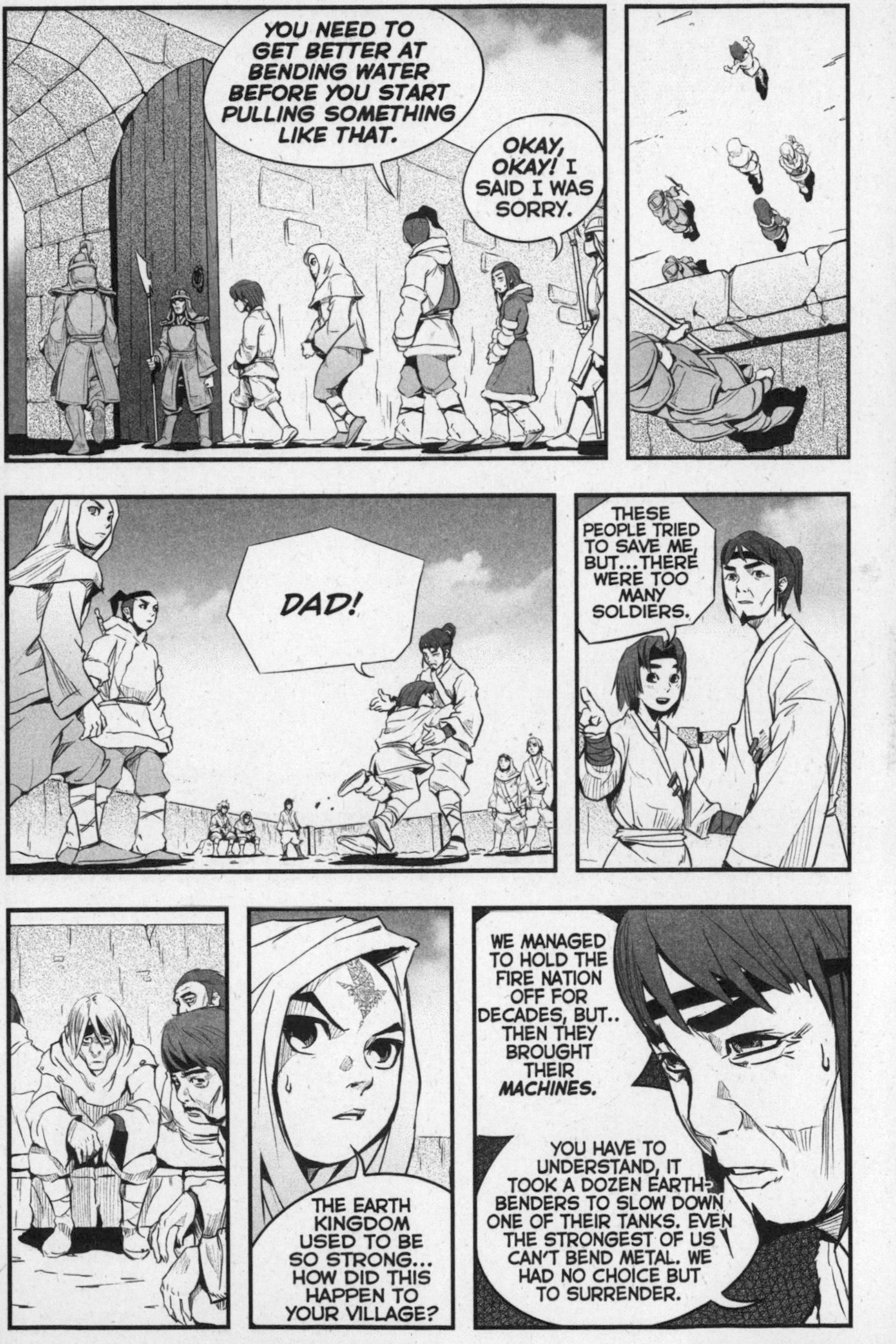
YOU NEED TO GET BETTER AT BENDING WATER BEFORE YOU START PULLING SOMETHING LIKE THAT.
OKAY, OKAY! I SAID I WAS SORRY.
DAD!
THESE PEOPLE TRIED TO SAVE ME, BUT...THERE WERE TOO MANY SOLDIERS.
THE EARTH KINGDOM USED TO BE SO STRONG... HOW DID THIS HAPPEN TO YOUR VILLAGE?
WE MANAGED TO HOLD THE FIRE NATION OFF FOR DECADES, BUT.. THEN THEY BROUGHT THEIR MACHINES.
YOU HAVE TO UNDERSTAND, IT TOOK A DOZEN EARTH-BENDERS TO SLOW DOWN ONE OF THEIR TANKS. EVEN THE STRONGEST OF US CAN'T BEND METAL. WE HAD NO CHOICE BUT TO SURRENDER.

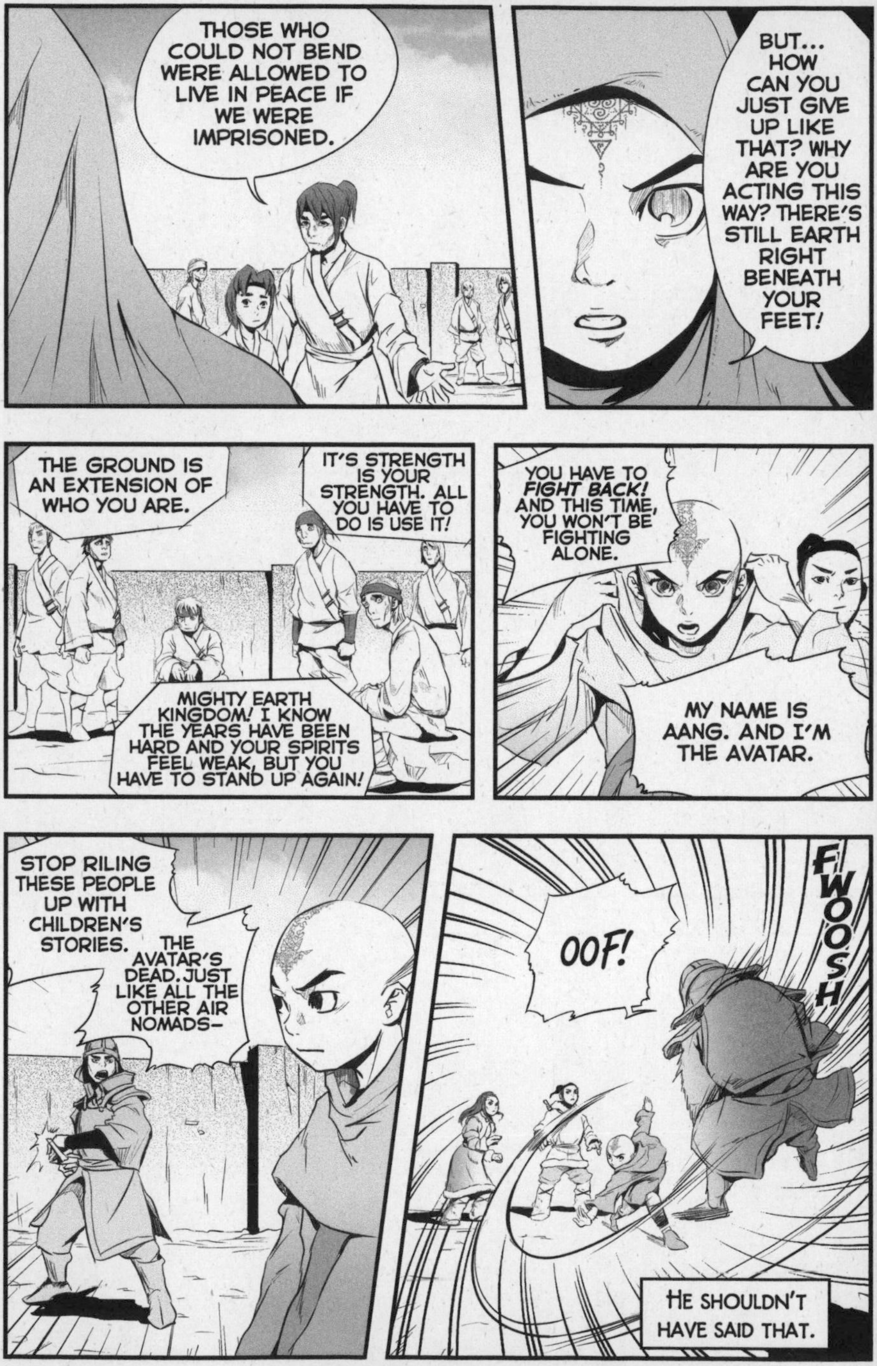
THOSE WHO COULD NOT BEND WERE ALLOWED TO LIVE IN PEACE IF WE WERE IMPRISONED.
BUT... HOW CAN YOU JUST GIVE UP LIKE THAT? WHY ARE YOU ACTING THIS WAY? THERE'S STILL EARTH RIGHT BENEATH YOUR FEET!
THE GROUND IS AN EXTENSION OF WHO YOU ARE.
IT'S STRENGTH IS YOUR STRENGTH. ALL YOU HAVE TO DO IS USE IT!
MIGHTY EARTH KINGDOM! I KNOW THE YEARS HAVE BEEN HARD AND YOUR SPIRITS FEEL WEAK, BUT YOU HAVE TO STAND UP AGAIN!
YOU HAVE TO *FIGHT BACK!* AND THIS TIME, YOU WON'T BE FIGHTING ALONE.
MY NAME IS AANG. AND I'M THE AVATAR.
STOP RILING THESE PEOPLE UP WITH CHILDREN'S STORIES.
THE AVATAR'S DEAD. JUST LIKE ALL THE OTHER AIR NOMADS–
OOF!
FWOOSH
HE SHOULDN'T HAVE SAID THAT.

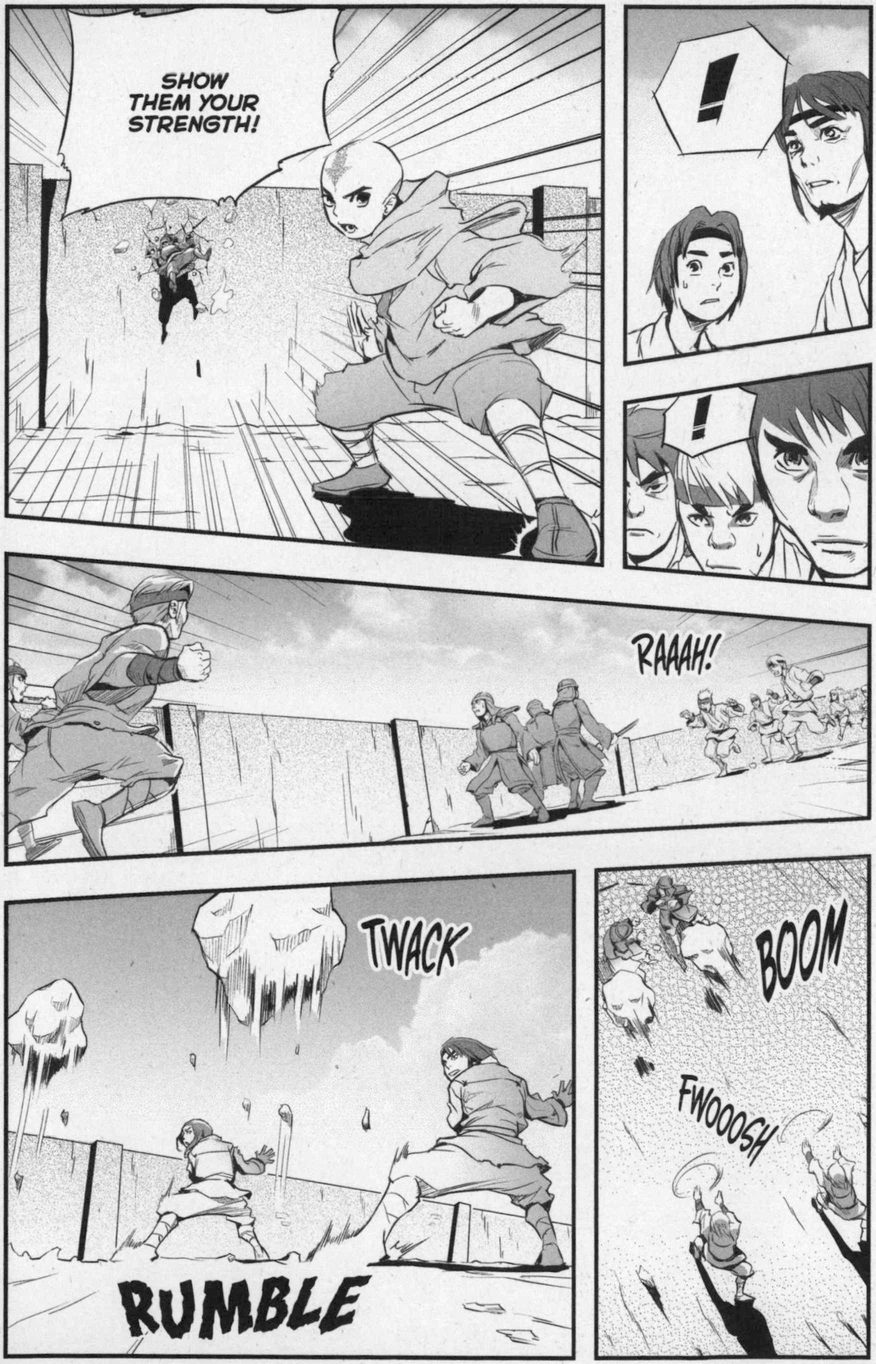
SHOW THEM YOUR STRENGTH!
!
!
RAAAH!
TWACK
RUMBLE
BOOM
FWOOOSH

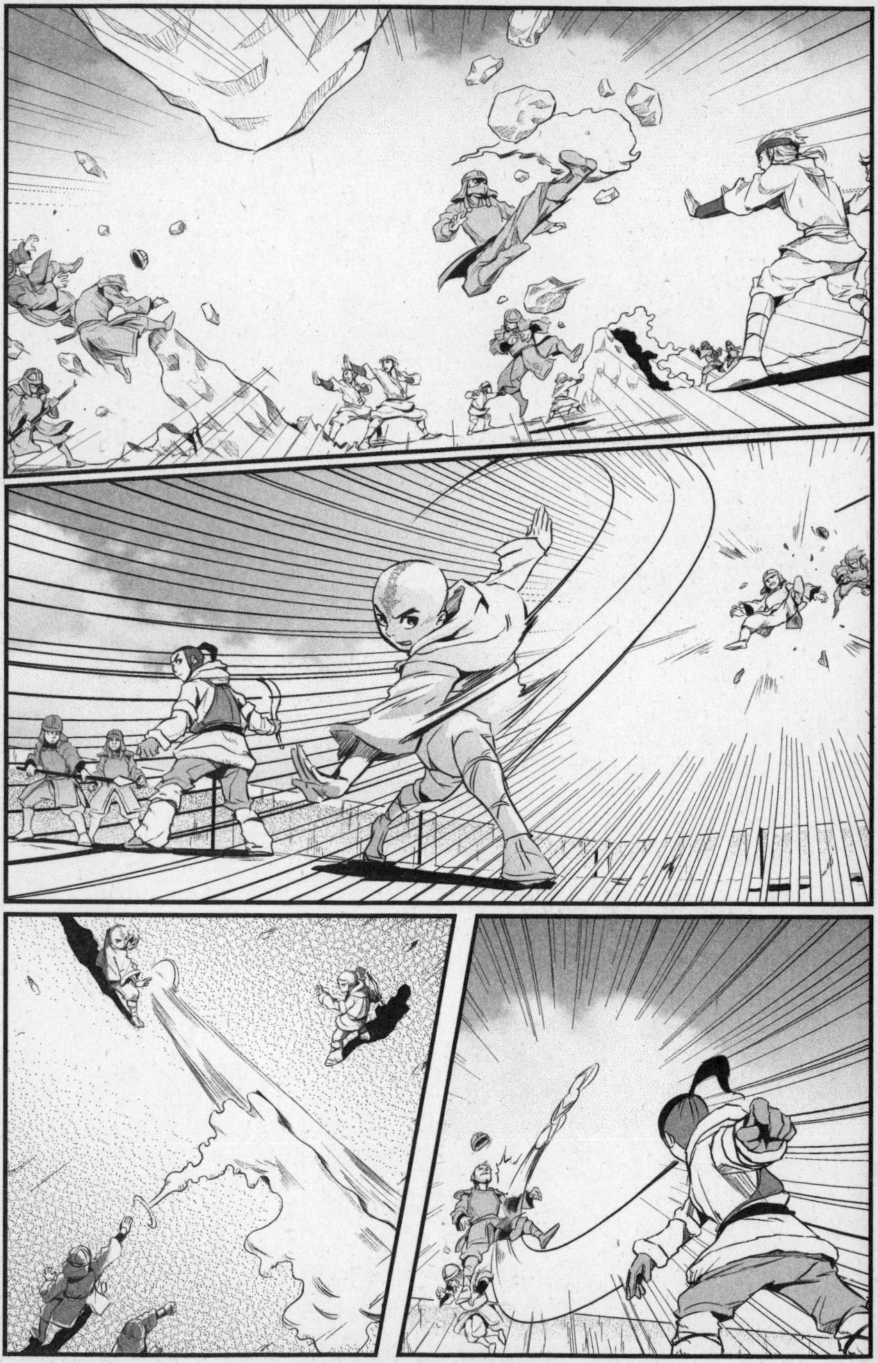

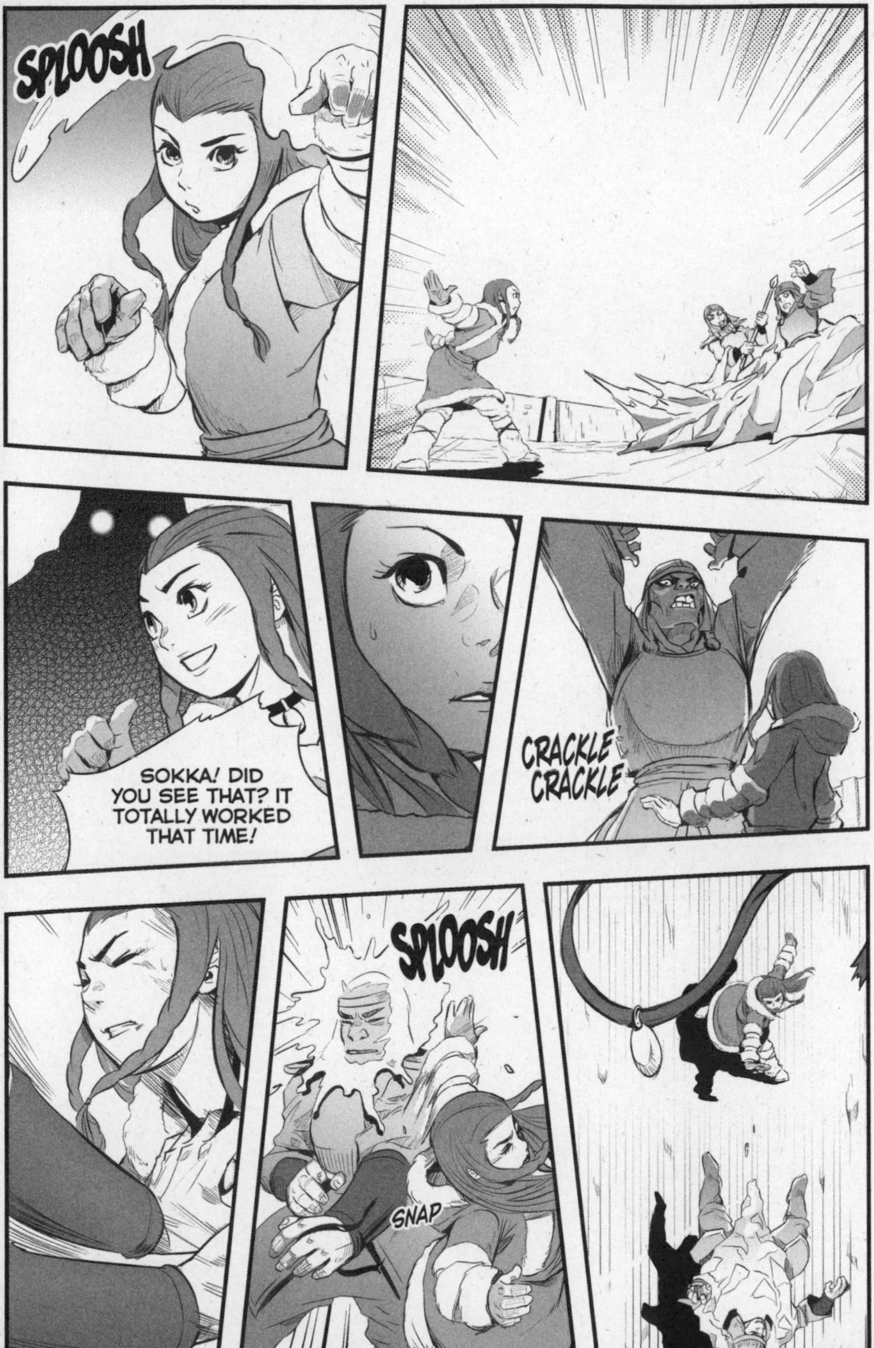
SPLOOSH
SOKKA! DID YOU SEE THAT? IT TOTALLY WORKED THAT TIME!
CRACKLE CRACKLE
SPLOOSH
SNAP

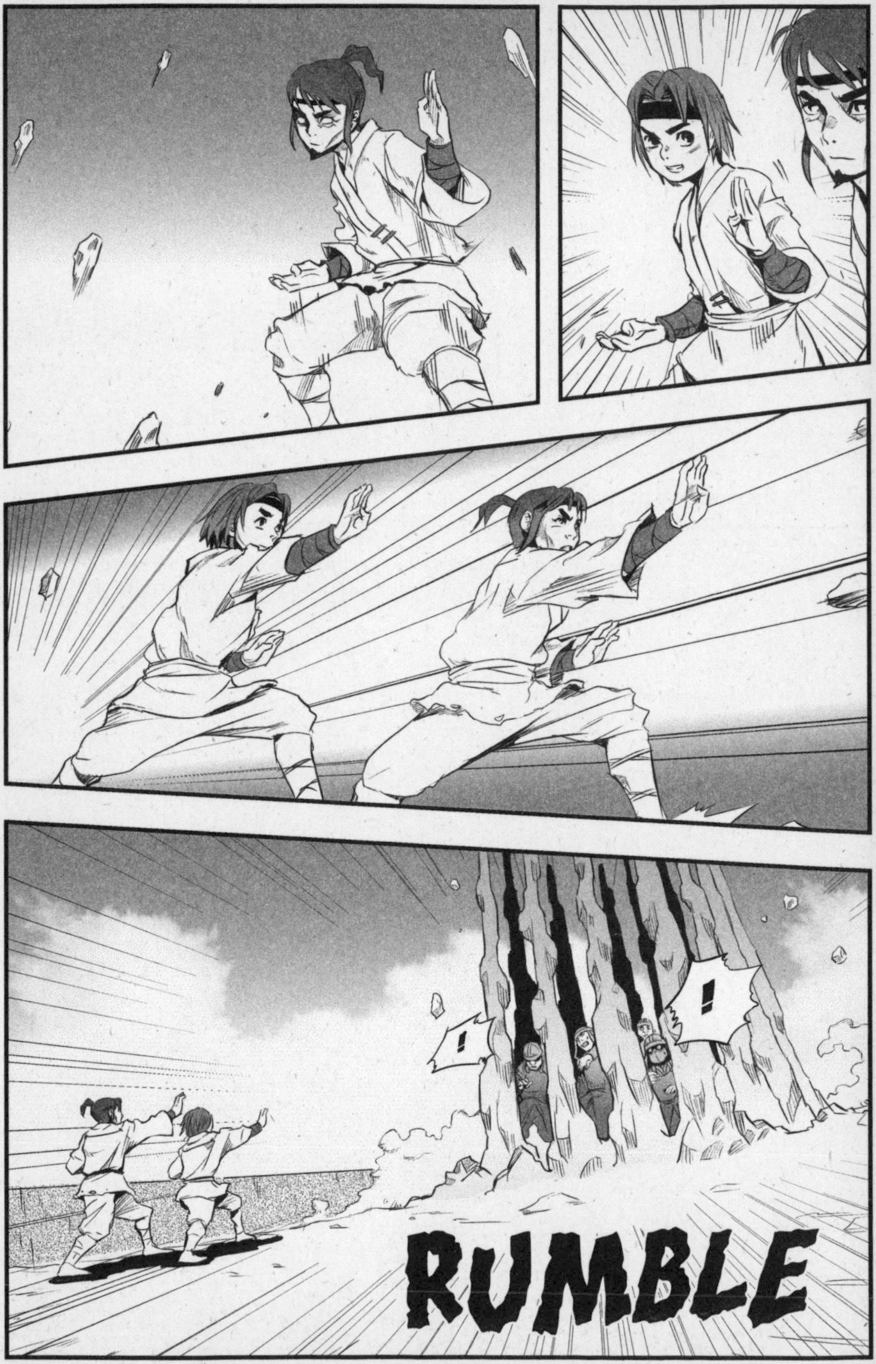
!
!
RUMBLE

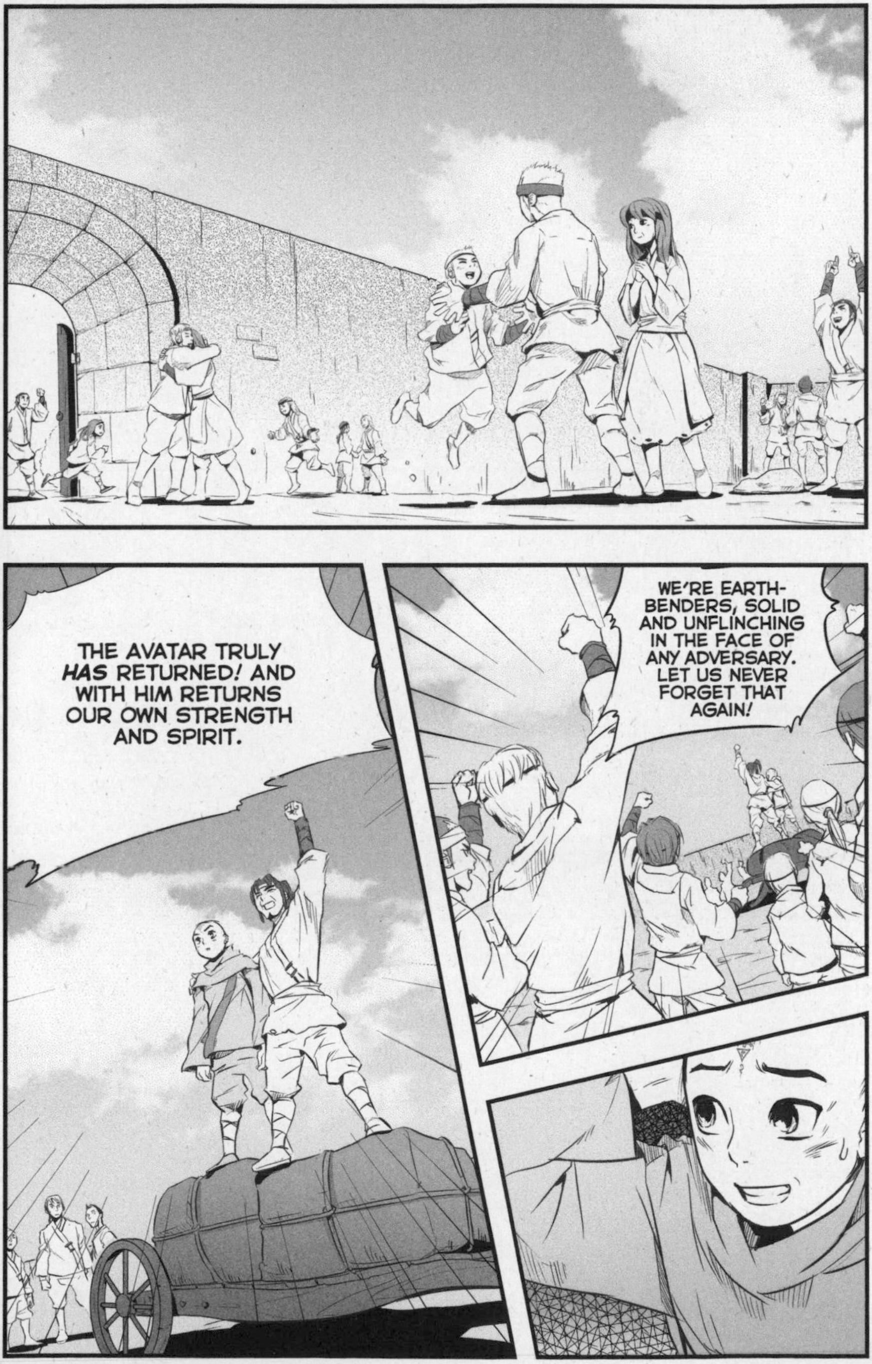
THE AVATAR TRULY HAS RETURNED! AND WITH HIM RETURNS OUR OWN STRENGTH AND SPIRIT.
WE'RE EARTH-BENDERS, SOLID AND UNFLINCHING IN THE FACE OF ANY ADVERSARY. LET US NEVER FORGET THAT AGAIN!

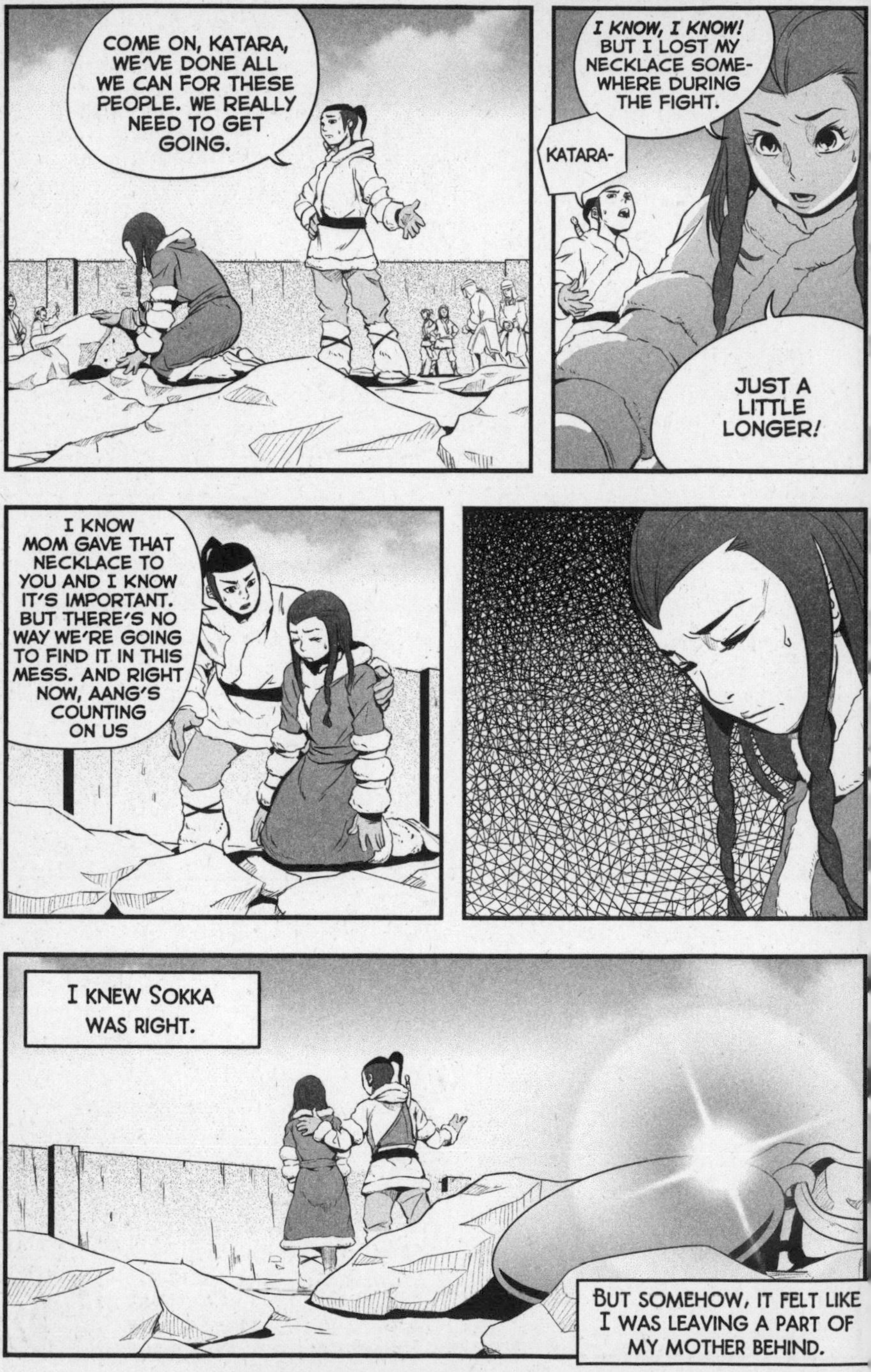
COME ON, KATARA, WE'VE DONE ALL WE CAN FOR THESE PEOPLE. WE REALLY NEED TO GET GOING.
I KNOW, I KNOW! BUT I LOST MY NECKLACE SOMEWHERE DURING THE FIGHT.
KATARA-
JUST A LITTLE LONGER!
I KNOW MOM GAVE THAT NECKLACE TO YOU AND I KNOW IT'S IMPORTANT. BUT THERE'S NO WAY WE'RE GOING TO FIND IT IN THIS MESS. AND RIGHT NOW, AANG'S COUNTING ON US
I KNEW SOKKA WAS RIGHT.
BUT SOMEHOW, IT FELT LIKE I WAS LEAVING A PART OF MY MOTHER BEHIND.

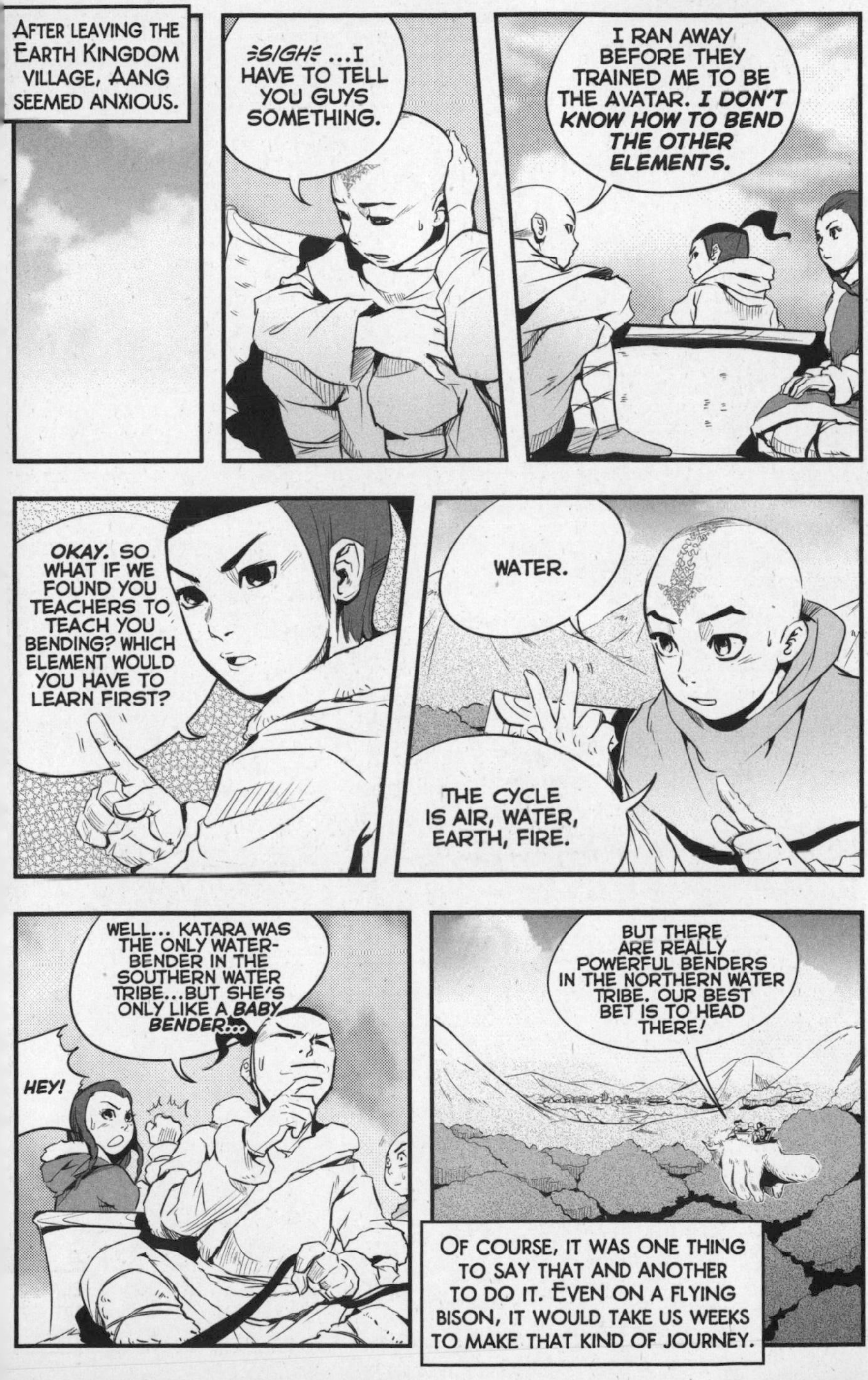
AFTER LEAVING THE EARTH KINGDOM VILLAGE, AANG SEEMED ANXIOUS.
SIGH ...I HAVE TO TELL YOU GUYS SOMETHING.
I RAN AWAY BEFORE THEY TRAINED ME TO BE THE AVATAR. I DON'T KNOW HOW TO BEND THE OTHER ELEMENTS.
OKAY. SO WHAT IF WE FOUND YOU TEACHERS TO TEACH YOU BENDING? WHICH ELEMENT WOULD YOU HAVE TO LEARN FIRST?
WATER.
THE CYCLE IS AIR, WATER, EARTH, FIRE.
WELL... KATARA WAS THE ONLY WATER-BENDER IN THE SOUTHERN WATER TRIBE...BUT SHE'S ONLY LIKE A BABY BENDER...
HEY!
BUT THERE ARE REALLY POWERFUL BENDERS IN THE NORTHERN WATER TRIBE. OUR BEST BET IS TO HEAD THERE!
OF COURSE, IT WAS ONE THING TO SAY THAT AND ANOTHER TO DO IT. EVEN ON A FLYING BISON, IT WOULD TAKE US WEEKS TO MAKE THAT KIND OF JOURNEY.

THE MOST IMPORTANT THING WAS FINDING A WATERBENDING MASTER FOR AANG. WE DIDN'T HAVE TIME TO HELP EVERY KID OR SAVE EVERY VILLAGE, ALTHOUGH WE WANTED TO. BUT AANG'S RETURN HAD AN EFFECT WE HADN'T COUNTED ON.

HE REMINDED PEOPLE OF HOW THINGS USED TO BE. HE INSPIRED THEM TO FIGHT FOR WHAT THE FIRE NATION HAD TAKEN FROM THEM.

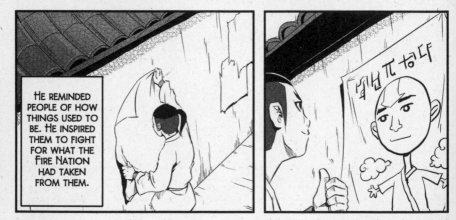

REBELLIONS SPREAD ACROSS THE EARTH KINGDOM, FOLLOWING US AS WE TRAVELED NORTH, AND THE FIRE NATION'S HOLD BEGAN TO WEAKEN.

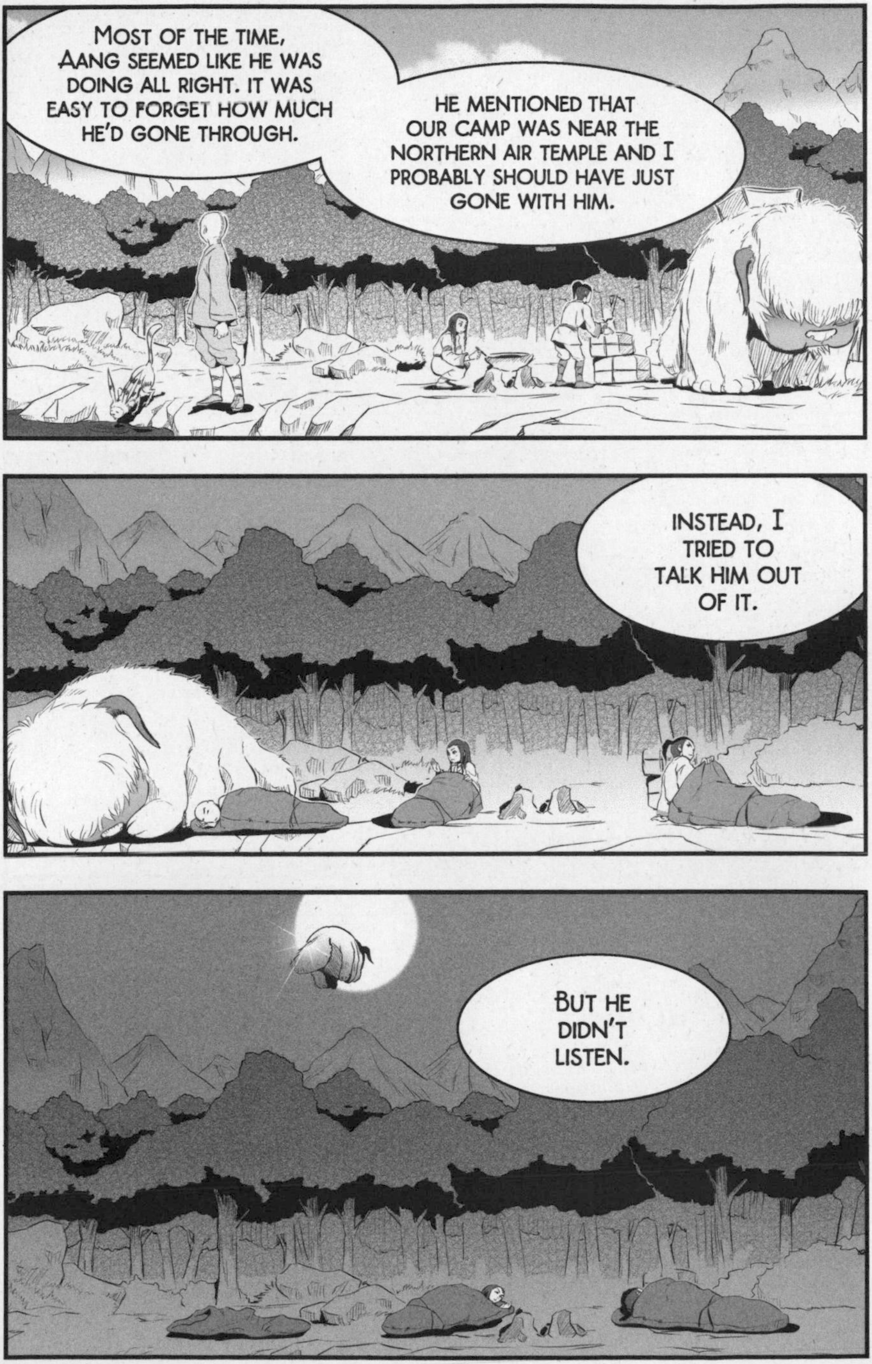
MOST OF THE TIME, AANG SEEMED LIKE HE WAS DOING ALL RIGHT. IT WAS EASY TO FORGET HOW MUCH HE'D GONE THROUGH.
HE MENTIONED THAT OUR CAMP WAS NEAR THE NORTHERN AIR TEMPLE AND I PROBABLY SHOULD HAVE JUST GONE WITH HIM.
INSTEAD, I TRIED TO TALK HIM OUT OF IT.
BUT HE DIDN'T LISTEN.

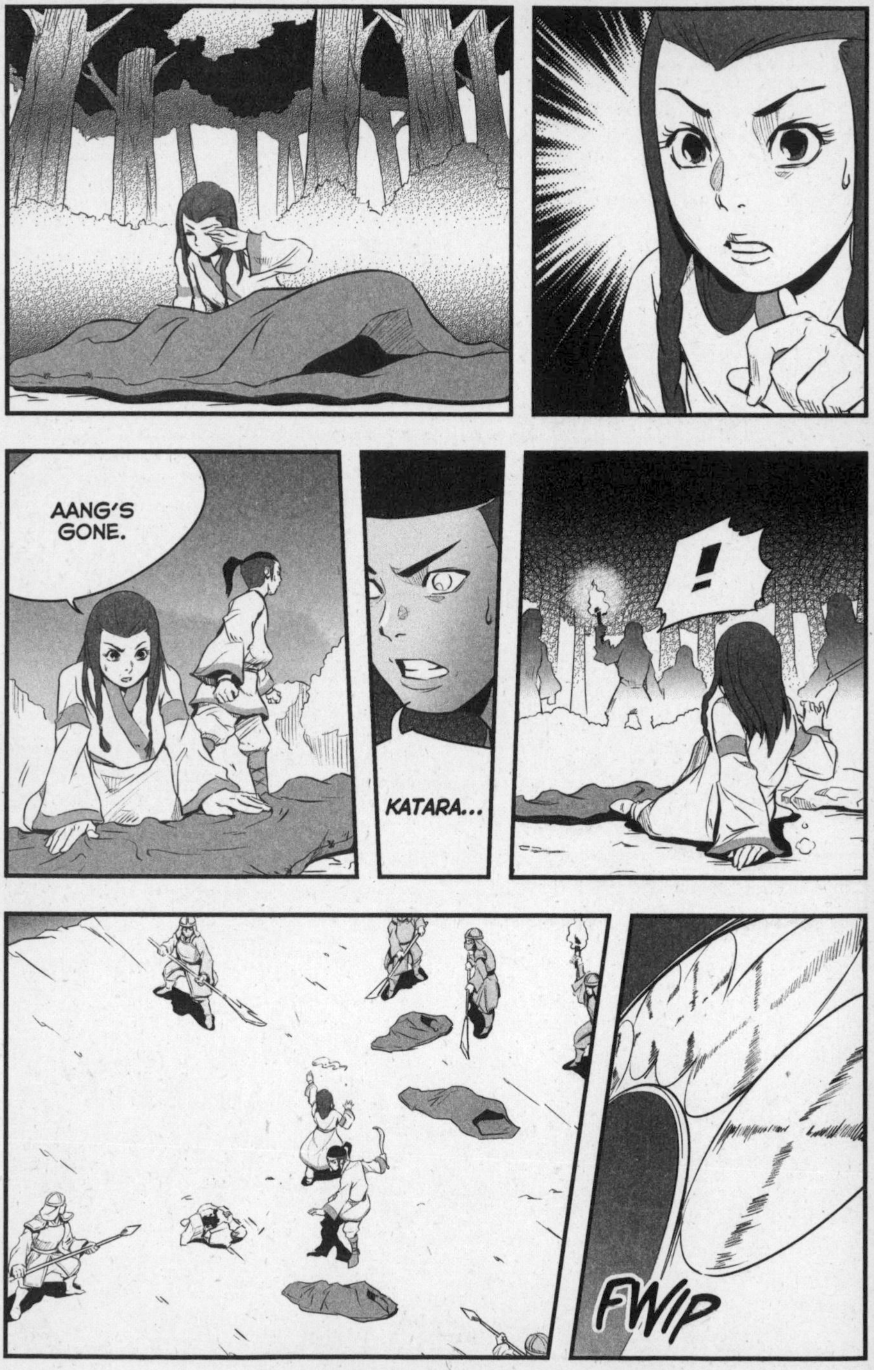
AANG'S GONE.
KATARA...
!
FWIP

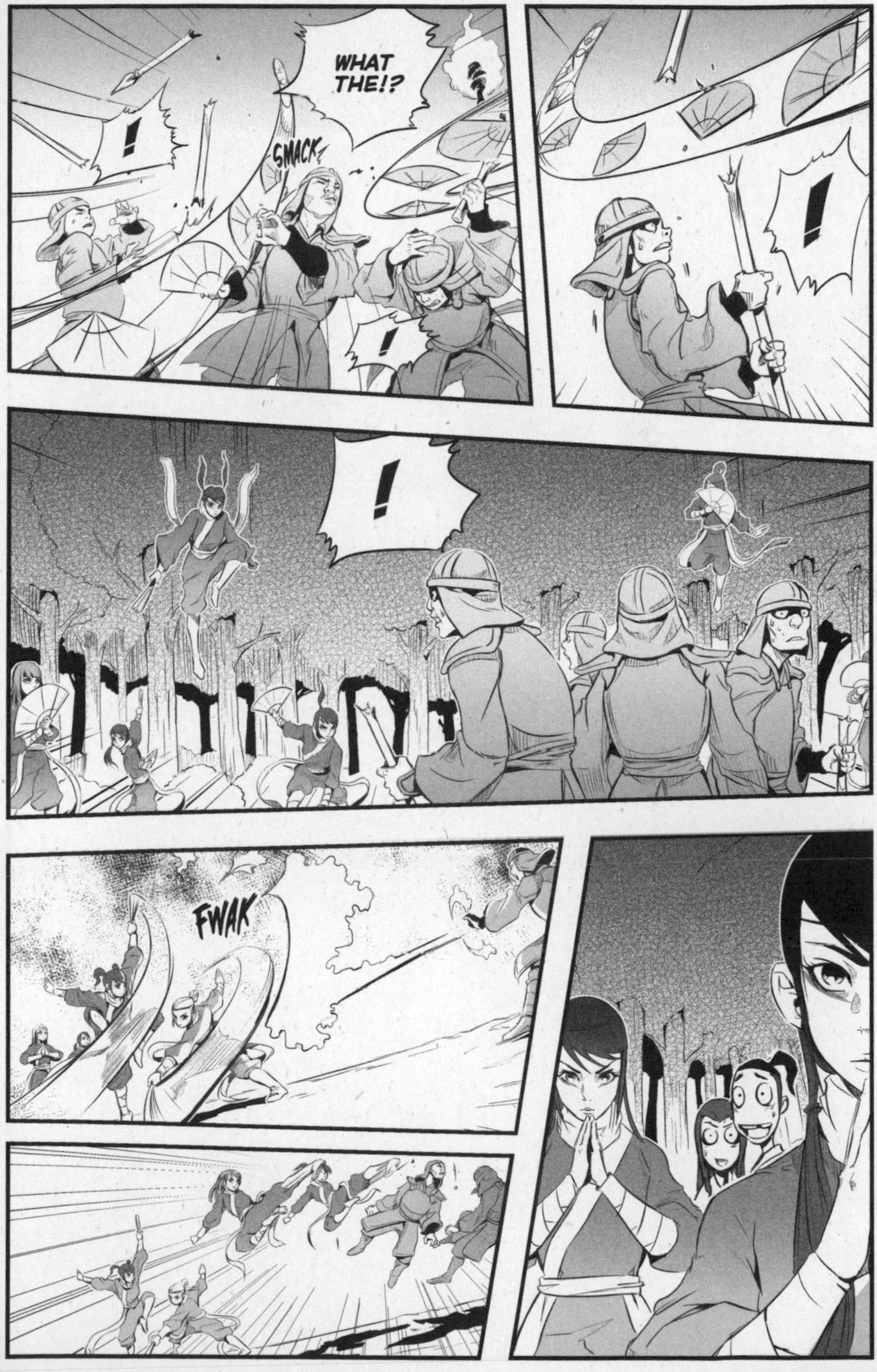
!
WHAT THE!?
SMACK
!
!
!
FWAK

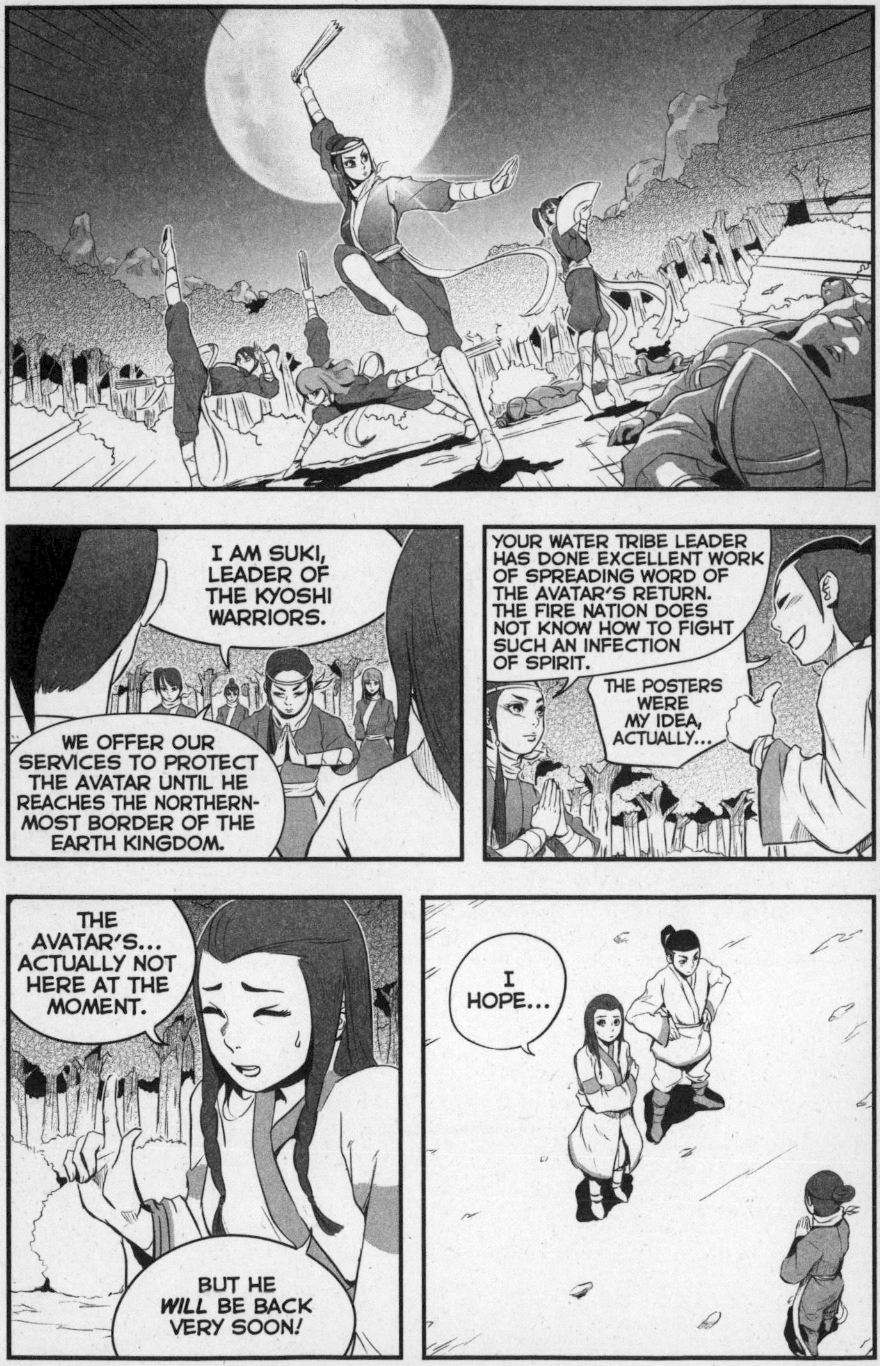
I AM SUKI, LEADER OF THE KYOSHI WARRIORS.
WE OFFER OUR SERVICES TO PROTECT THE AVATAR UNTIL HE REACHES THE NORTHERN-MOST BORDER OF THE EARTH KINGDOM.
YOUR WATER TRIBE LEADER HAS DONE EXCELLENT WORK OF SPREADING WORD OF THE AVATAR'S RETURN. THE FIRE NATION DOES NOT KNOW HOW TO FIGHT SUCH AN INFECTION OF SPIRIT.
THE POSTERS WERE MY IDEA, ACTUALLY...
THE AVATAR'S... ACTUALLY NOT HERE AT THE MOMENT.
BUT HE *WILL* BE BACK VERY SOON!
I HOPE...

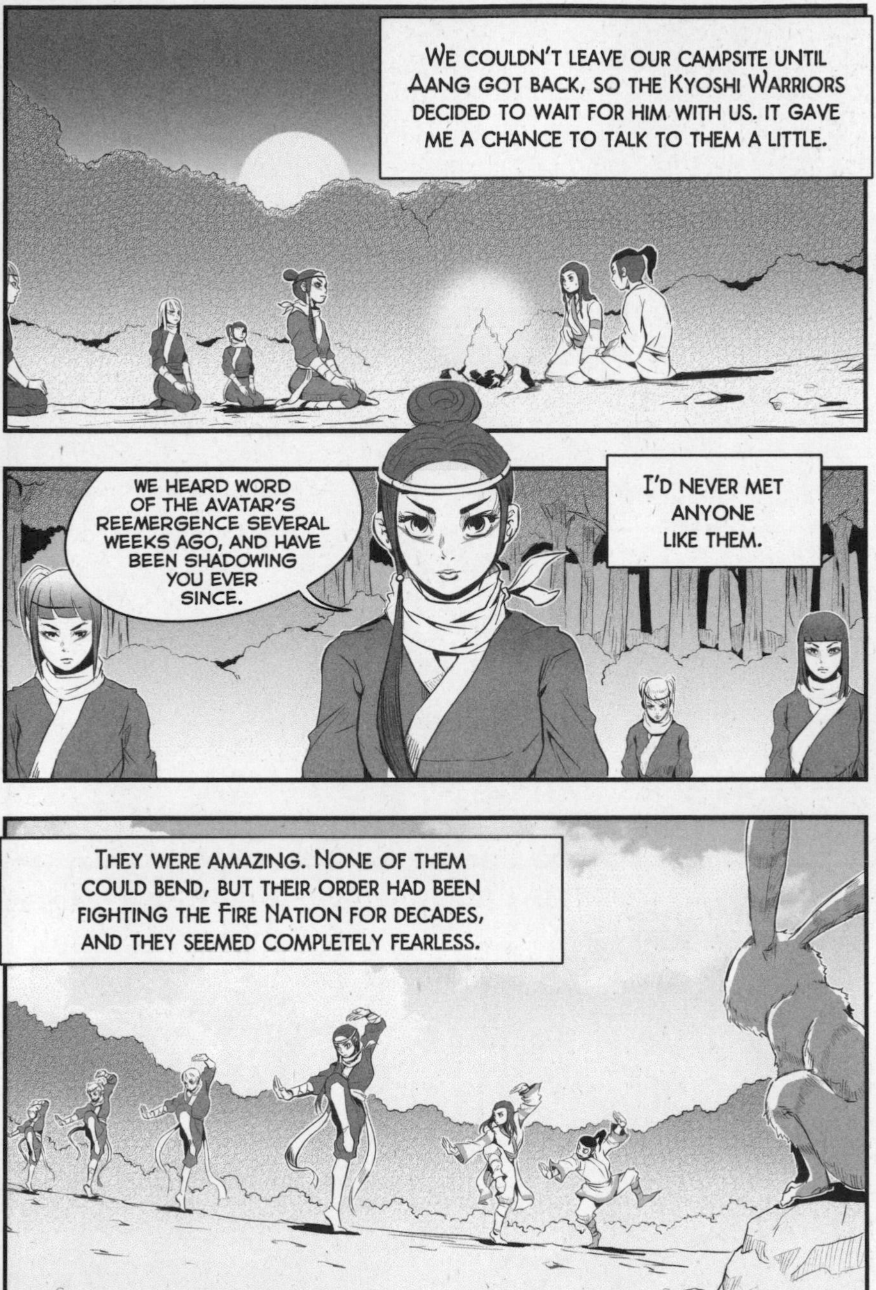

WE COULDN'T LEAVE OUR CAMPSITE UNTIL AANG GOT BACK, SO THE KYOSHI WARRIORS DECIDED TO WAIT FOR HIM WITH US. IT GAVE ME A CHANCE TO TALK TO THEM A LITTLE.
WE HEARD WORD OF THE AVATAR'S REEMERGENCE SEVERAL WEEKS AGO, AND HAVE BEEN SHADOWING YOU EVER SINCE.
I'D NEVER MET ANYONE LIKE THEM.
THEY WERE AMAZING. NONE OF THEM COULD BEND, BUT THEIR ORDER HAD BEEN FIGHTING THE FIRE NATION FOR DECADES, AND THEY SEEMED COMPLETELY FEARLESS.

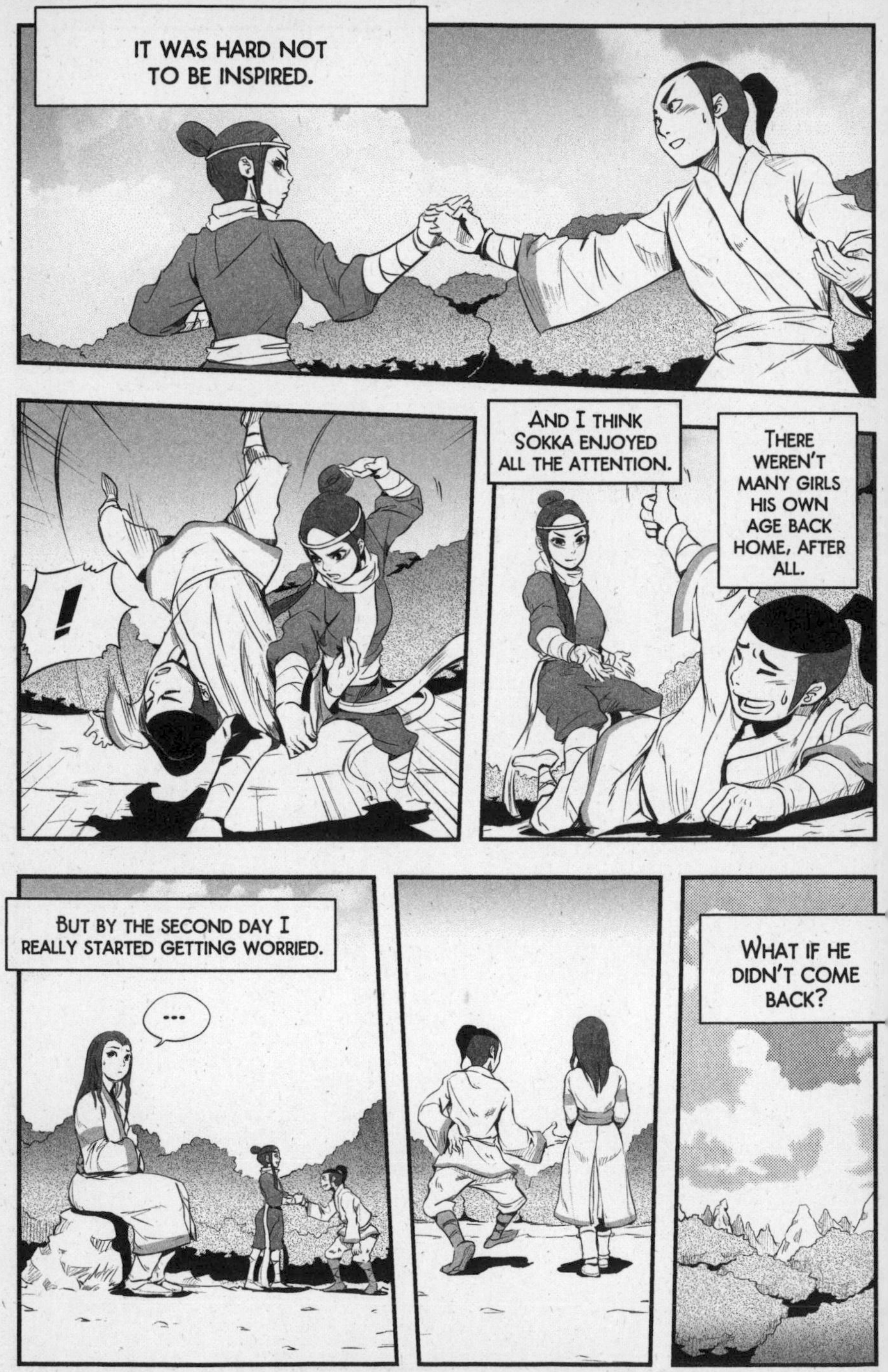
IT WAS HARD NOT TO BE INSPIRED.
!
AND I THINK SOKKA ENJOYED ALL THE ATTENTION.
THERE WEREN'T MANY GIRLS HIS OWN AGE BACK HOME, AFTER ALL.
BUT BY THE SECOND DAY I REALLY STARTED GETTING WORRIED.
...
WHAT IF HE DIDN'T COME BACK?

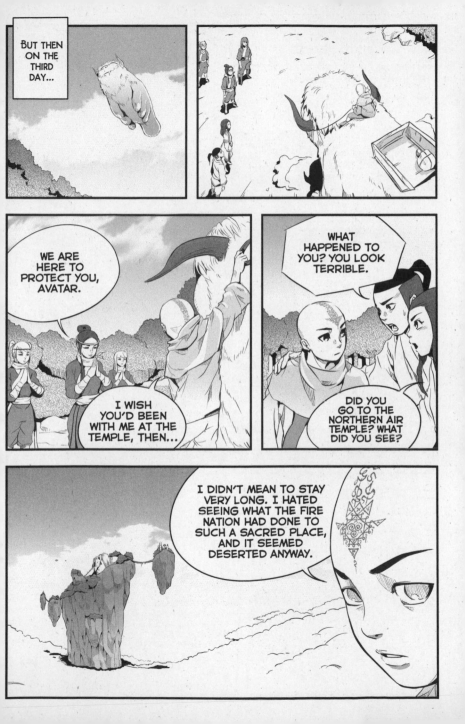

BUT THEN ON THE THIRD DAY...

WE ARE HERE TO PROTECT YOU, AVATAR.

I WISH YOU'D BEEN WITH ME AT THE TEMPLE, THEN...

WHAT HAPPENED TO YOU? YOU LOOK TERRIBLE.

DID YOU GO TO THE NORTHERN AIR TEMPLE? WHAT DID YOU SEE?

I DIDN'T MEAN TO STAY VERY LONG. I HATED SEEING WHAT THE FIRE NATION HAD DONE TO SUCH A SACRED PLACE, AND IT SEEMED DESERTED ANYWAY.

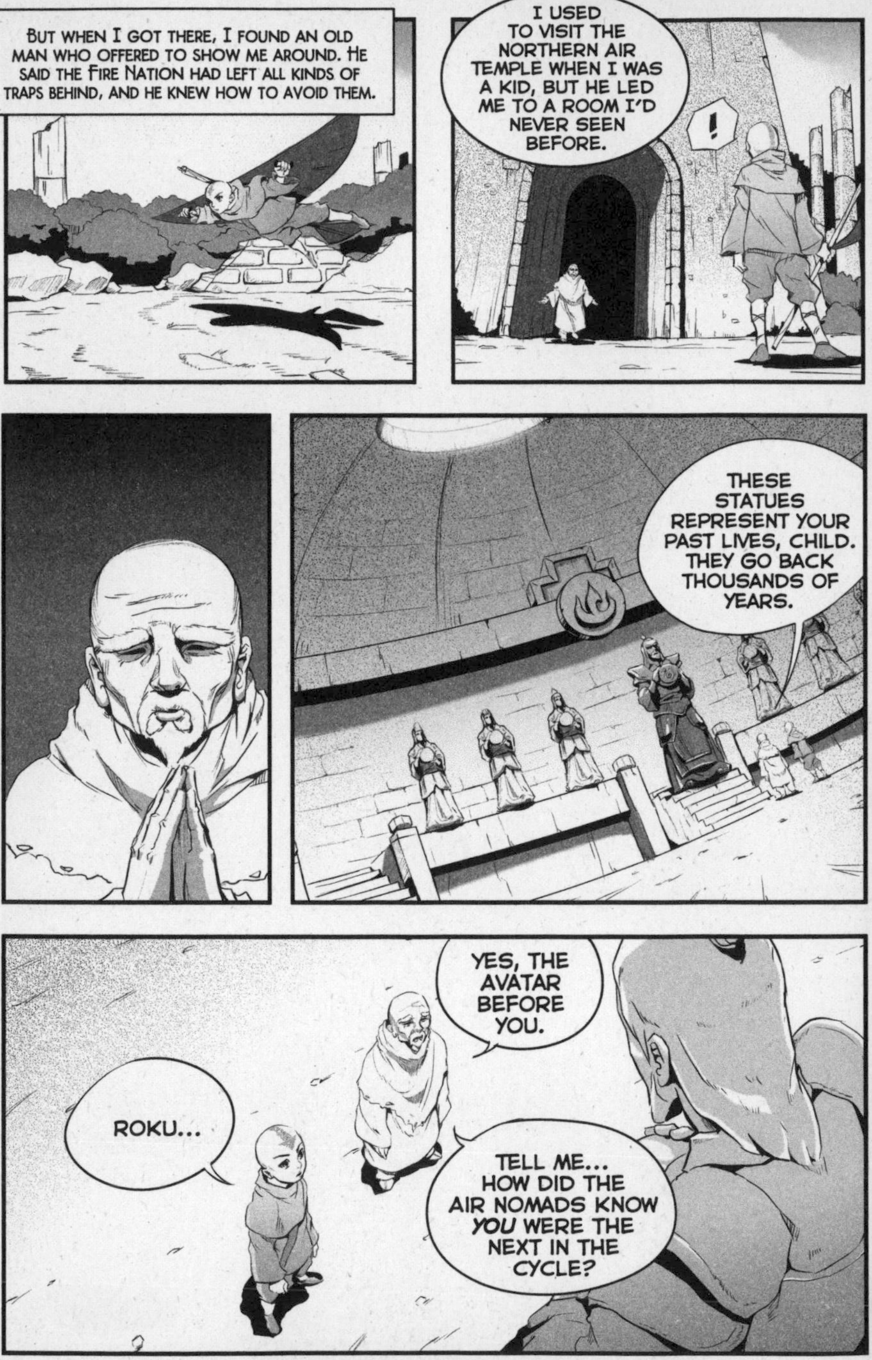
BUT WHEN I GOT THERE, I FOUND AN OLD MAN WHO OFFERED TO SHOW ME AROUND. HE SAID THE FIRE NATION HAD LEFT ALL KINDS OF TRAPS BEHIND, AND HE KNEW HOW TO AVOID THEM.
I USED TO VISIT THE NORTHERN AIR TEMPLE WHEN I WAS A KID, BUT HE LED ME TO A ROOM I'D NEVER SEEN BEFORE.
!
THESE STATUES REPRESENT YOUR PAST LIVES, CHILD. THEY GO BACK THOUSANDS OF YEARS.
ROKU...
YES, THE AVATAR BEFORE YOU.
TELL ME... HOW DID THE AIR NOMADS KNOW *YOU* WERE THE NEXT IN THE CYCLE?

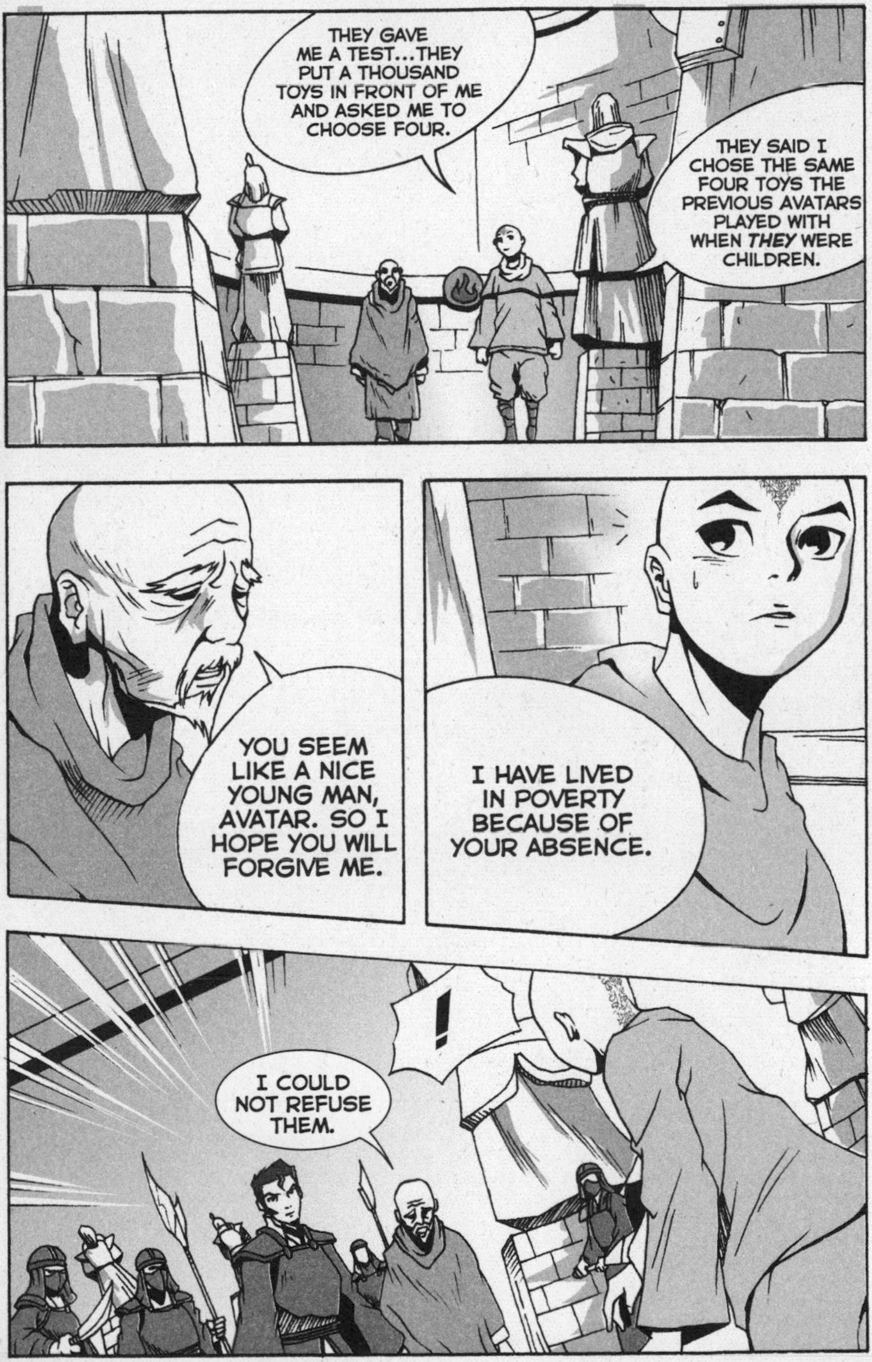
THEY GAVE ME A TEST...THEY PUT A THOUSAND TOYS IN FRONT OF ME AND ASKED ME TO CHOOSE FOUR.
THEY SAID I CHOSE THE SAME FOUR TOYS THE PREVIOUS AVATARS PLAYED WITH WHEN *THEY* WERE CHILDREN.
YOU SEEM LIKE A NICE YOUNG MAN, AVATAR. SO I HOPE YOU WILL FORGIVE ME.
I HAVE LIVED IN POVERTY BECAUSE OF YOUR ABSENCE.
!
I COULD NOT REFUSE THEM.

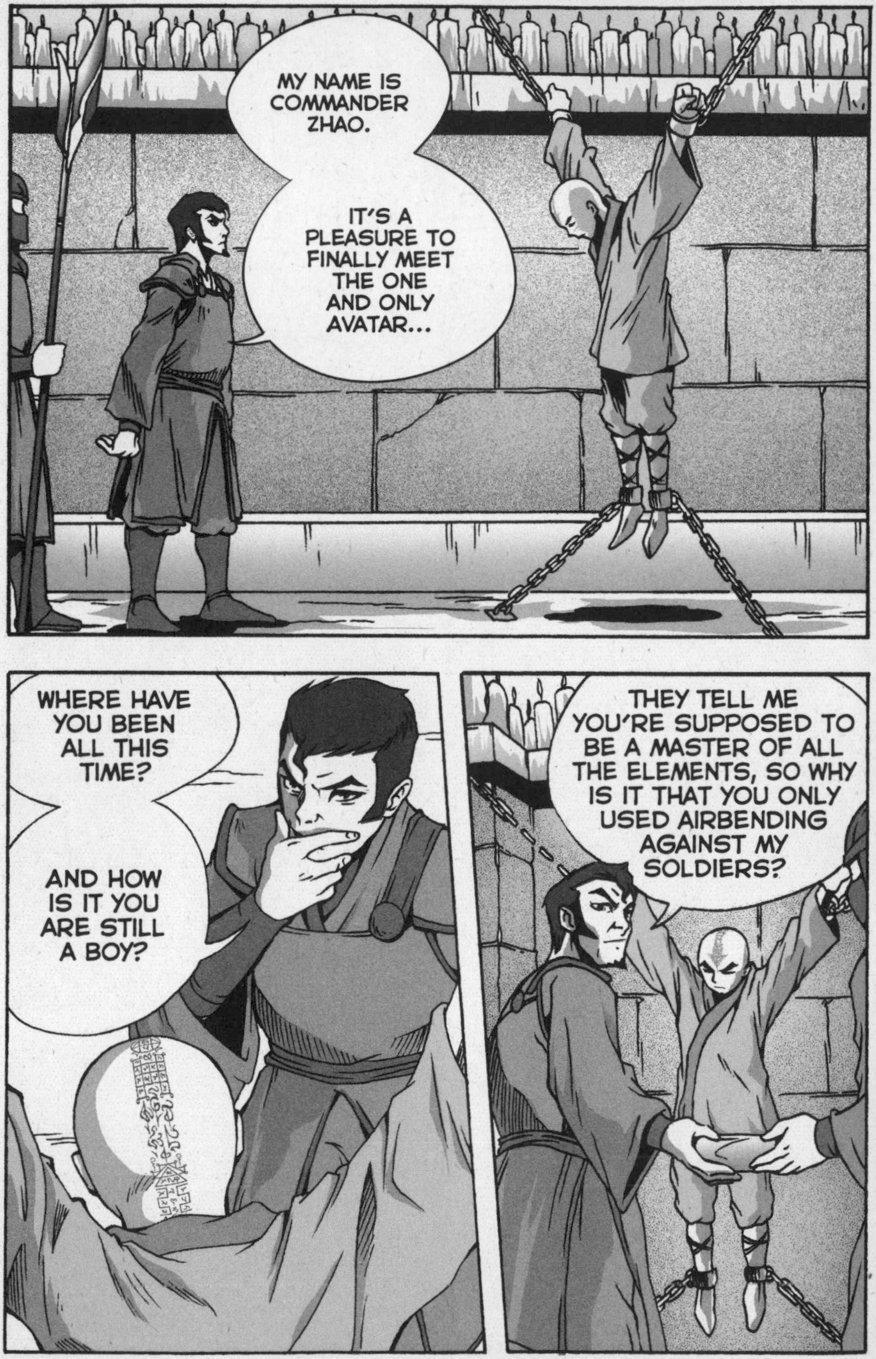
MY NAME IS COMMANDER ZHAO.
IT'S A PLEASURE TO FINALLY MEET THE ONE AND ONLY AVATAR...
WHERE HAVE YOU BEEN ALL THIS TIME?
AND HOW IS IT YOU ARE STILL A BOY?
THEY TELL ME YOU'RE SUPPOSED TO BE A MASTER OF ALL THE ELEMENTS, SO WHY IS IT THAT YOU ONLY USED AIRBENDING AGAINST MY SOLDIERS?

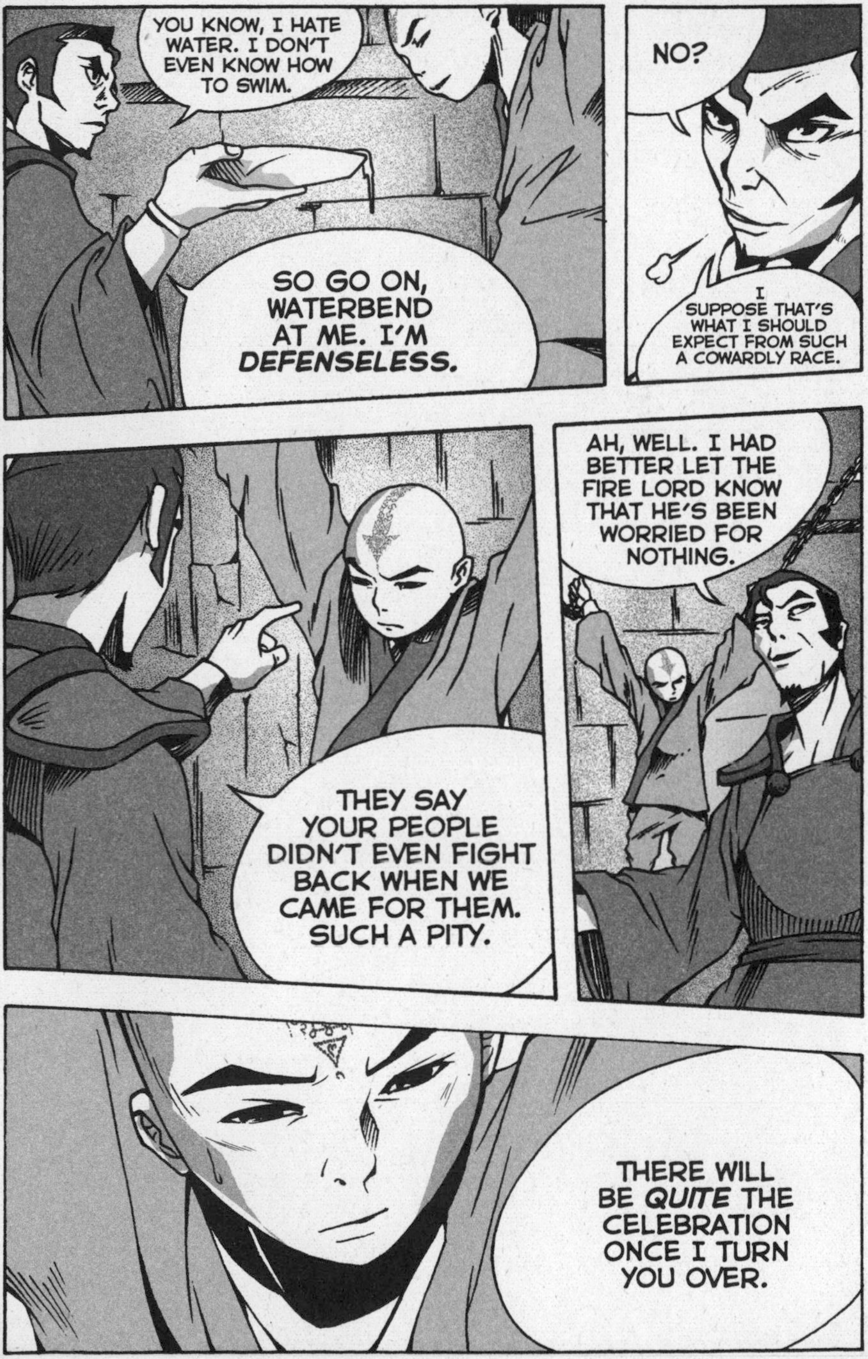
YOU KNOW, I HATE WATER. I DON'T EVEN KNOW HOW TO SWIM.
SO GO ON, WATERBEND AT ME. I'M *DEFENSELESS.*
NO?
I SUPPOSE THAT'S WHAT I SHOULD EXPECT FROM SUCH A COWARDLY RACE.
THEY SAY YOUR PEOPLE DIDN'T EVEN FIGHT BACK WHEN WE CAME FOR THEM. SUCH A PITY.
AH, WELL. I HAD BETTER LET THE FIRE LORD KNOW THAT HE'S BEEN WORRIED FOR NOTHING.
THERE WILL BE *QUITE* THE CELEBRATION ONCE I TURN YOU OVER.

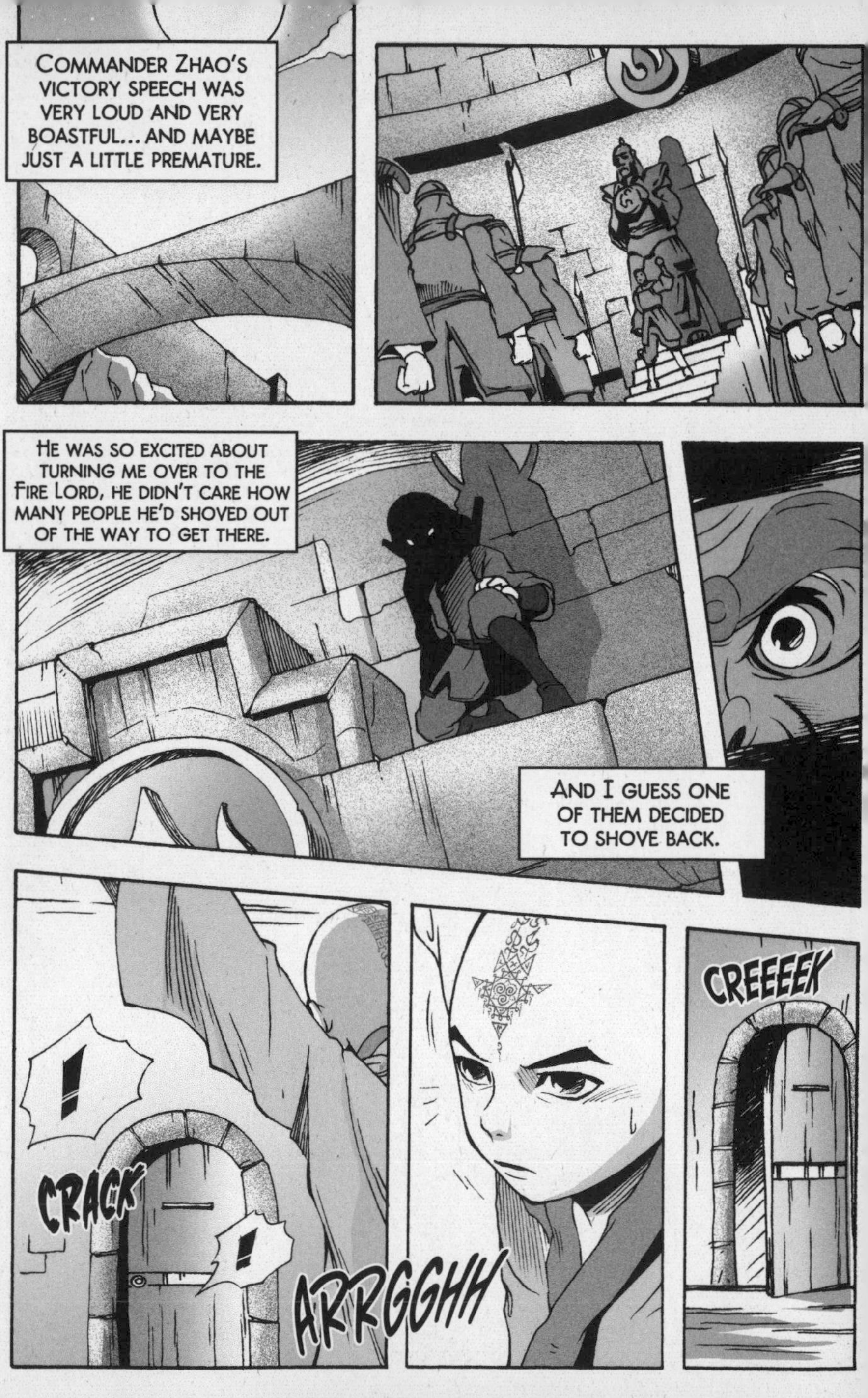
COMMANDER ZHAO'S VICTORY SPEECH WAS VERY LOUD AND VERY BOASTFUL... AND MAYBE JUST A LITTLE PREMATURE.
HE WAS SO EXCITED ABOUT TURNING ME OVER TO THE FIRE LORD, HE DIDN'T CARE HOW MANY PEOPLE HE'D SHOVED OUT OF THE WAY TO GET THERE.
AND I GUESS ONE OF THEM DECIDED TO SHOVE BACK.
!
CRACK
!
ARRGGHH
CREEEEK

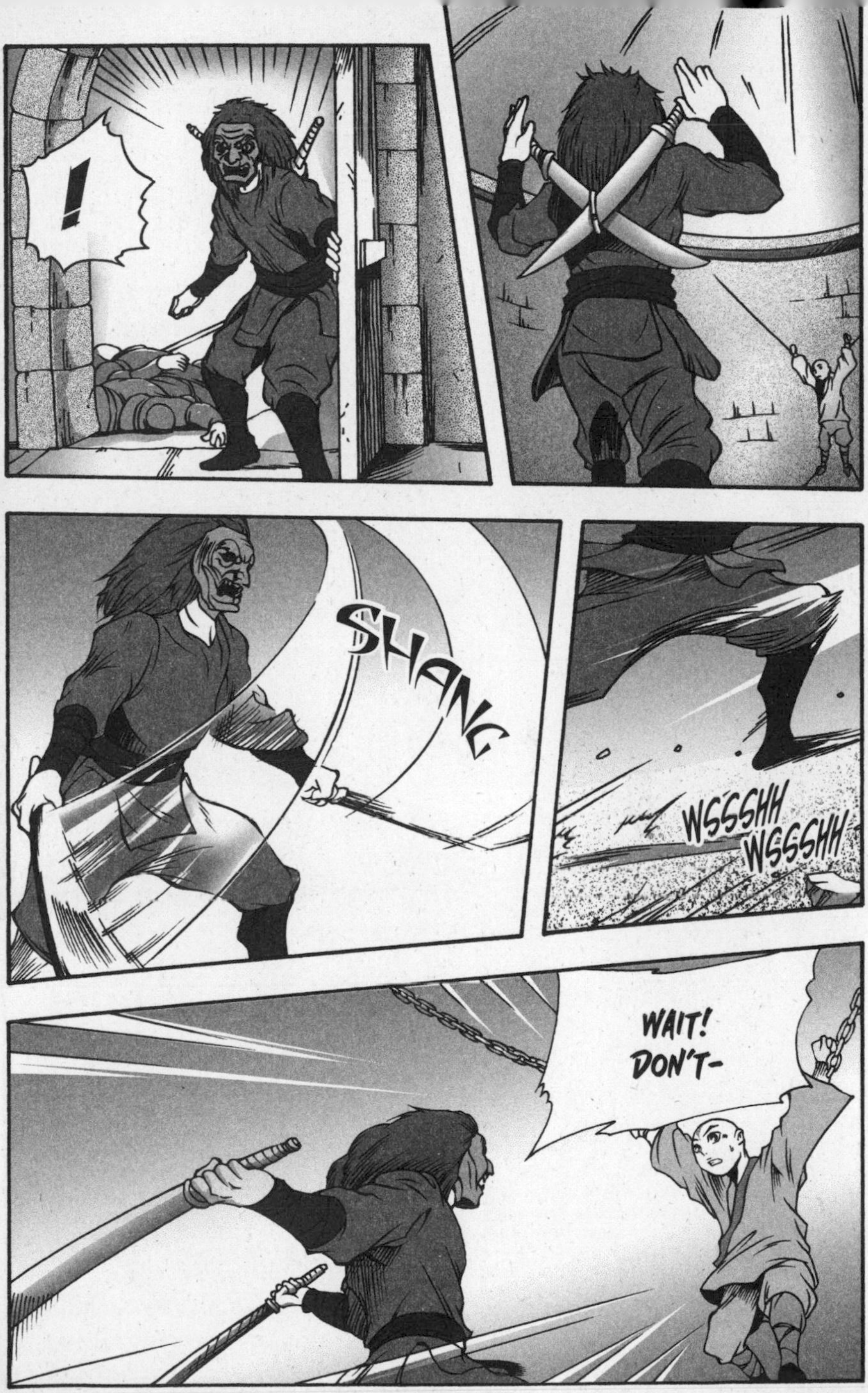
!
SHANG
WSSSHH
WSSSHH
WAIT! DON'T-

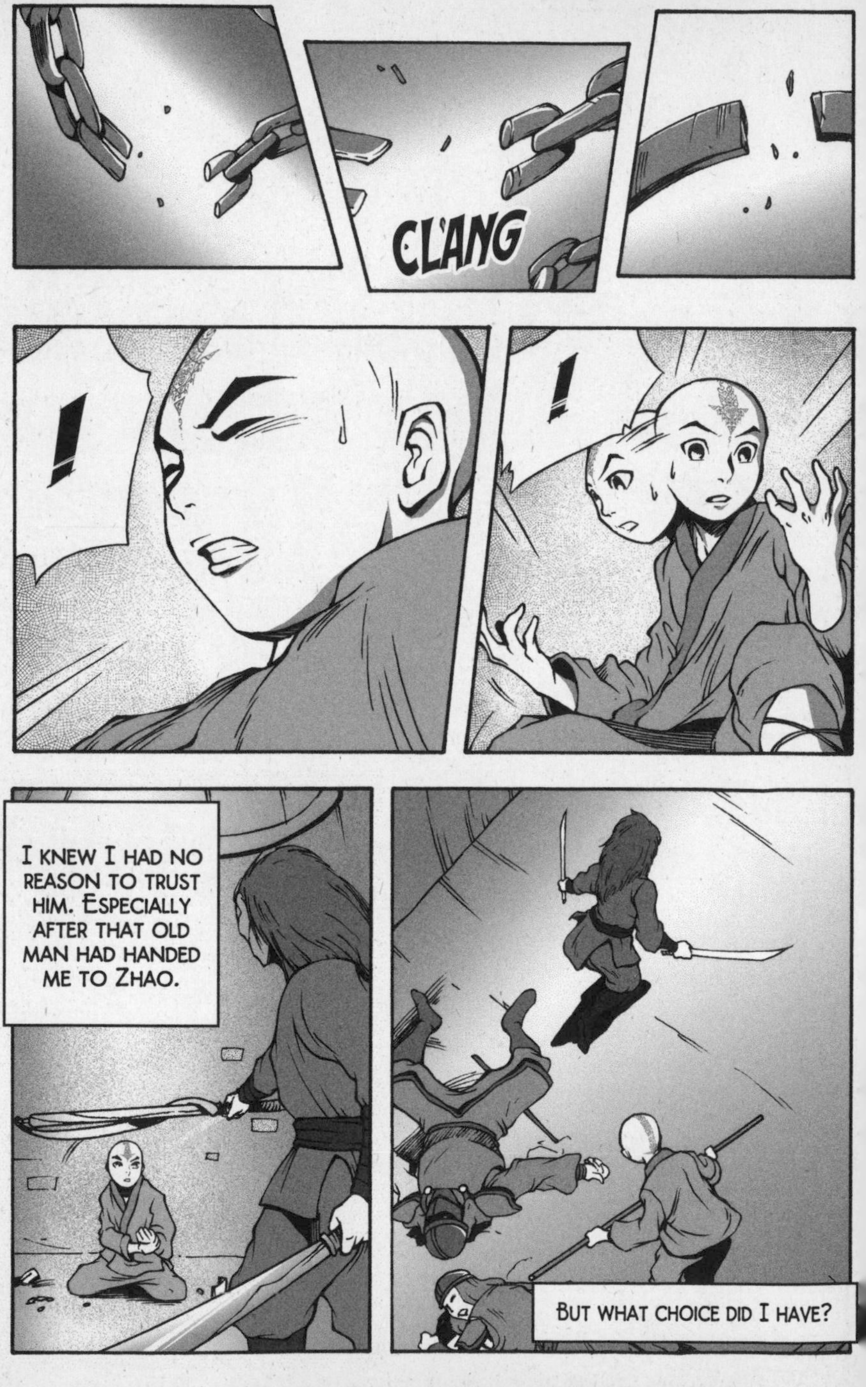
CLANG
!
!
I KNEW I HAD NO REASON TO TRUST HIM. ESPECIALLY AFTER THAT OLD MAN HAD HANDED ME TO ZHAO.
BUT WHAT CHOICE DID I HAVE?

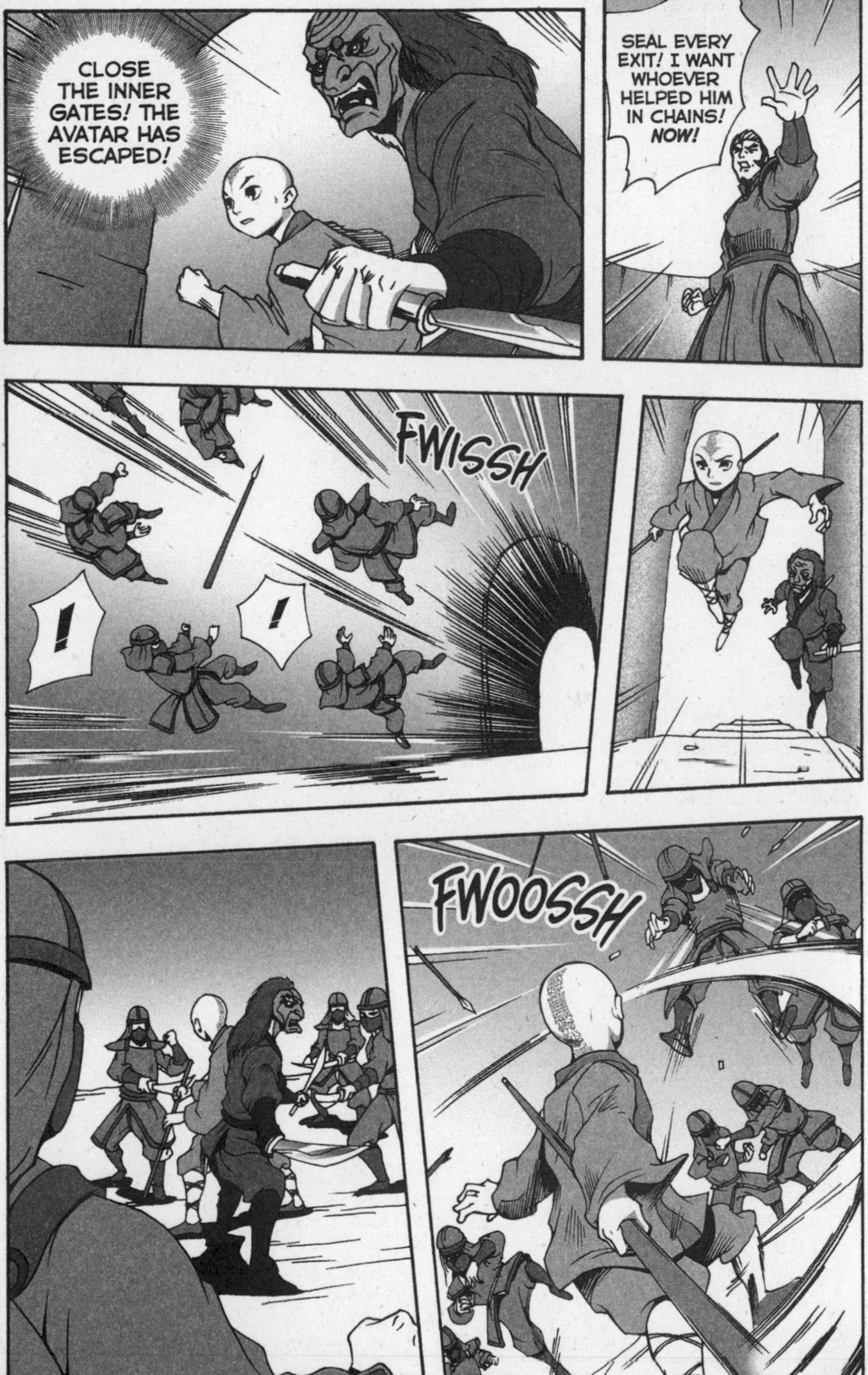
CLOSE THE INNER GATES! THE AVATAR HAS ESCAPED!
SEAL EVERY EXIT! I WANT WHOEVER HELPED HIM IN CHAINS! NOW!
FWISSH
!
!
FWOOSSH

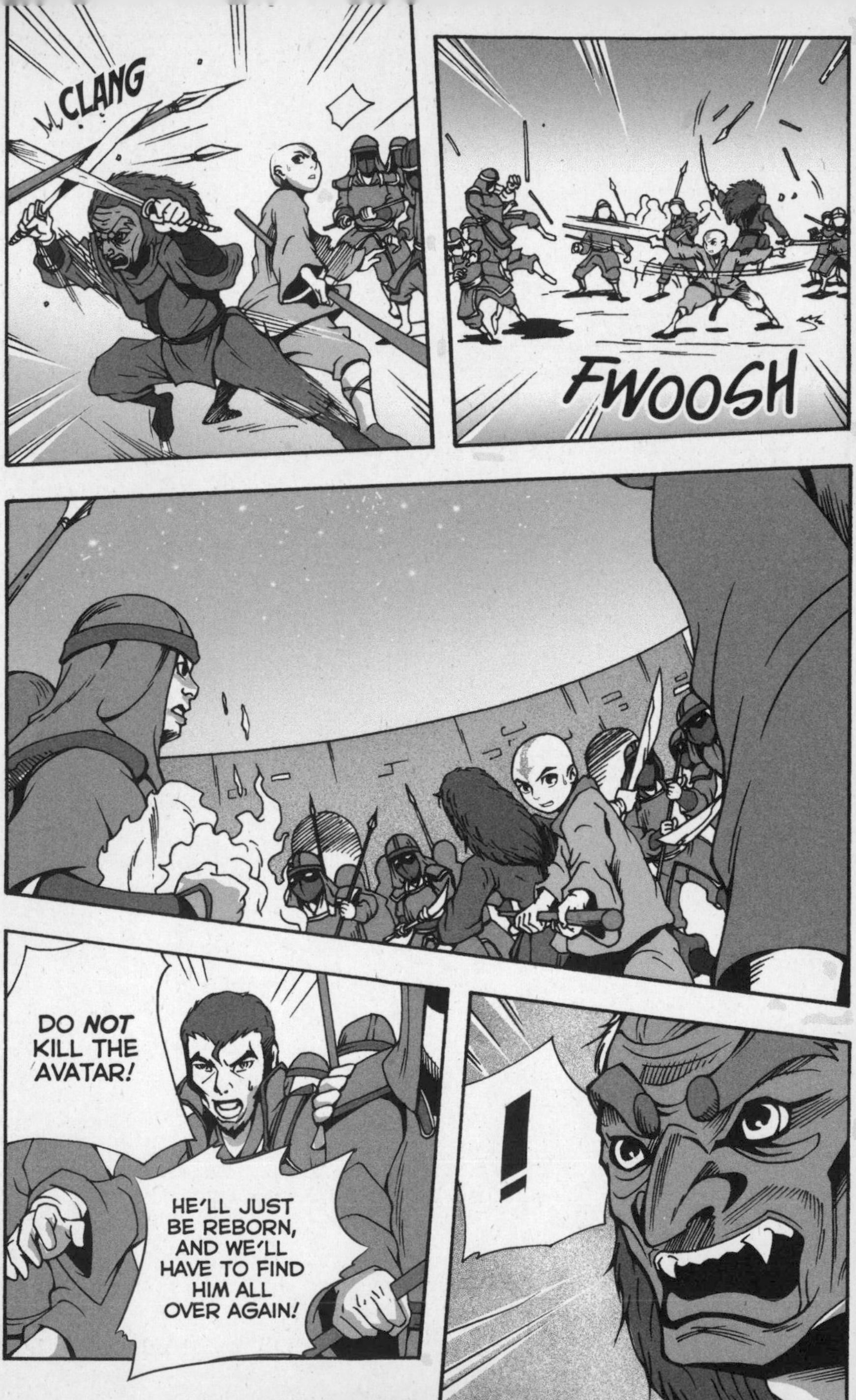
CLANG
FWOOSH
DO NOT KILL THE AVATAR!
HE'LL JUST BE REBORN, AND WE'LL HAVE TO FIND HIM ALL OVER AGAIN!
!

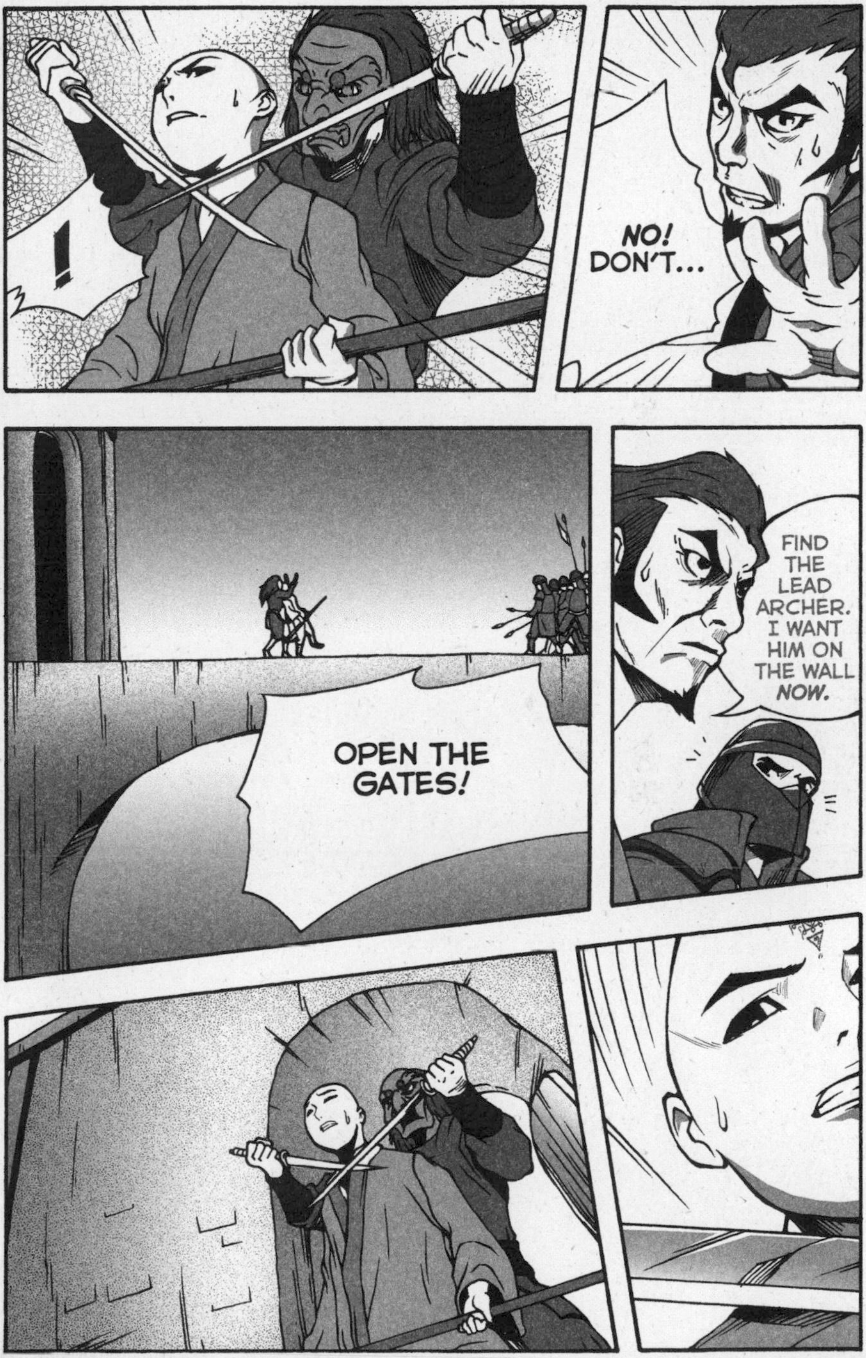
!
NO! DON'T...
OPEN THE GATES!
FIND THE LEAD ARCHER. I WANT HIM ON THE WALL NOW.

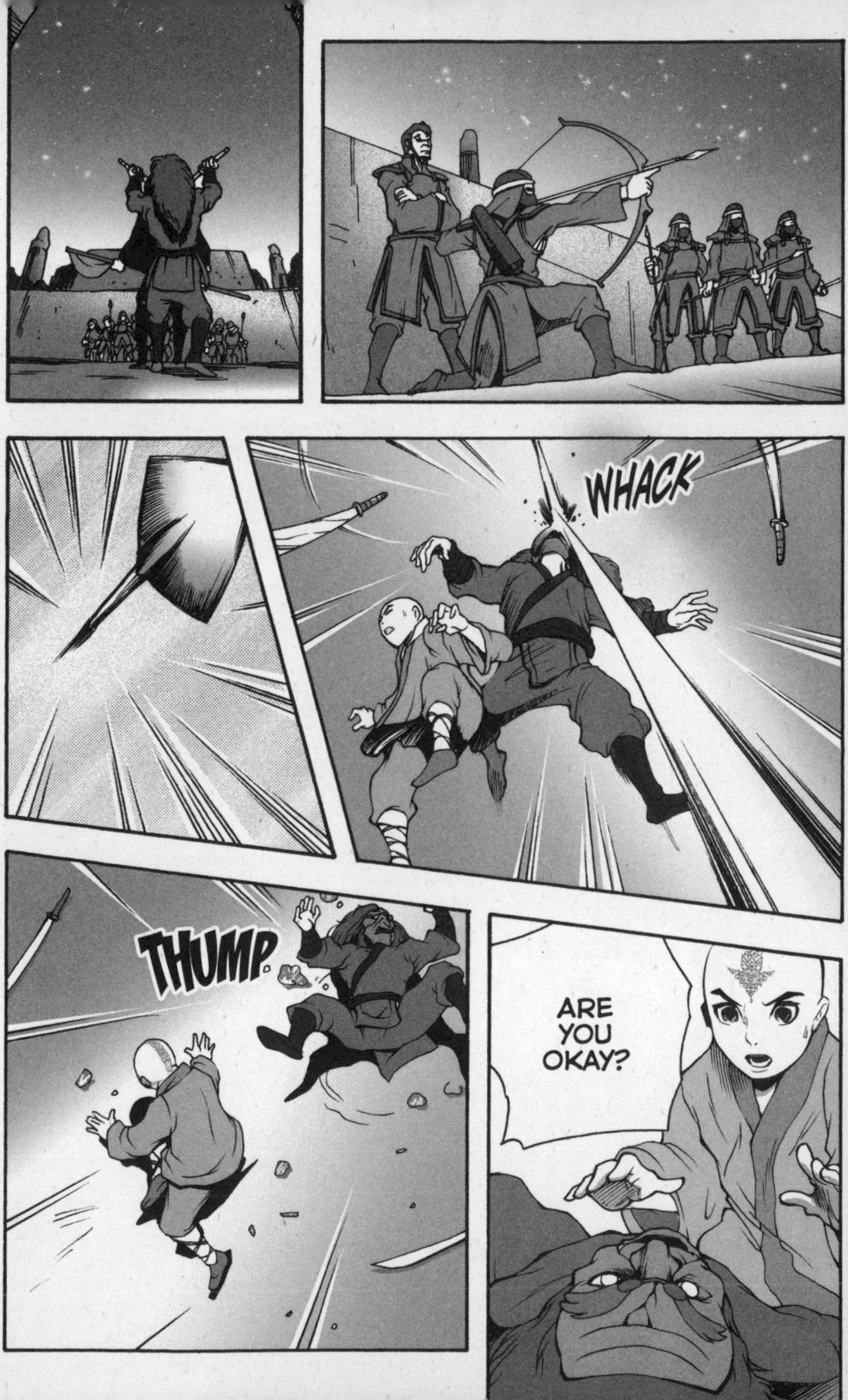
WHACK
THUMP
ARE YOU OKAY?

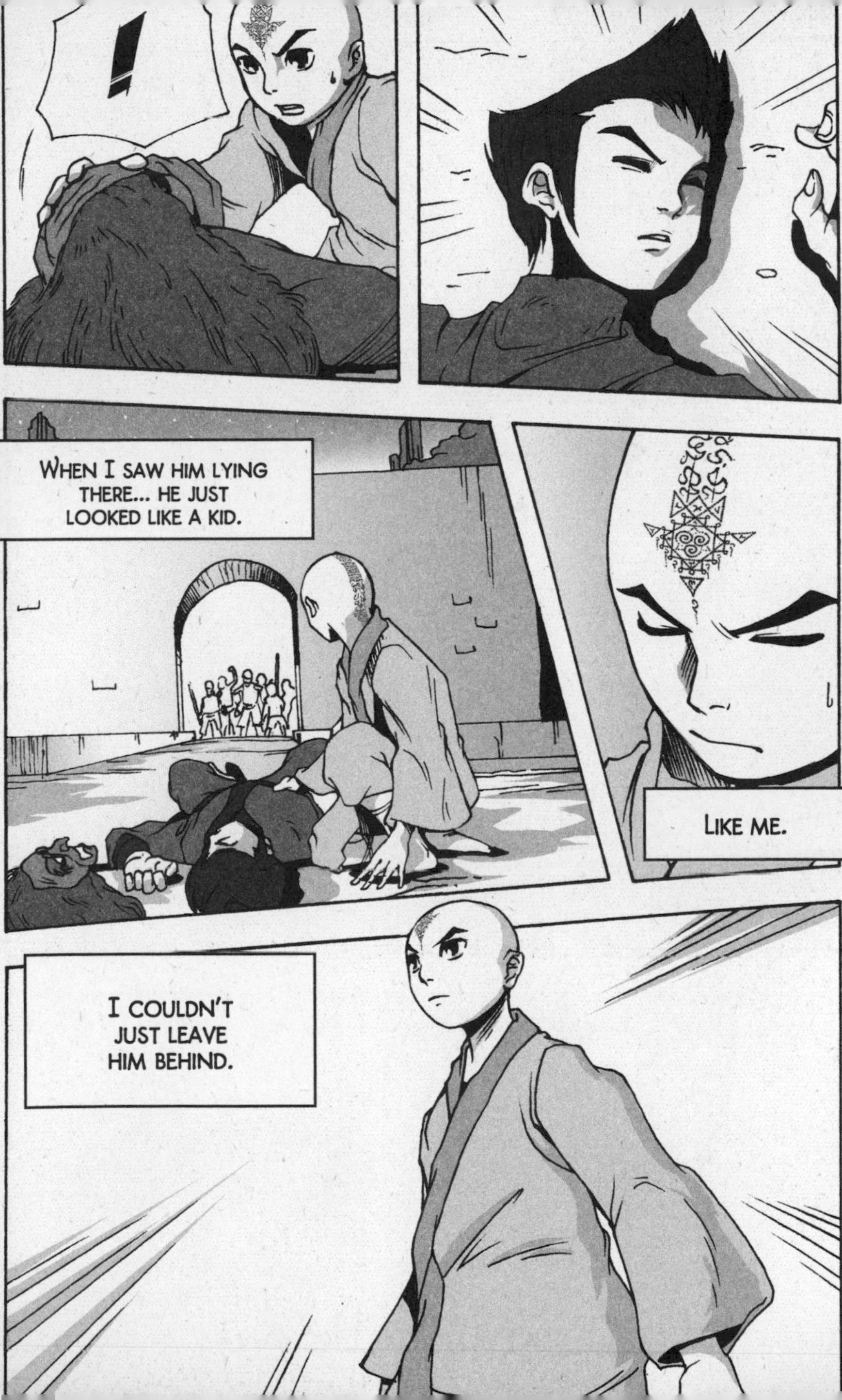
!
WHEN I SAW HIM LYING THERE... HE JUST LOOKED LIKE A KID.
LIKE ME.
I COULDN'T JUST LEAVE HIM BEHIND.

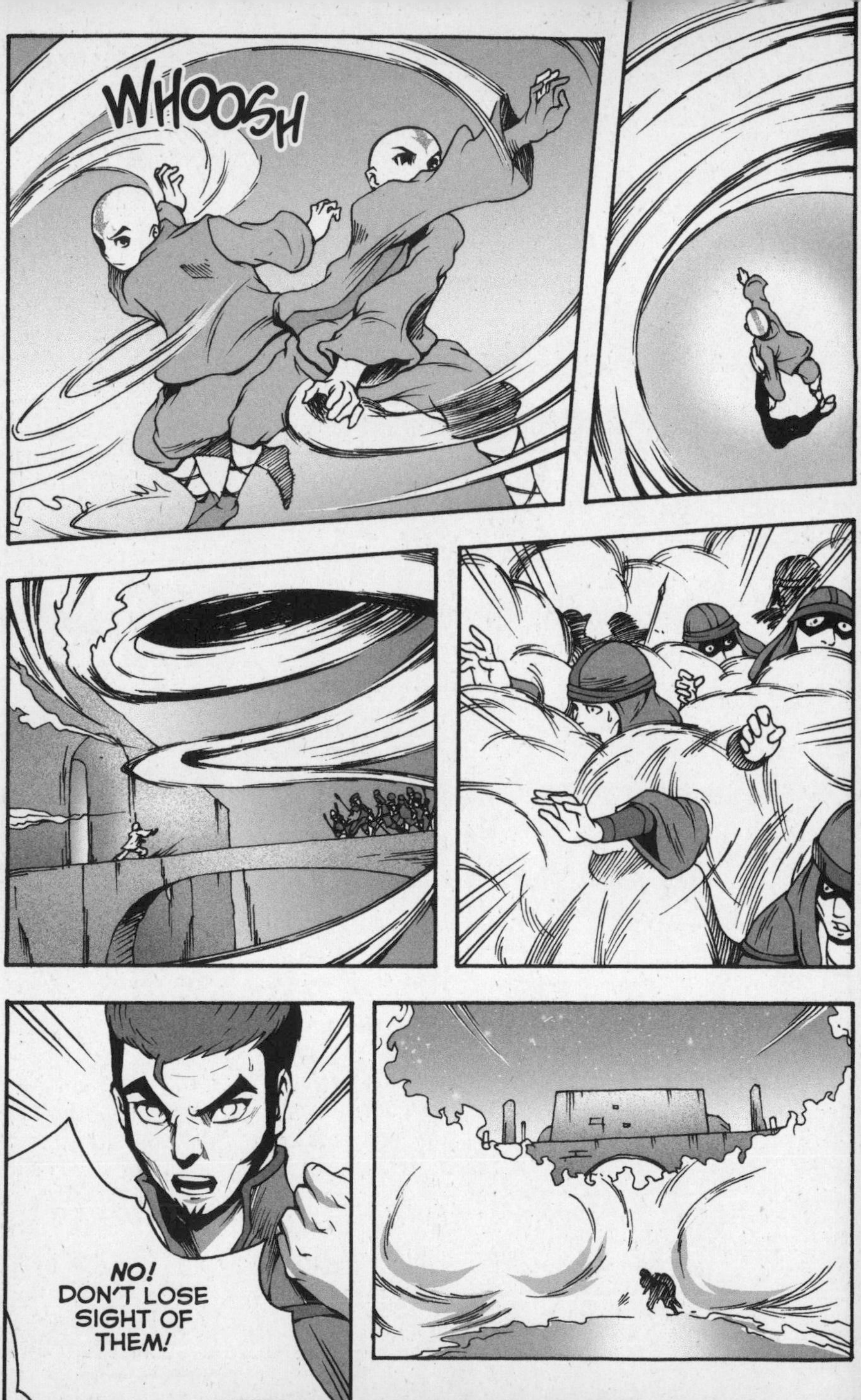
WHOOSH
NO! DON'T LOSE SIGHT OF THEM!

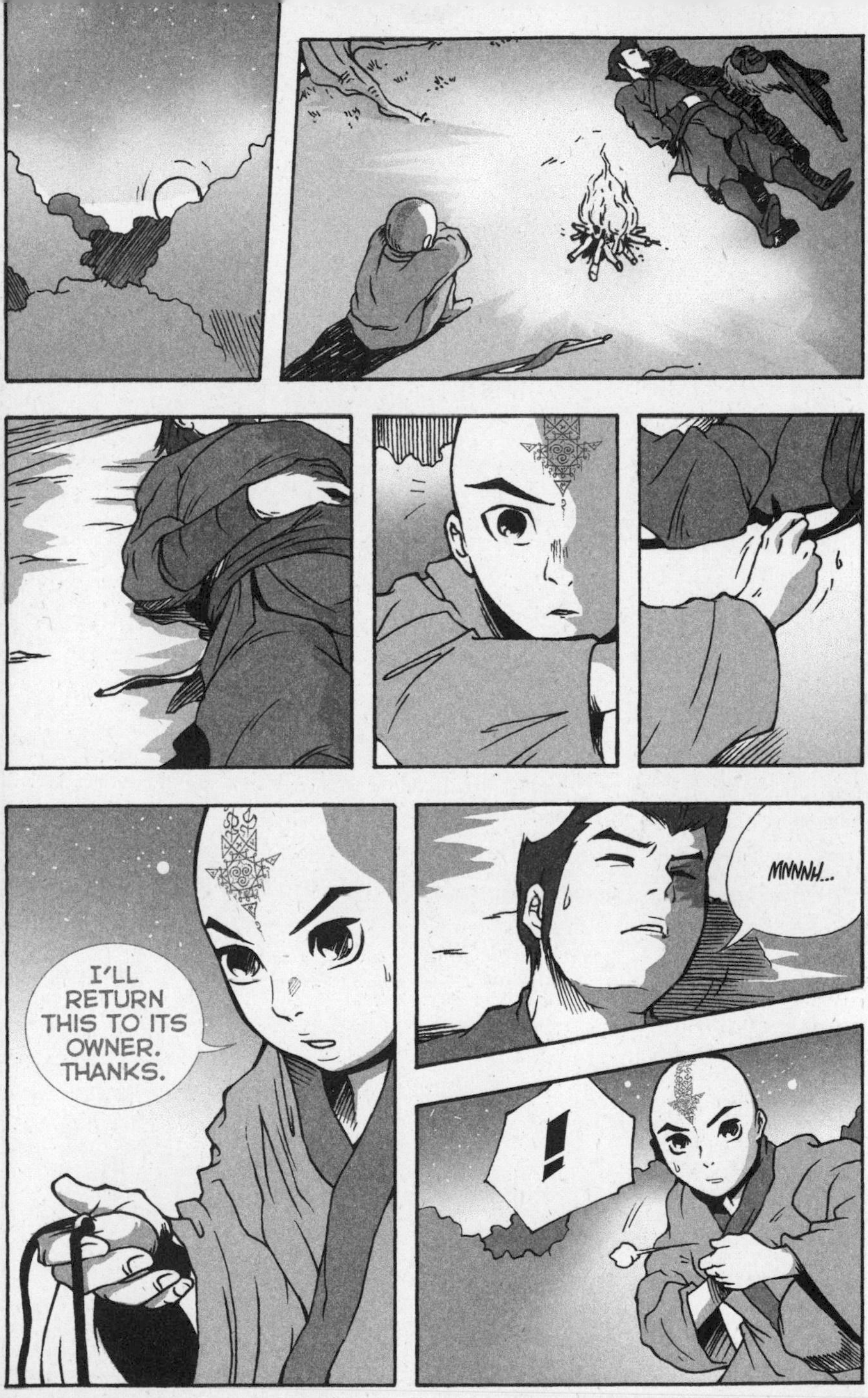
I'LL RETURN THIS TO ITS OWNER. THANKS.
MNNNH...
!

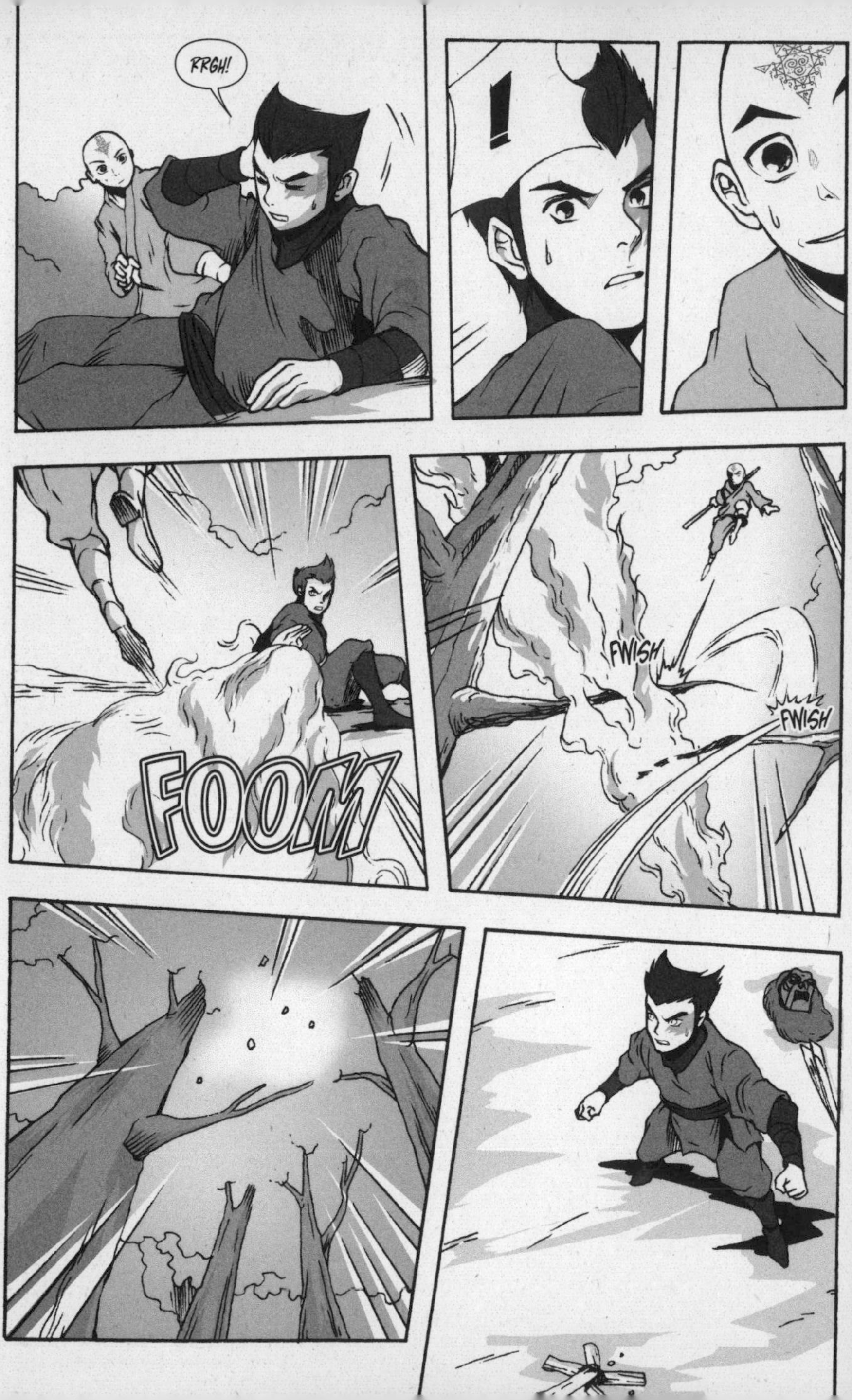
RRGH!
!
FOOM
FWISH
FWISH

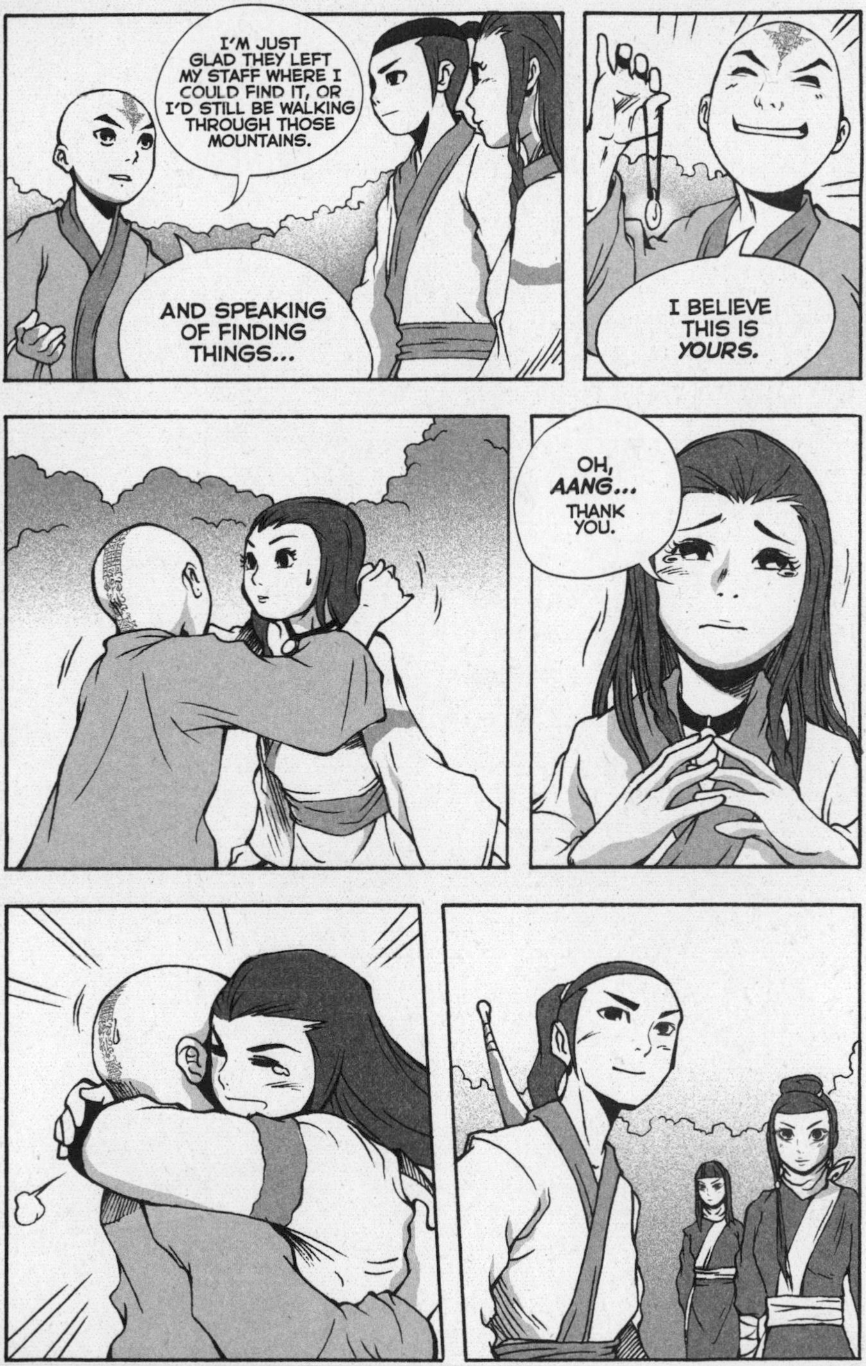
I'M JUST GLAD THEY LEFT MY STAFF WHERE I COULD FIND IT, OR I'D STILL BE WALKING THROUGH THOSE MOUNTAINS.
AND SPEAKING OF FINDING THINGS...
I BELIEVE THIS IS *YOURS.*
OH, *AANG*... THANK YOU.

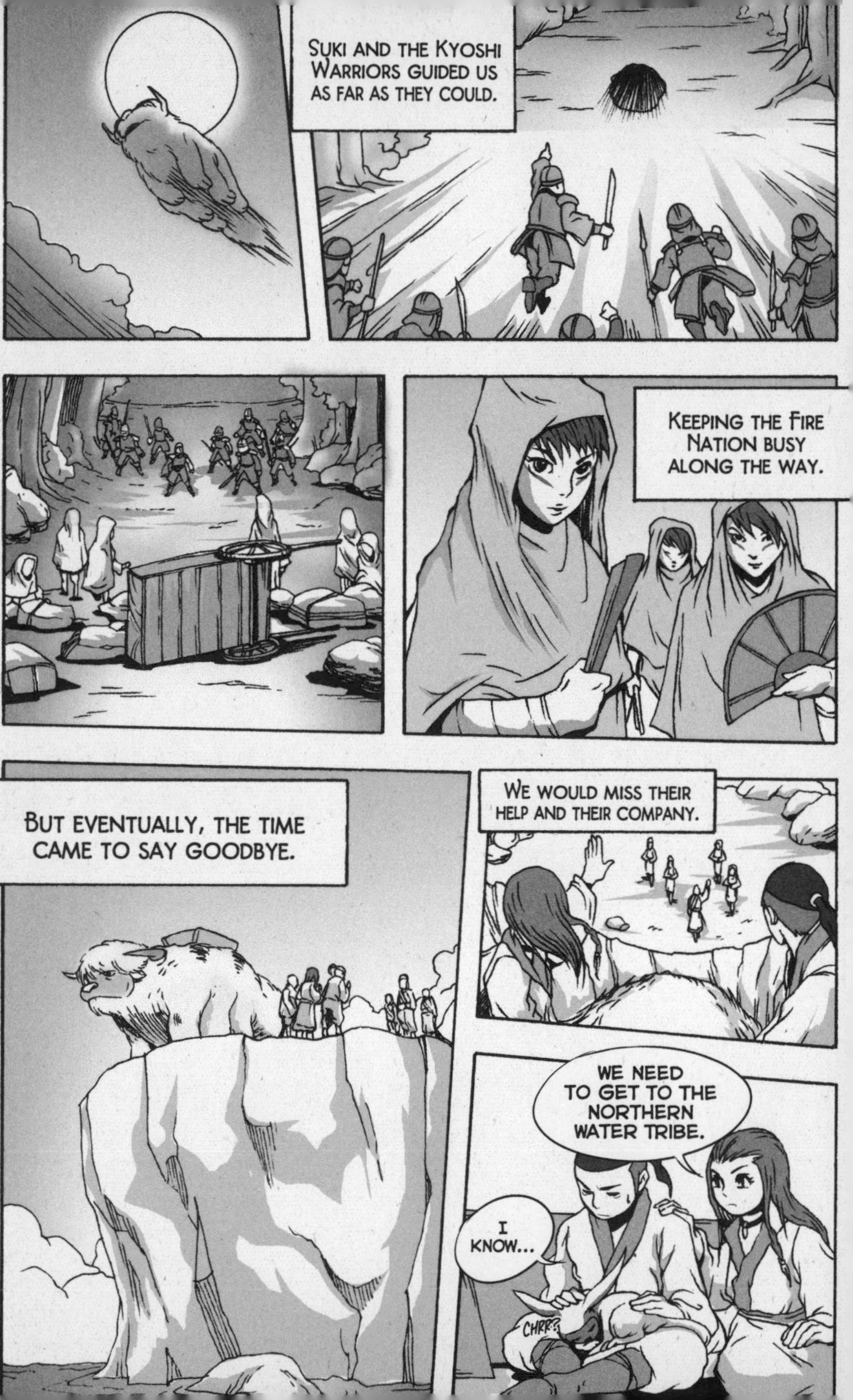

SUKI AND THE KYOSHI WARRIORS GUIDED US AS FAR AS THEY COULD.
KEEPING THE FIRE NATION BUSY ALONG THE WAY.
BUT EVENTUALLY, THE TIME CAME TO SAY GOODBYE.
WE WOULD MISS THEIR HELP AND THEIR COMPANY.
WE NEED TO GET TO THE NORTHERN WATER TRIBE.
I KNOW...
CHRR?

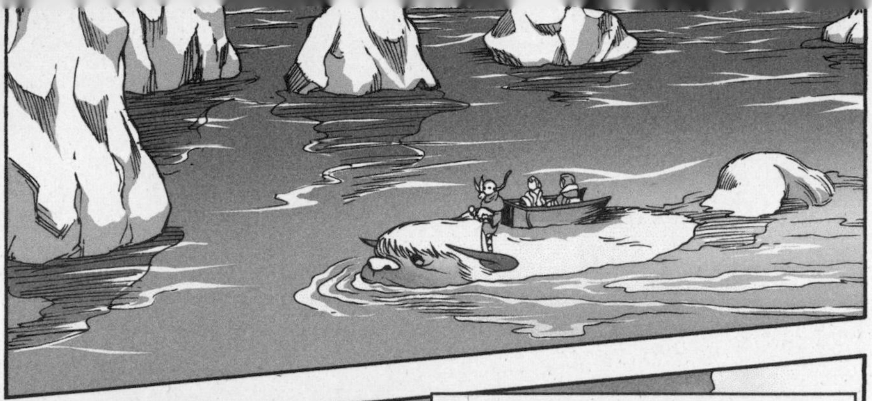

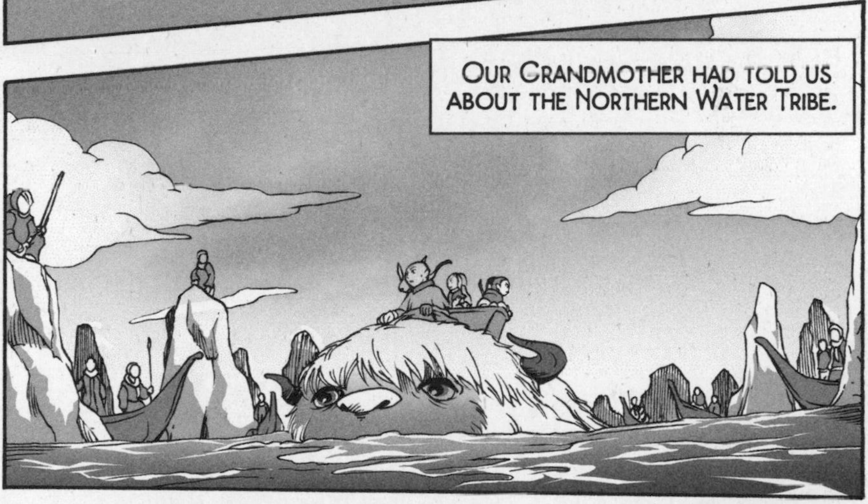
Our Grandmother had told us about the Northern Water Tribe.

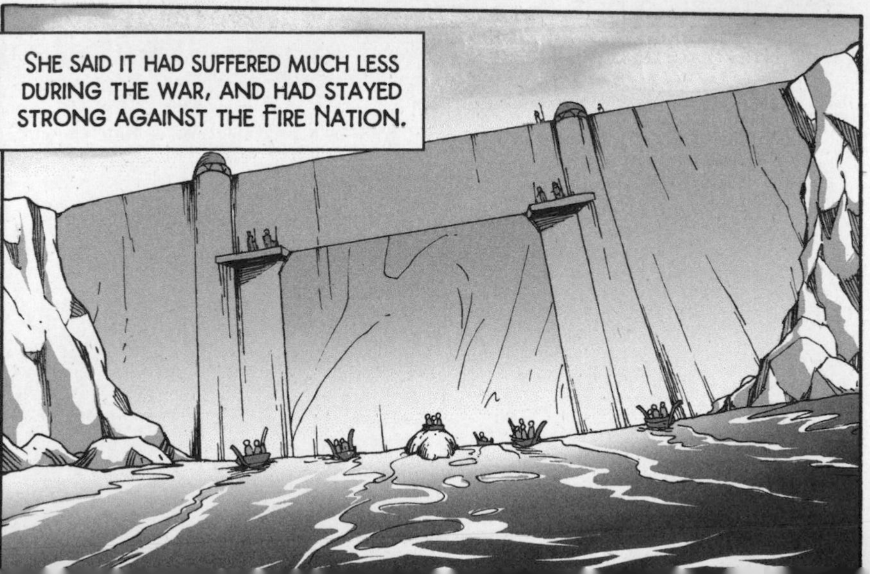
She said it had suffered much less during the war, and had stayed strong against the Fire Nation.

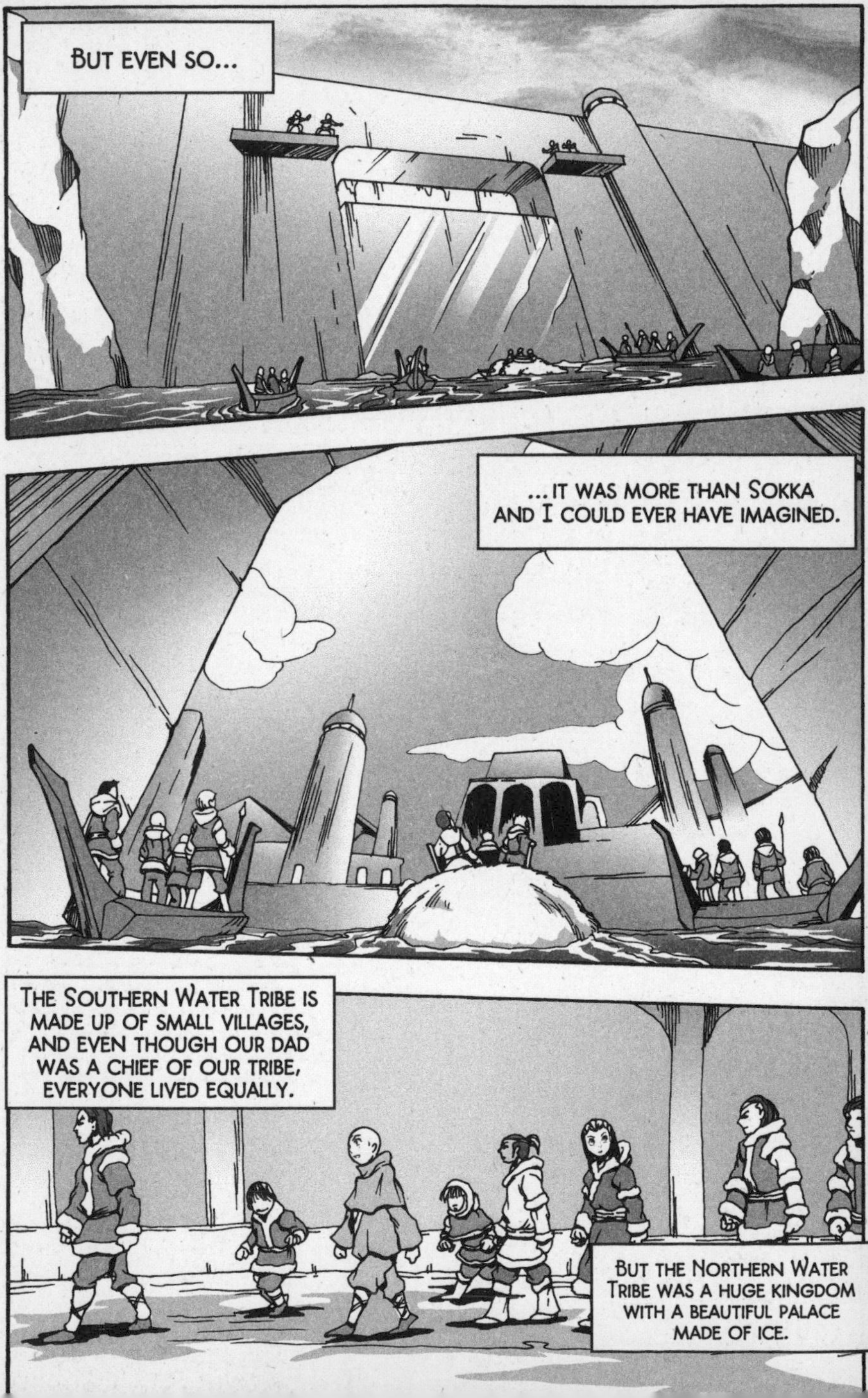
BUT EVEN SO...
...IT WAS MORE THAN SOKKA AND I COULD EVER HAVE IMAGINED.
THE SOUTHERN WATER TRIBE IS MADE UP OF SMALL VILLAGES, AND EVEN THOUGH OUR DAD WAS A CHIEF OF OUR TRIBE, EVERYONE LIVED EQUALLY.
BUT THE NORTHERN WATER TRIBE WAS A HUGE KINGDOM WITH A BEAUTIFUL PALACE MADE OF ICE.

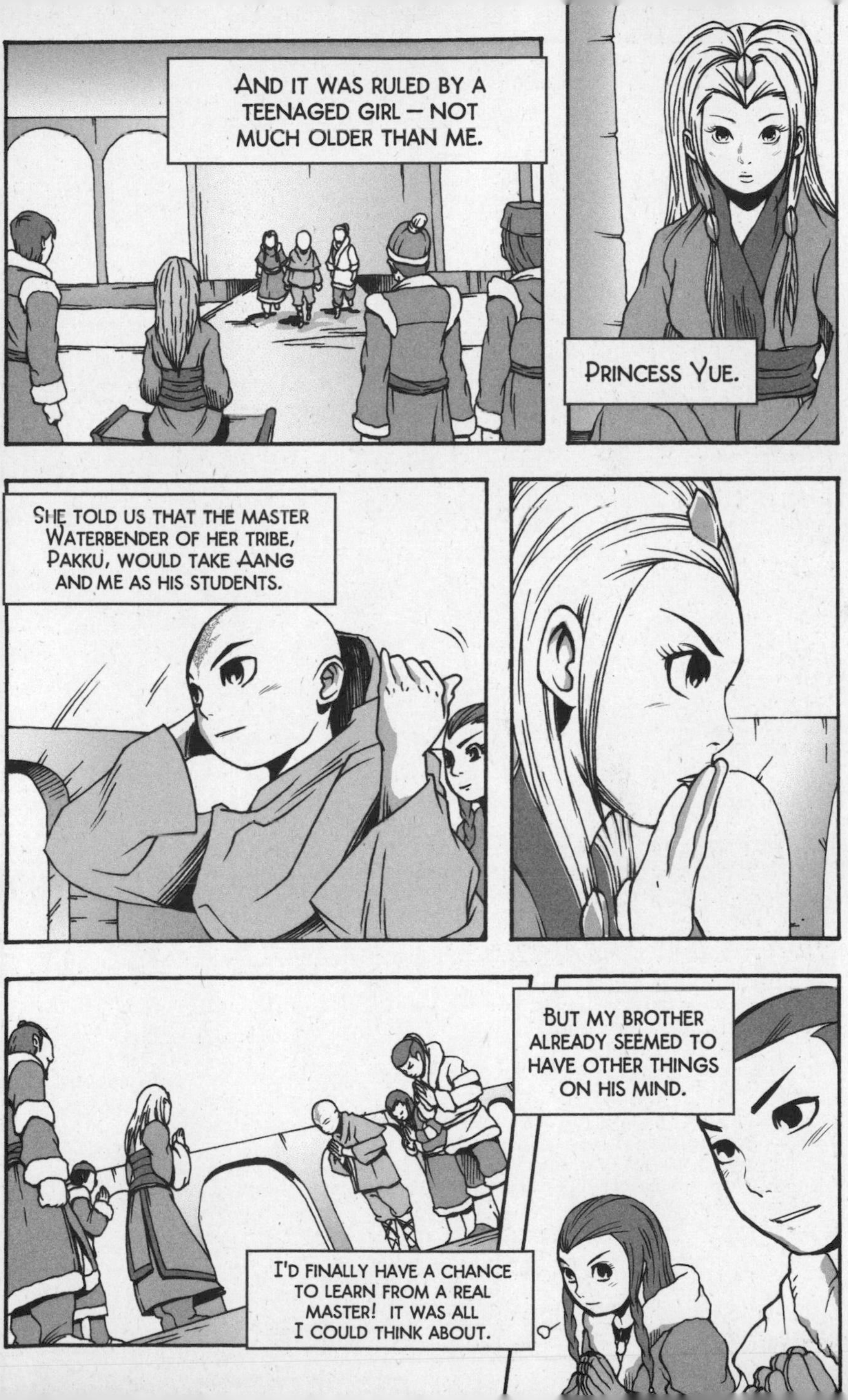
AND IT WAS RULED BY A TEENAGED GIRL — NOT MUCH OLDER THAN ME.
PRINCESS YUE.
SHE TOLD US THAT THE MASTER WATERBENDER OF HER TRIBE, PAKKU, WOULD TAKE AANG AND ME AS HIS STUDENTS.
I'D FINALLY HAVE A CHANCE TO LEARN FROM A REAL MASTER! IT WAS ALL I COULD THINK ABOUT.
BUT MY BROTHER ALREADY SEEMED TO HAVE OTHER THINGS ON HIS MIND.

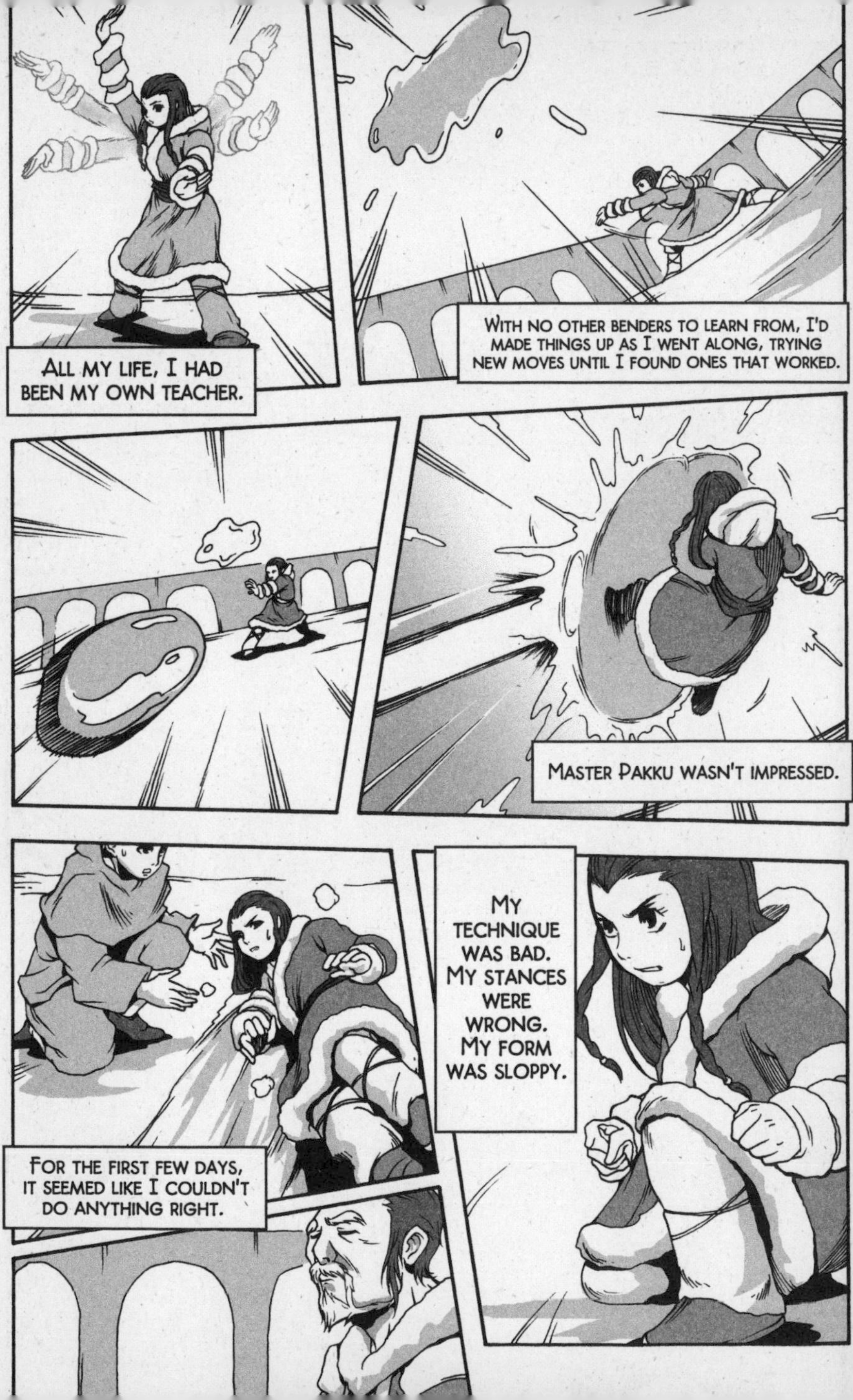
ALL MY LIFE, I HAD BEEN MY OWN TEACHER.
WITH NO OTHER BENDERS TO LEARN FROM, I'D MADE THINGS UP AS I WENT ALONG, TRYING NEW MOVES UNTIL I FOUND ONES THAT WORKED.
MASTER PAKKU WASN'T IMPRESSED.
FOR THE FIRST FEW DAYS, IT SEEMED LIKE I COULDN'T DO ANYTHING RIGHT.
MY TECHNIQUE WAS BAD. MY STANCES WERE WRONG. MY FORM WAS SLOPPY.

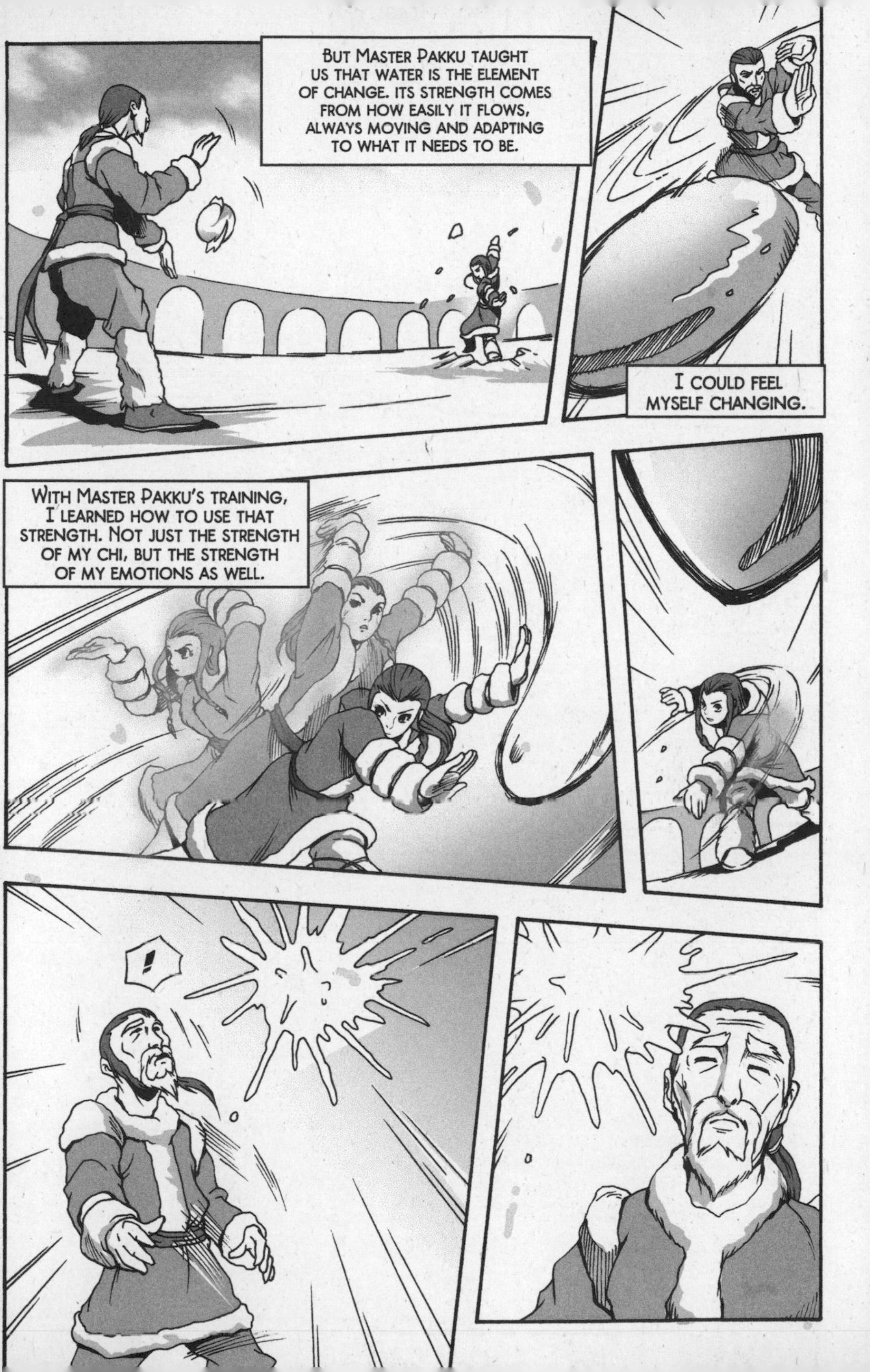
BUT MASTER PAKKU TAUGHT US THAT WATER IS THE ELEMENT OF CHANGE. ITS STRENGTH COMES FROM HOW EASILY IT FLOWS, ALWAYS MOVING AND ADAPTING TO WHAT IT NEEDS TO BE.
I COULD FEEL MYSELF CHANGING.
WITH MASTER PAKKU'S TRAINING, I LEARNED HOW TO USE THAT STRENGTH. NOT JUST THE STRENGTH OF MY CHI, BUT THE STRENGTH OF MY EMOTIONS AS WELL.
!

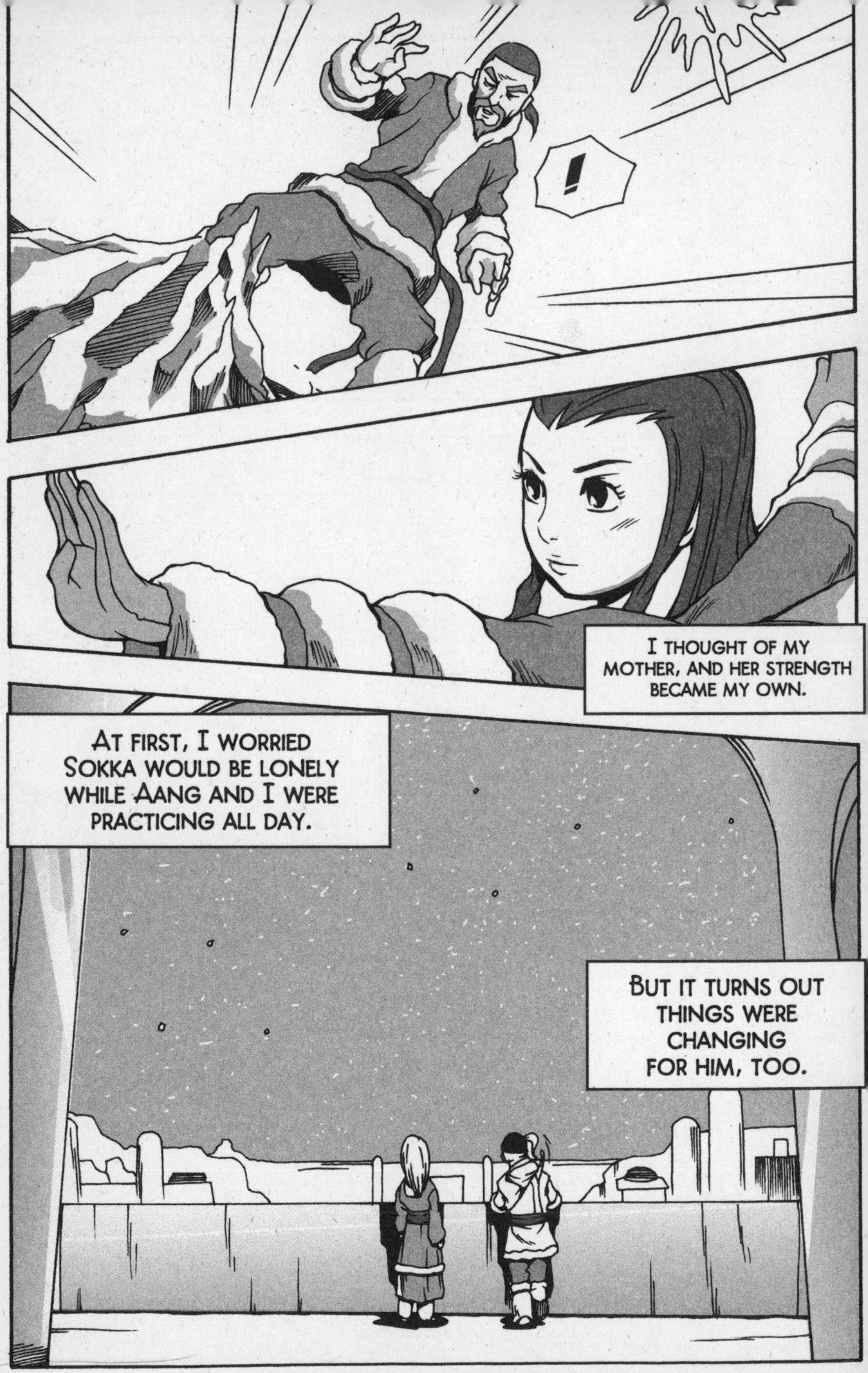
I THOUGHT OF MY MOTHER, AND HER STRENGTH BECAME MY OWN.
AT FIRST, I WORRIED SOKKA WOULD BE LONELY WHILE AANG AND I WERE PRACTICING ALL DAY.
BUT IT TURNS OUT THINGS WERE CHANGING FOR HIM, TOO.

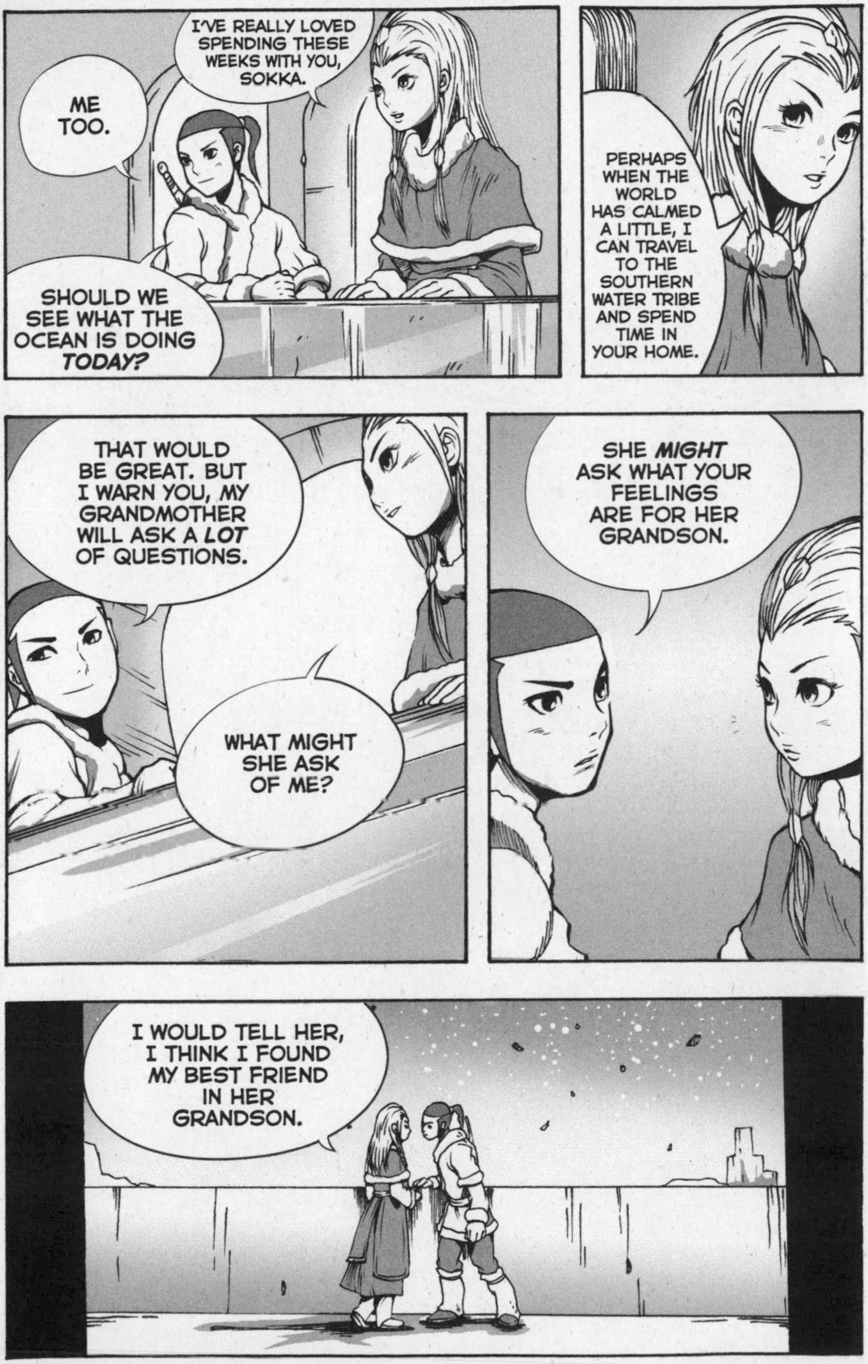
I'VE REALLY LOVED SPENDING THESE WEEKS WITH YOU, SOKKA.
ME TOO.
SHOULD WE SEE WHAT THE OCEAN IS DOING *TODAY?*
PERHAPS WHEN THE WORLD HAS CALMED A LITTLE, I CAN TRAVEL TO THE SOUTHERN WATER TRIBE AND SPEND TIME IN YOUR HOME.
THAT WOULD BE GREAT. BUT I WARN YOU, MY GRANDMOTHER WILL ASK A *LOT* OF QUESTIONS.
WHAT MIGHT SHE ASK OF ME?
SHE *MIGHT* ASK WHAT YOUR FEELINGS ARE FOR HER GRANDSON.
I WOULD TELL HER, I THINK I FOUND MY BEST FRIEND IN HER GRANDSON.

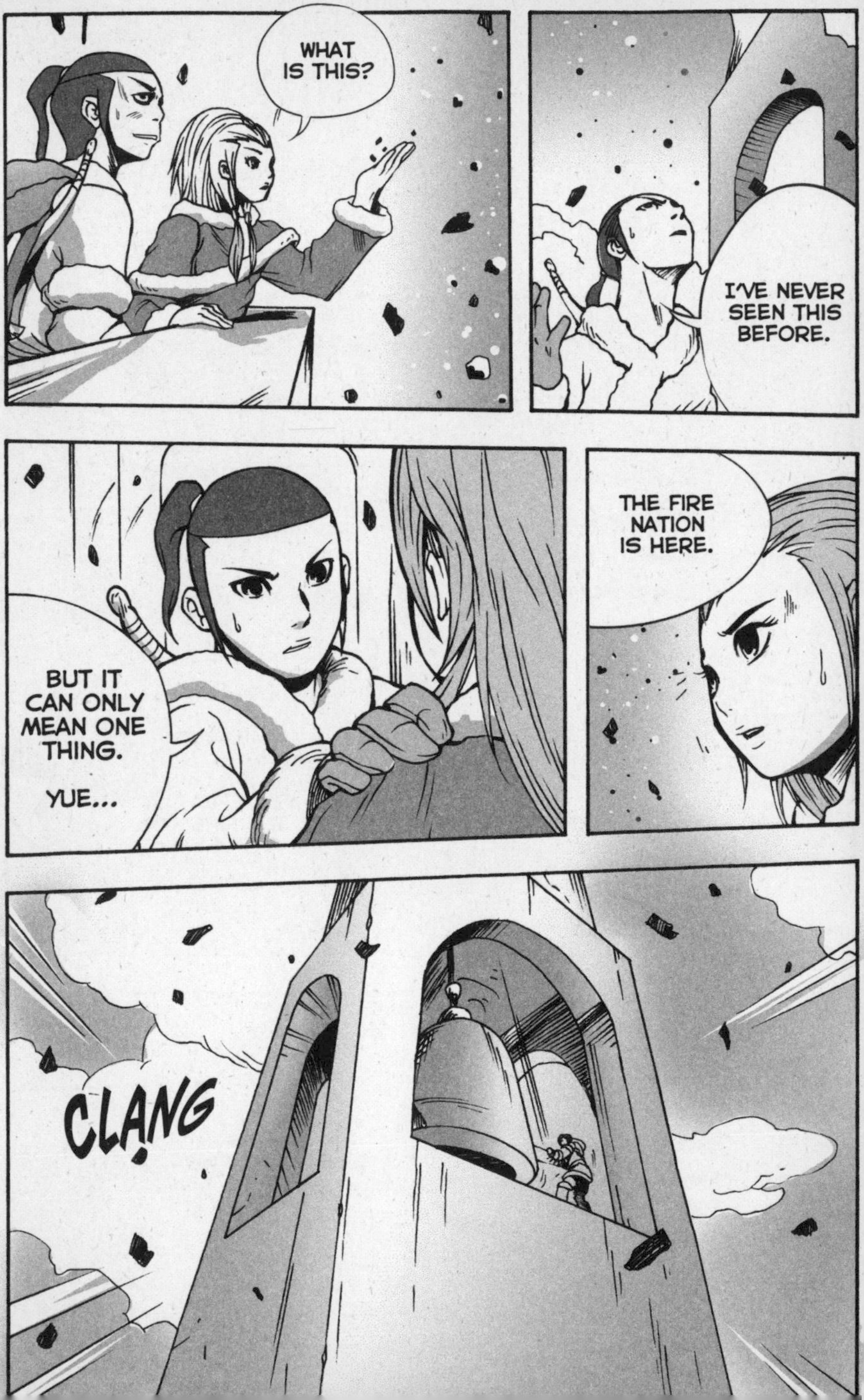
WHAT IS THIS?
I'VE NEVER SEEN THIS BEFORE.
BUT IT CAN ONLY MEAN ONE THING.
YUE...
THE FIRE NATION IS HERE.
CLANG

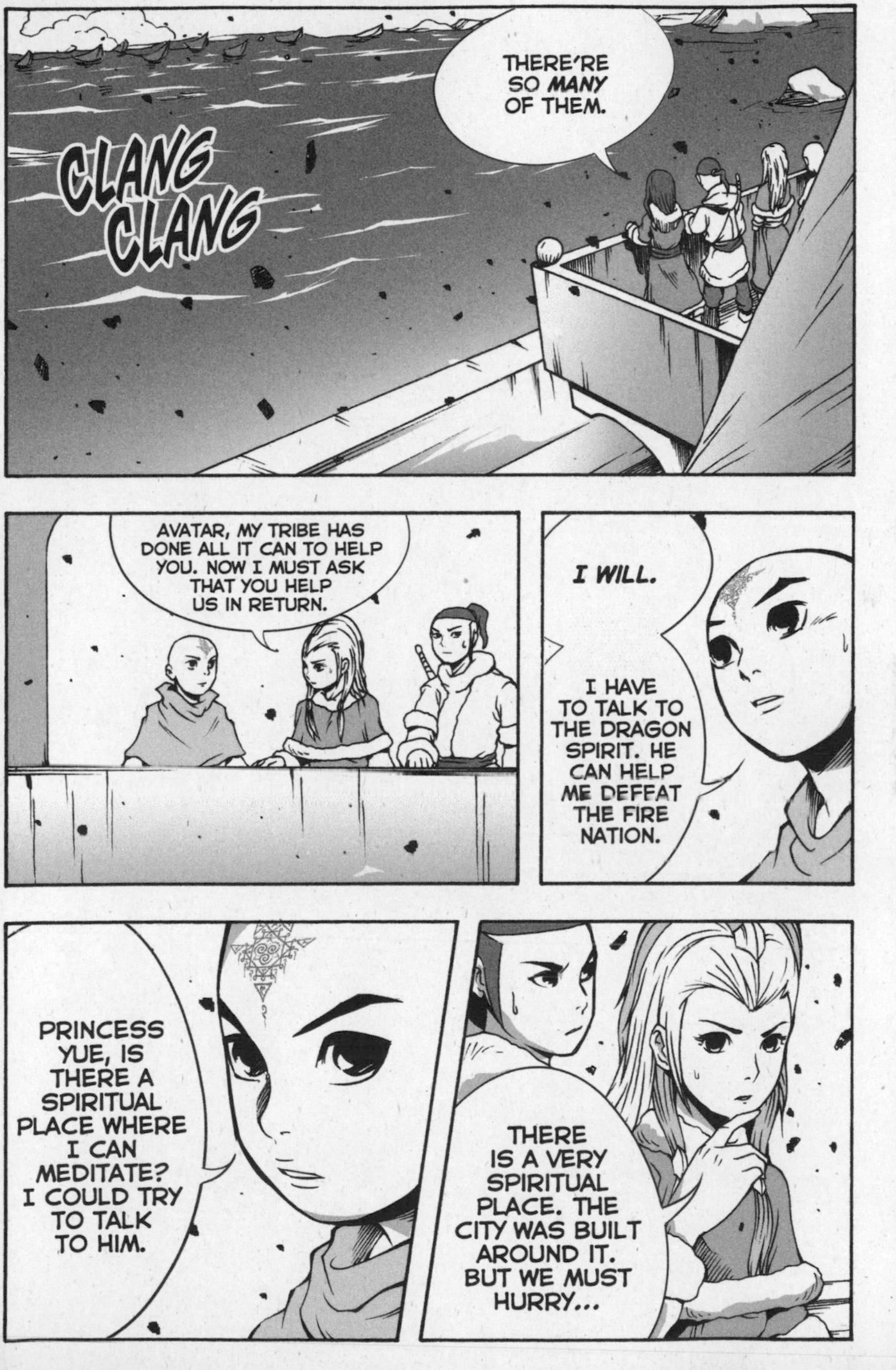
CLANG CLANG
THERE'RE SO *MANY* OF THEM.
AVATAR, MY TRIBE HAS DONE ALL IT CAN TO HELP YOU. NOW I MUST ASK THAT YOU HELP US IN RETURN.
*I WILL.*
I HAVE TO TALK TO THE DRAGON SPIRIT. HE CAN HELP ME DEFEAT THE FIRE NATION.
PRINCESS YUE, IS THERE A SPIRITUAL PLACE WHERE I CAN MEDITATE? I COULD TRY TO TALK TO HIM.
THERE IS A VERY SPIRITUAL PLACE. THE CITY WAS BUILT AROUND IT. BUT WE MUST HURRY...

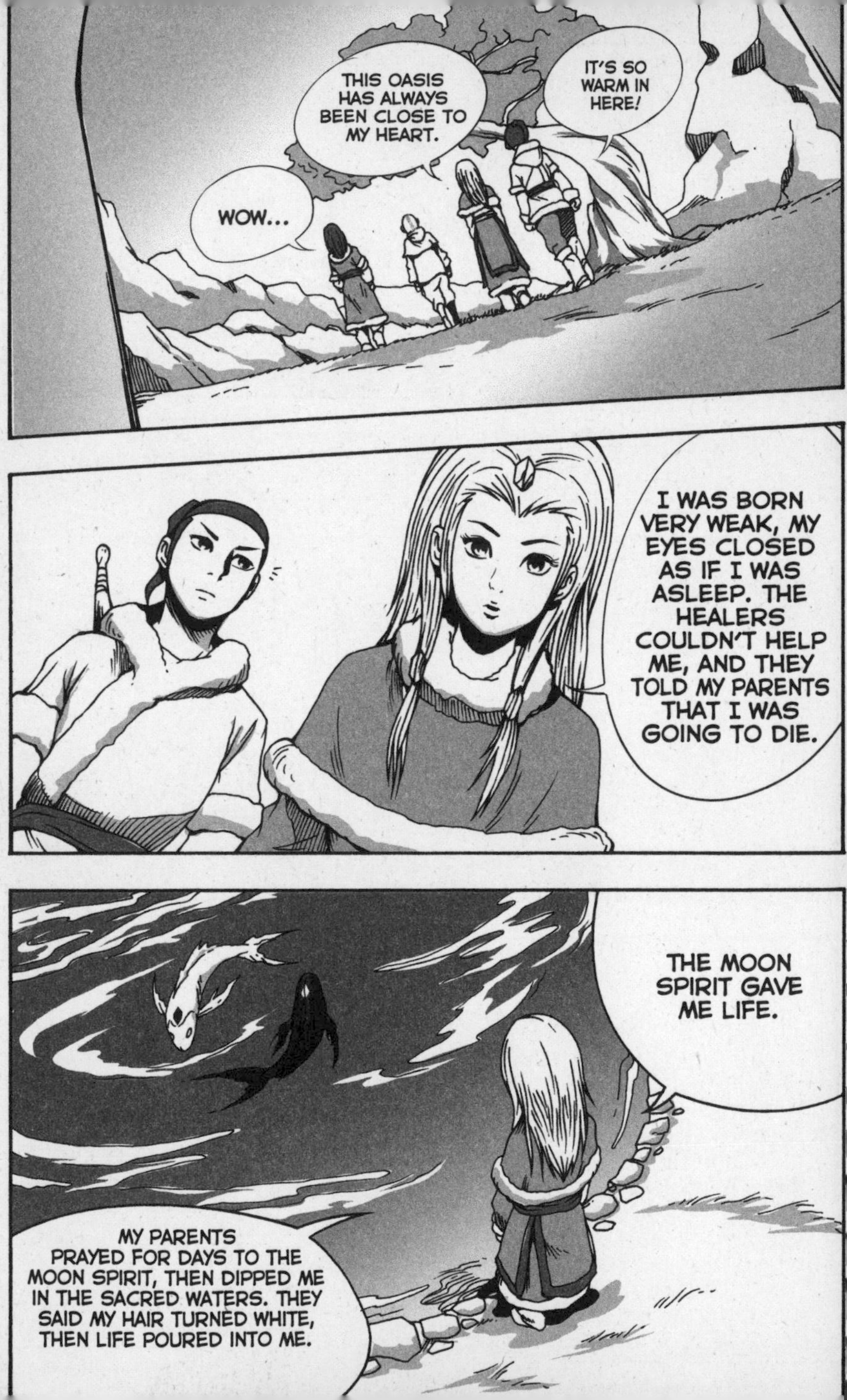
WOW...
THIS OASIS HAS ALWAYS BEEN CLOSE TO MY HEART.
IT'S SO WARM IN HERE!
I WAS BORN VERY WEAK, MY EYES CLOSED AS IF I WAS ASLEEP. THE HEALERS COULDN'T HELP ME, AND THEY TOLD MY PARENTS THAT I WAS GOING TO DIE.
THE MOON SPIRIT GAVE ME LIFE.
MY PARENTS PRAYED FOR DAYS TO THE MOON SPIRIT, THEN DIPPED ME IN THE SACRED WATERS. THEY SAID MY HAIR TURNED WHITE, THEN LIFE POURED INTO ME.

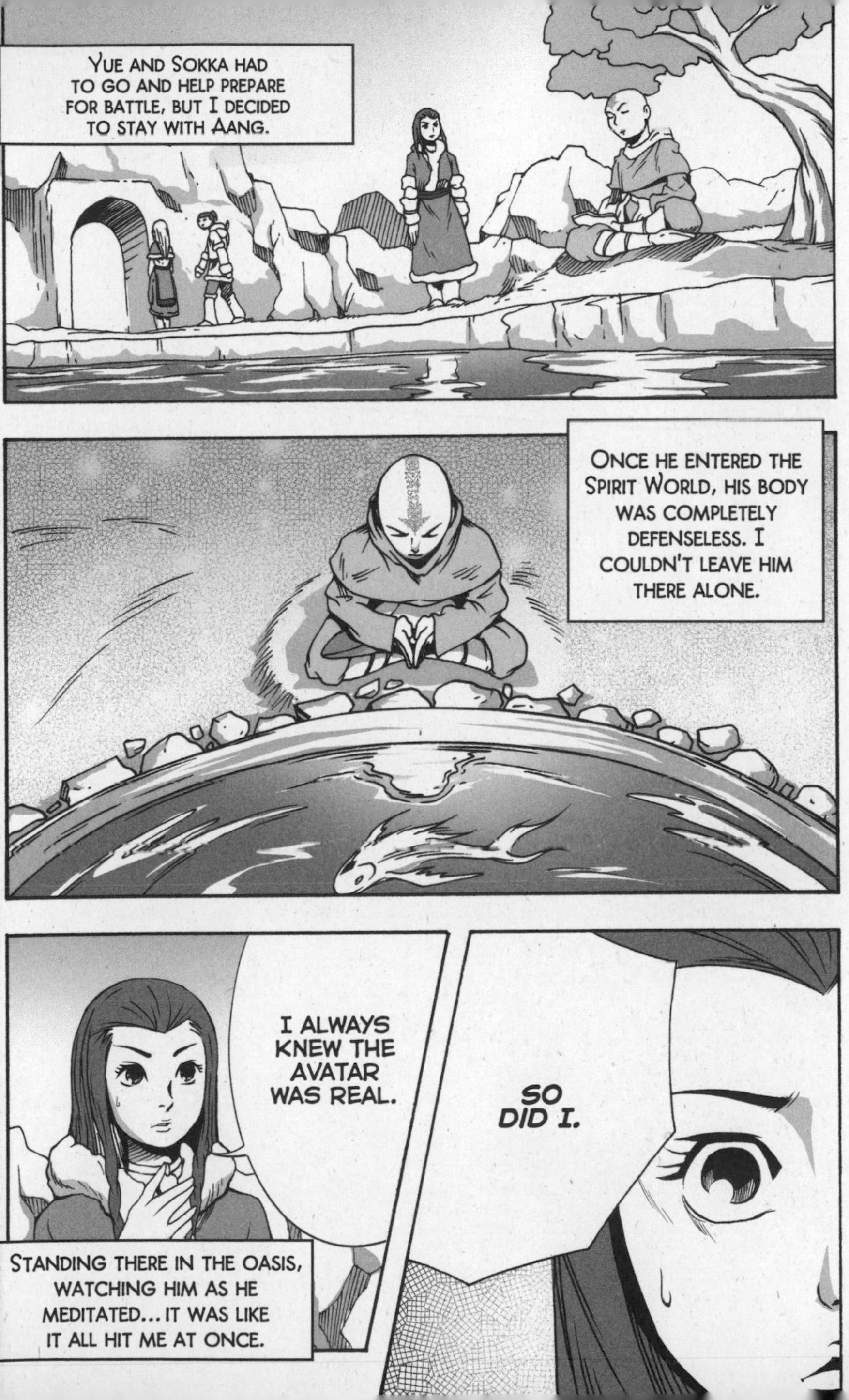

YUE AND SOKKA HAD TO GO AND HELP PREPARE FOR BATTLE, BUT I DECIDED TO STAY WITH AANG.
ONCE HE ENTERED THE SPIRIT WORLD, HIS BODY WAS COMPLETELY DEFENSELESS. I COULDN'T LEAVE HIM THERE ALONE.
I ALWAYS KNEW THE AVATAR WAS REAL.
STANDING THERE IN THE OASIS, WATCHING HIM AS HE MEDITATED... IT WAS LIKE IT ALL HIT ME AT ONCE.
SO DID I.

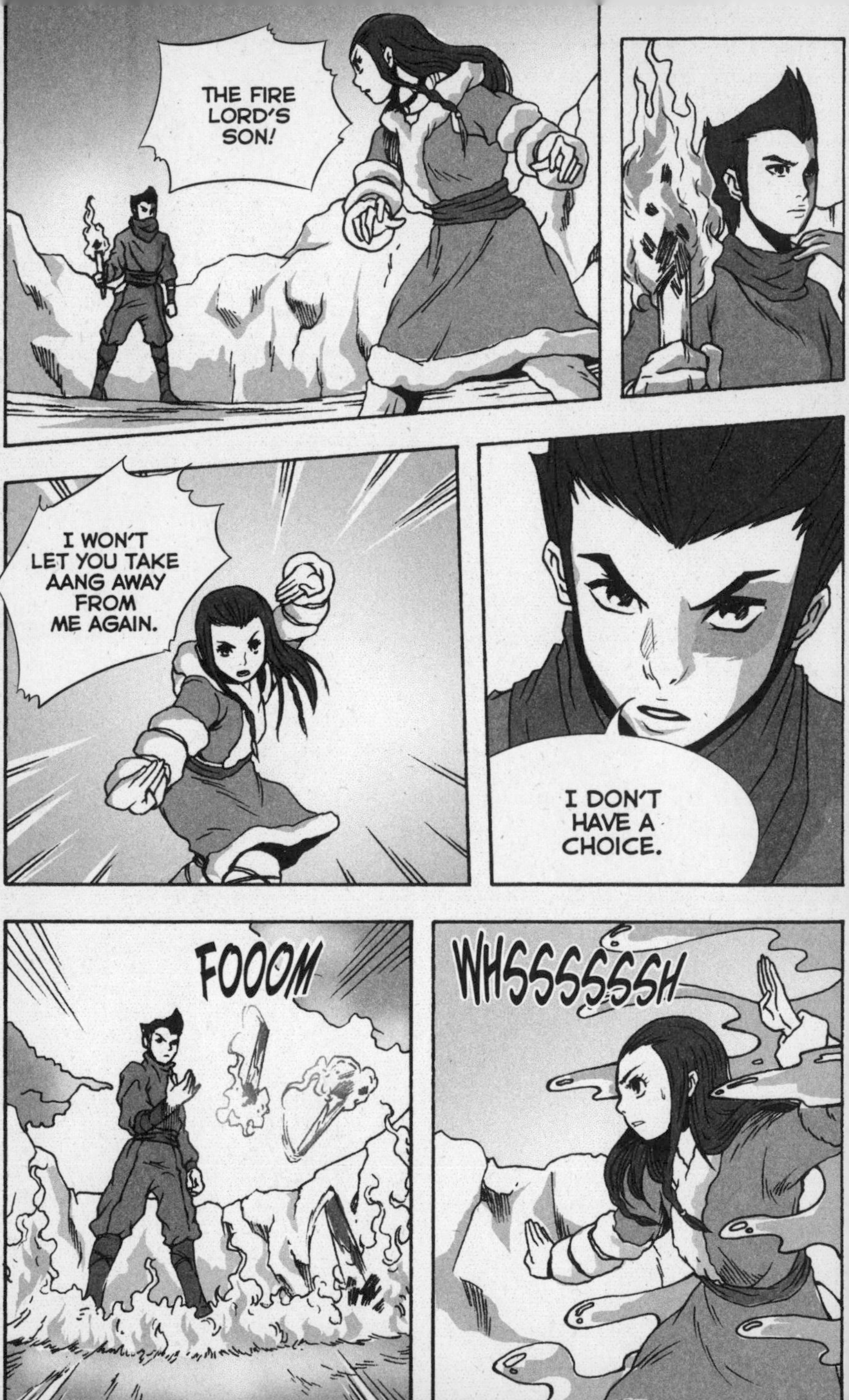
THE FIRE LORD'S SON!
I WON'T LET YOU TAKE AANG AWAY FROM ME AGAIN.
I DON'T HAVE A CHOICE.
FOOOM
WHSSSSSSSH

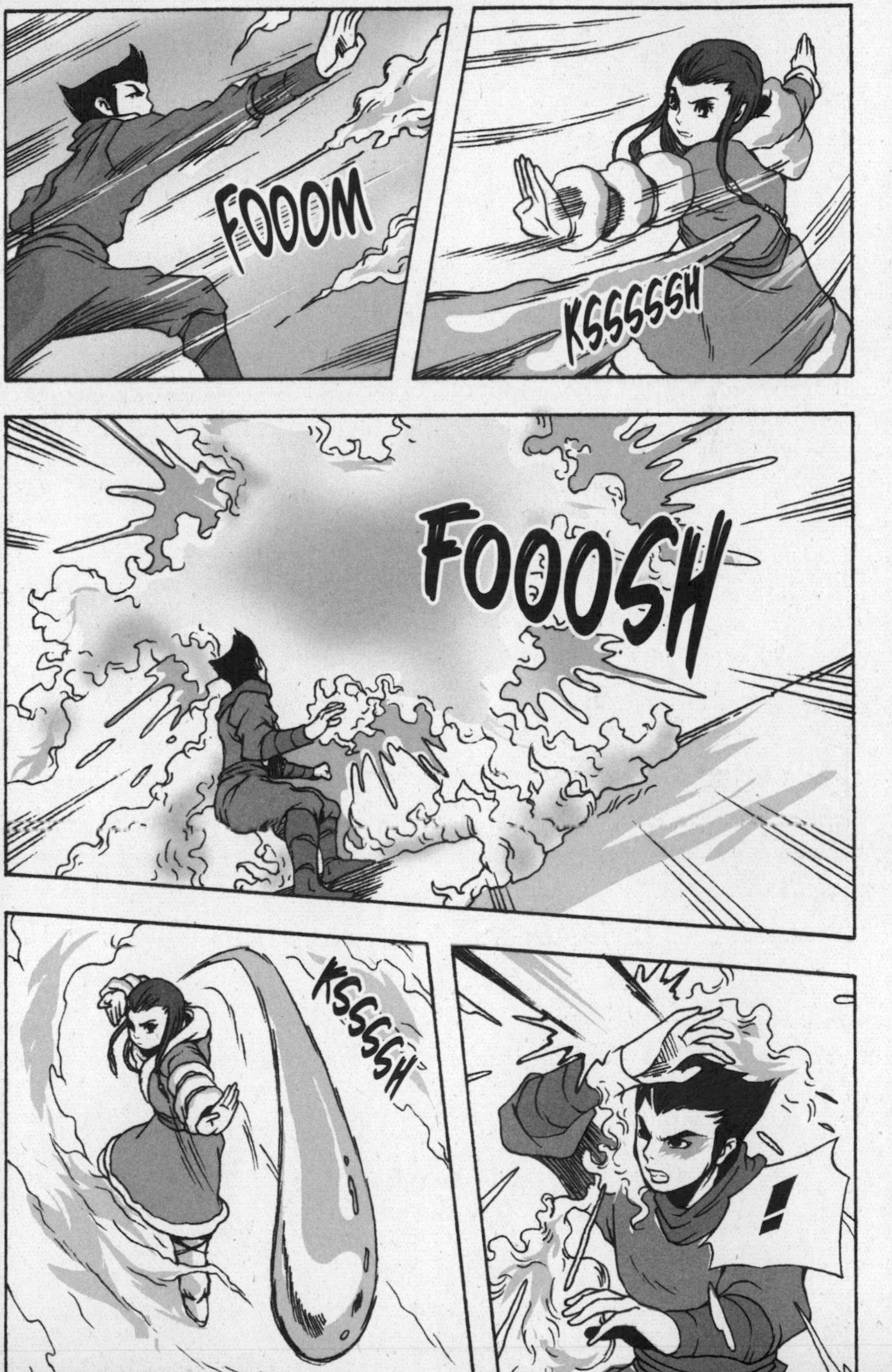
FOOOM
KSSSSSH
FOOOSH
KSSSSSH
!

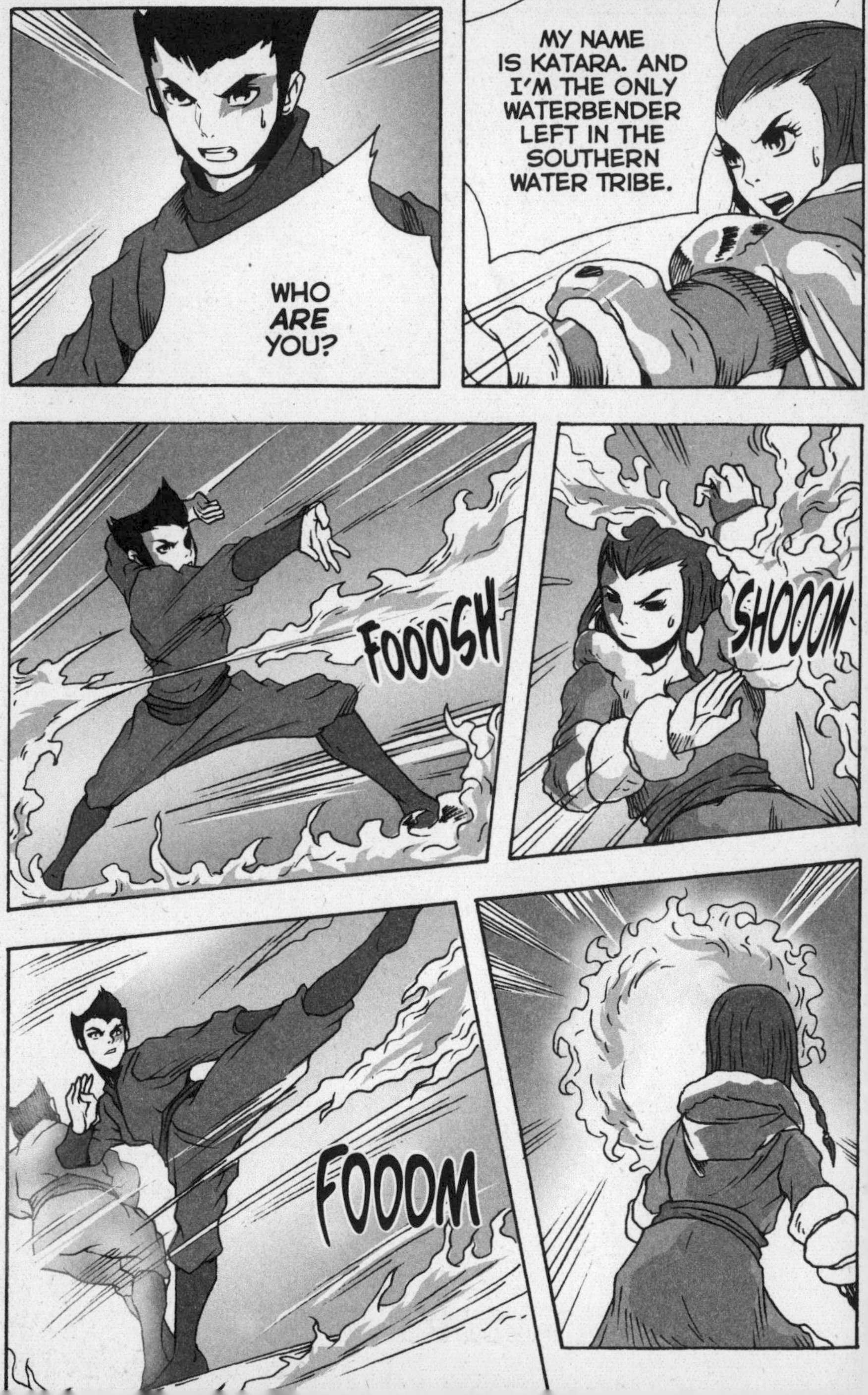

WHO ARE YOU?
MY NAME IS KATARA. AND I'M THE ONLY WATERBENDER LEFT IN THE SOUTHERN WATER TRIBE.
FOOOSH
SHOOOM
FOOOM

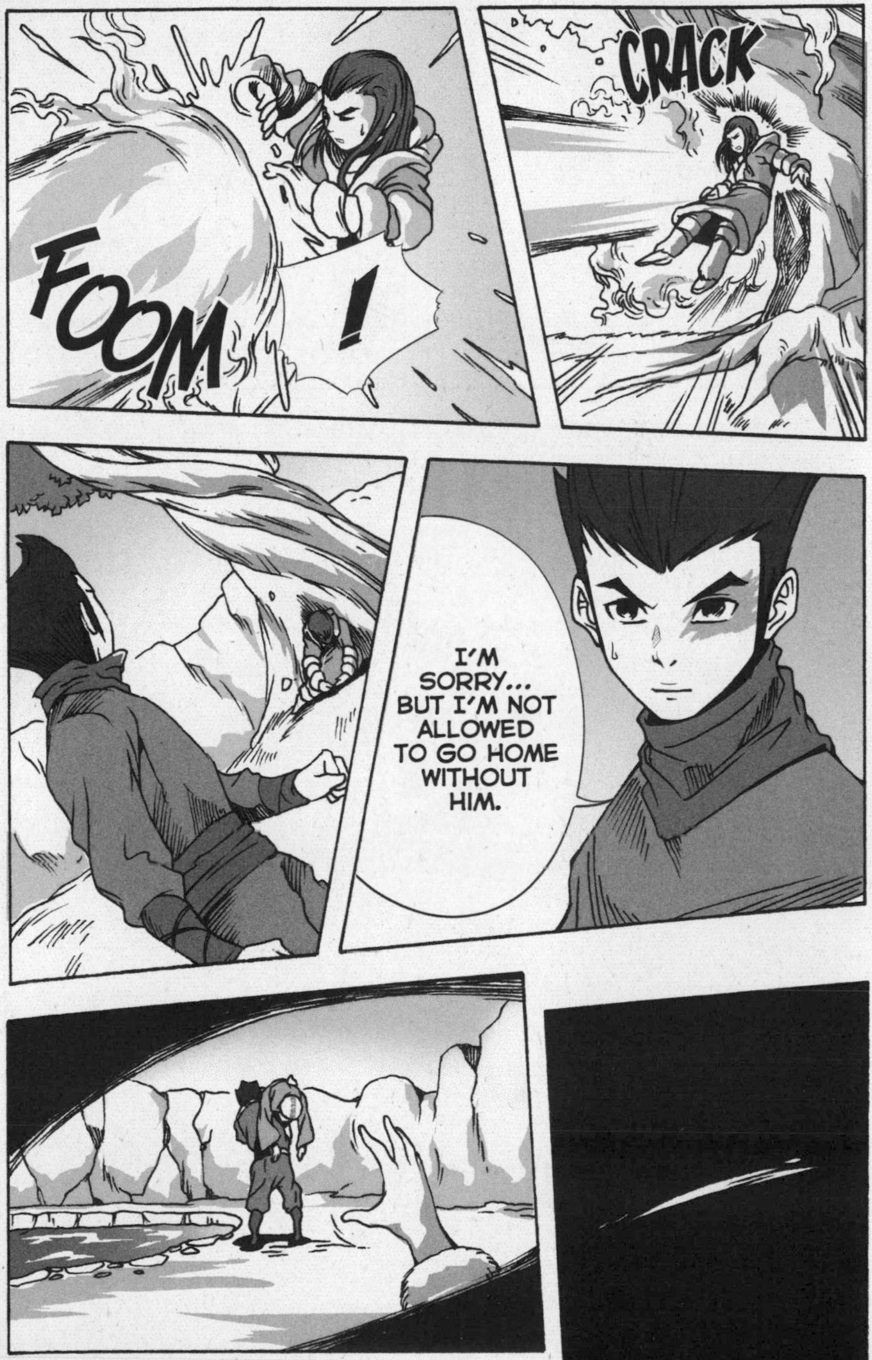
FOOM
!
CRACK
I'M SORRY... BUT I'M NOT ALLOWED TO GO HOME WITHOUT HIM.

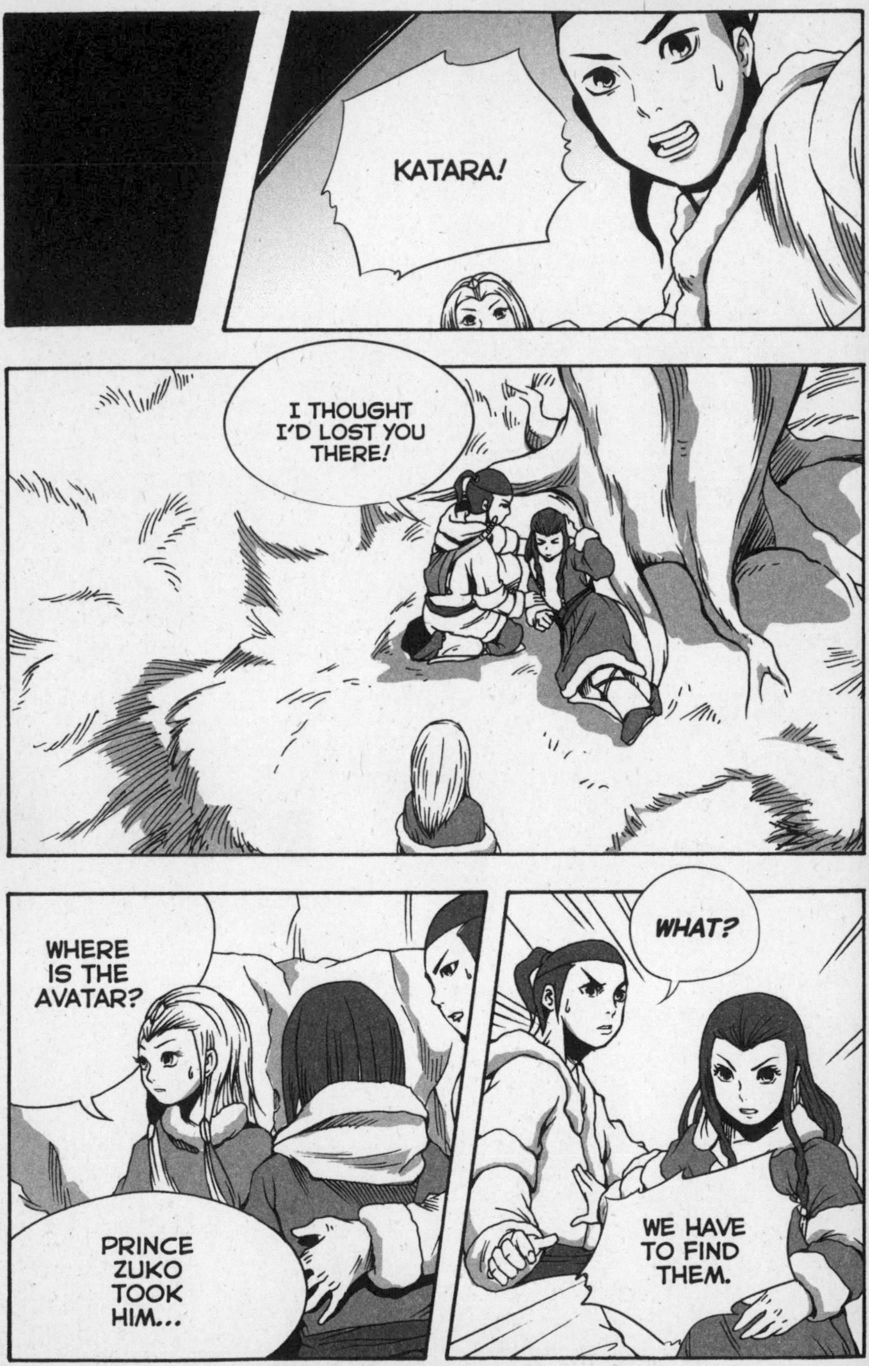
KATARA!
I THOUGHT I'D LOST YOU THERE!
WHERE IS THE AVATAR?
PRINCE ZUKO TOOK HIM...
WHAT?
WE HAVE TO FIND THEM.

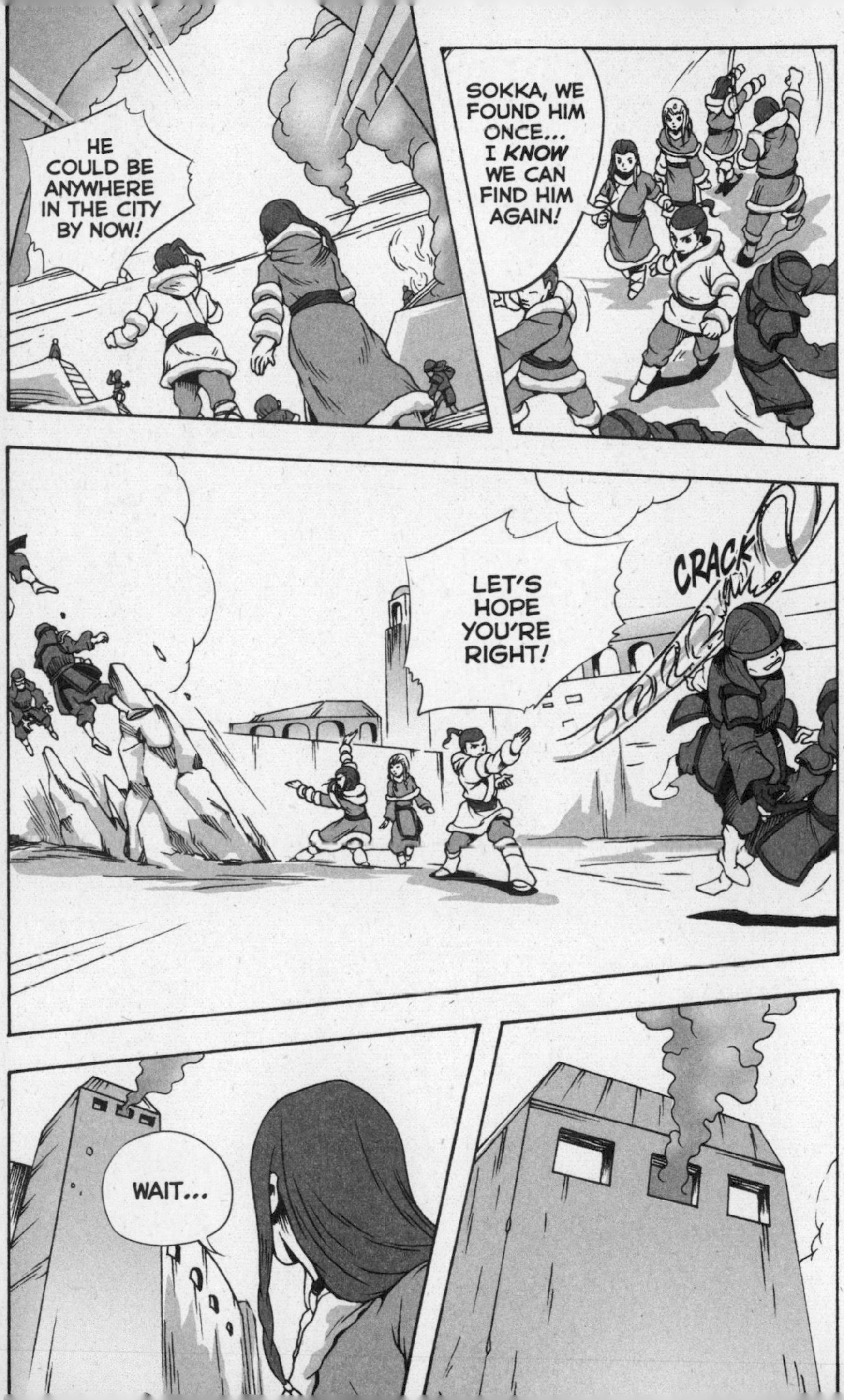
HE COULD BE ANYWHERE IN THE CITY BY NOW!
SOKKA, WE FOUND HIM ONCE... I *KNOW* WE CAN FIND HIM AGAIN!
LET'S HOPE YOU'RE RIGHT!
CRACK
WAIT...

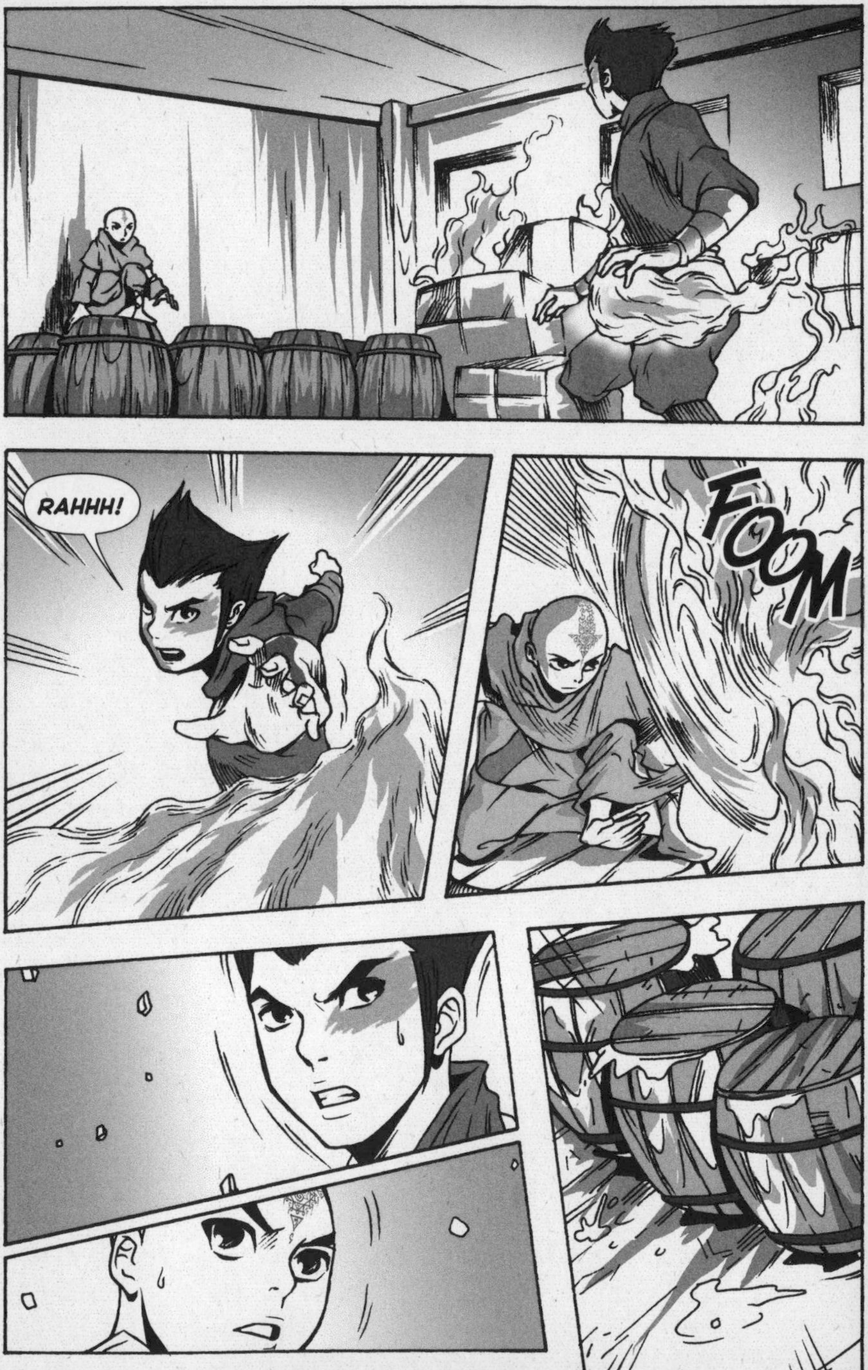
RAHHH!
FOOM

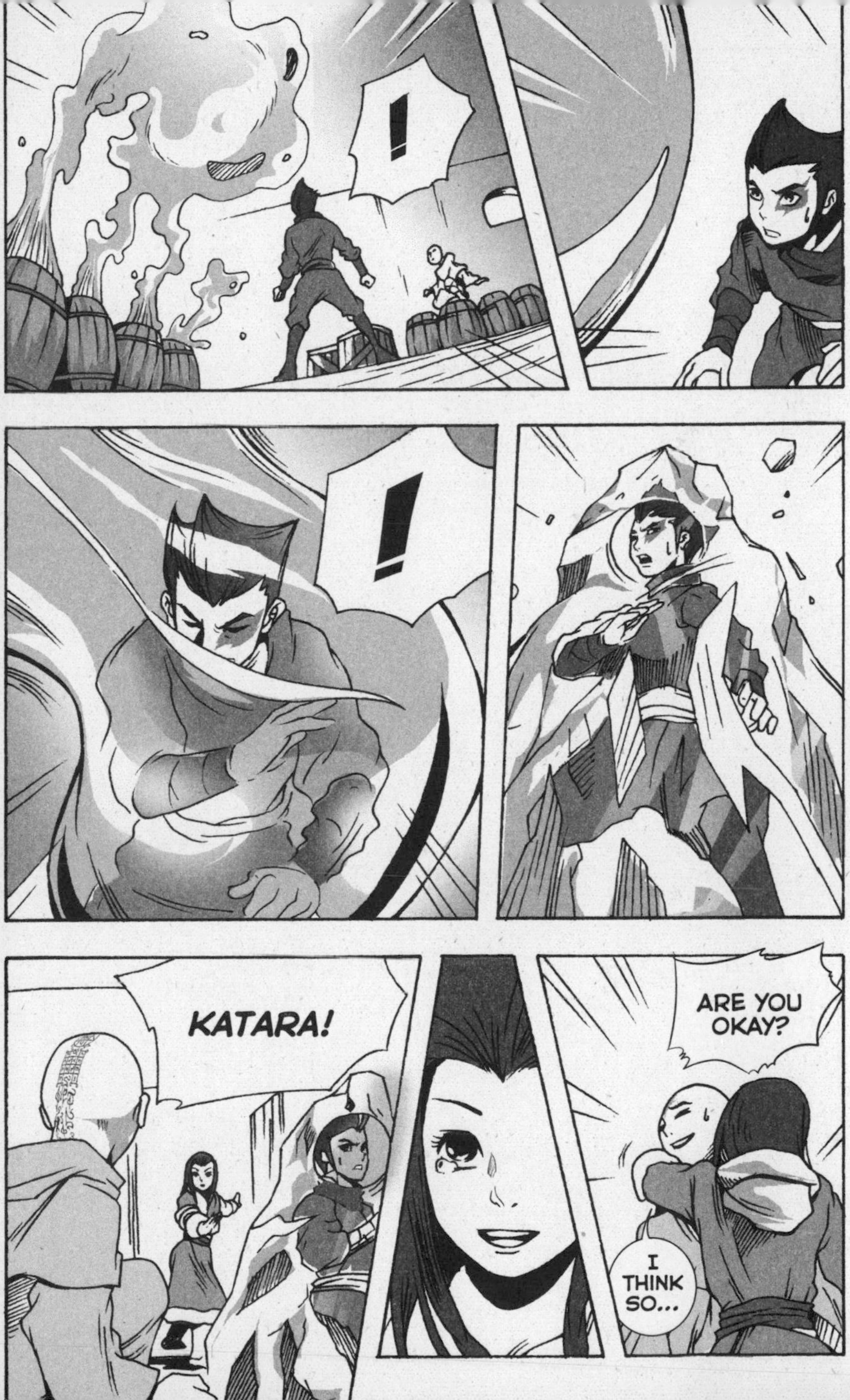
!
!
KATARA!
ARE YOU OKAY?
I THINK SO...

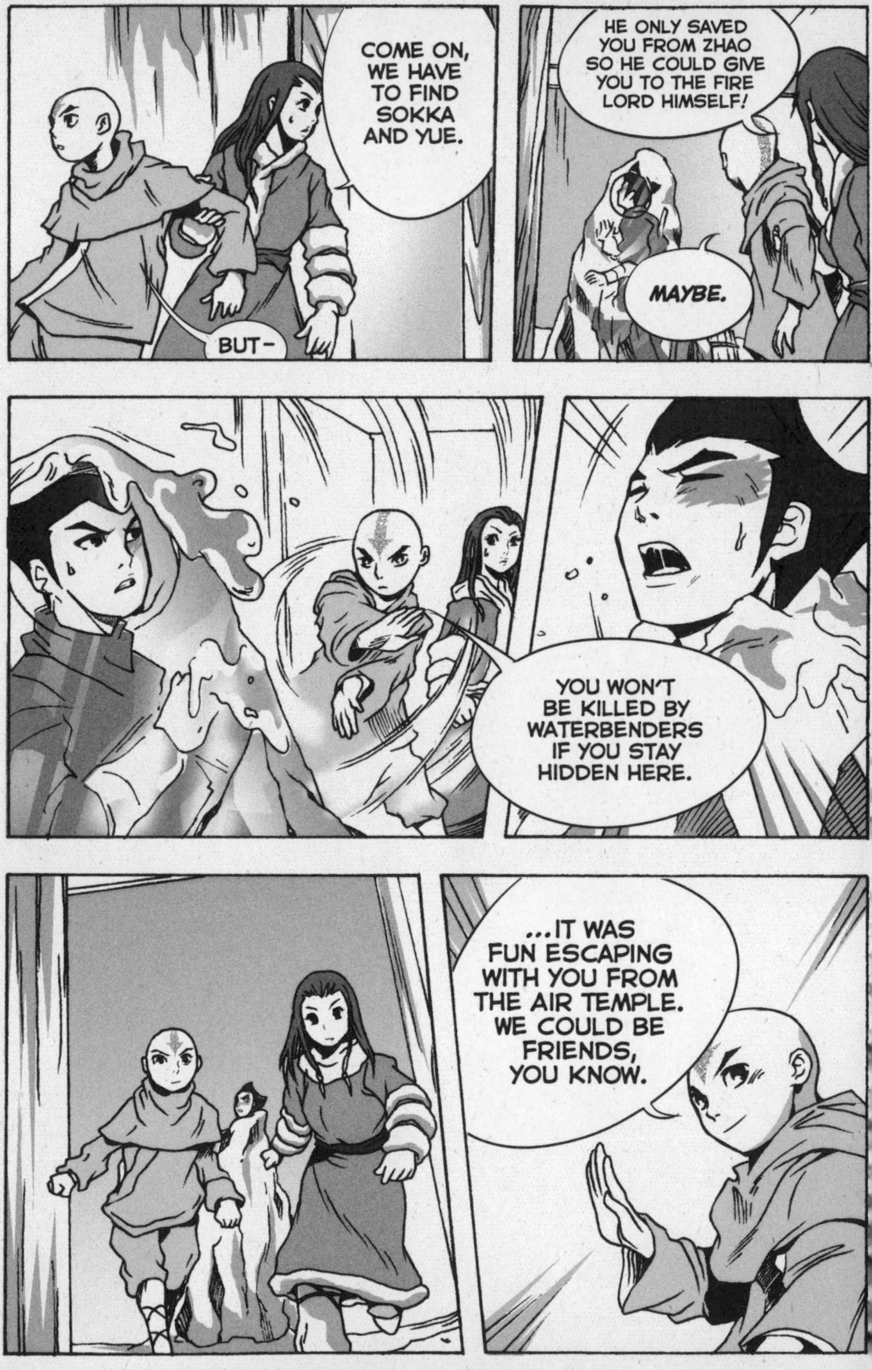
COME ON, WE HAVE TO FIND SOKKA AND YUE.
BUT-
HE ONLY SAVED YOU FROM ZHAO SO HE COULD GIVE YOU TO THE FIRE LORD HIMSELF!
MAYBE.
YOU WON'T BE KILLED BY WATERBENDERS IF YOU STAY HIDDEN HERE.
...IT WAS FUN ESCAPING WITH YOU FROM THE AIR TEMPLE. WE COULD BE FRIENDS, YOU KNOW.

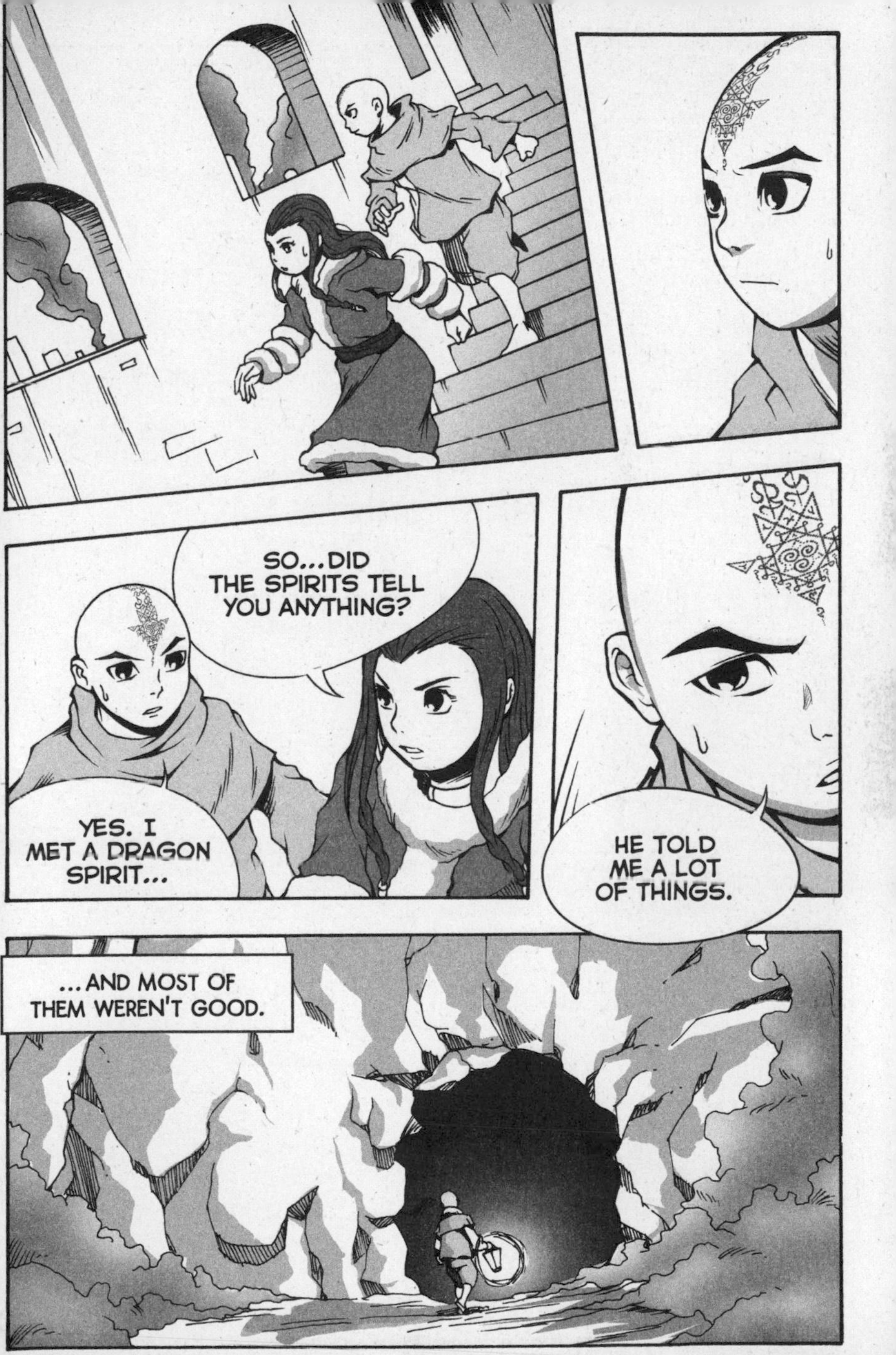
SO...DID THE SPIRITS TELL YOU ANYTHING?
YES. I MET A DRAGON SPIRIT...
HE TOLD ME A LOT OF THINGS.
...AND MOST OF THEM WEREN'T GOOD.

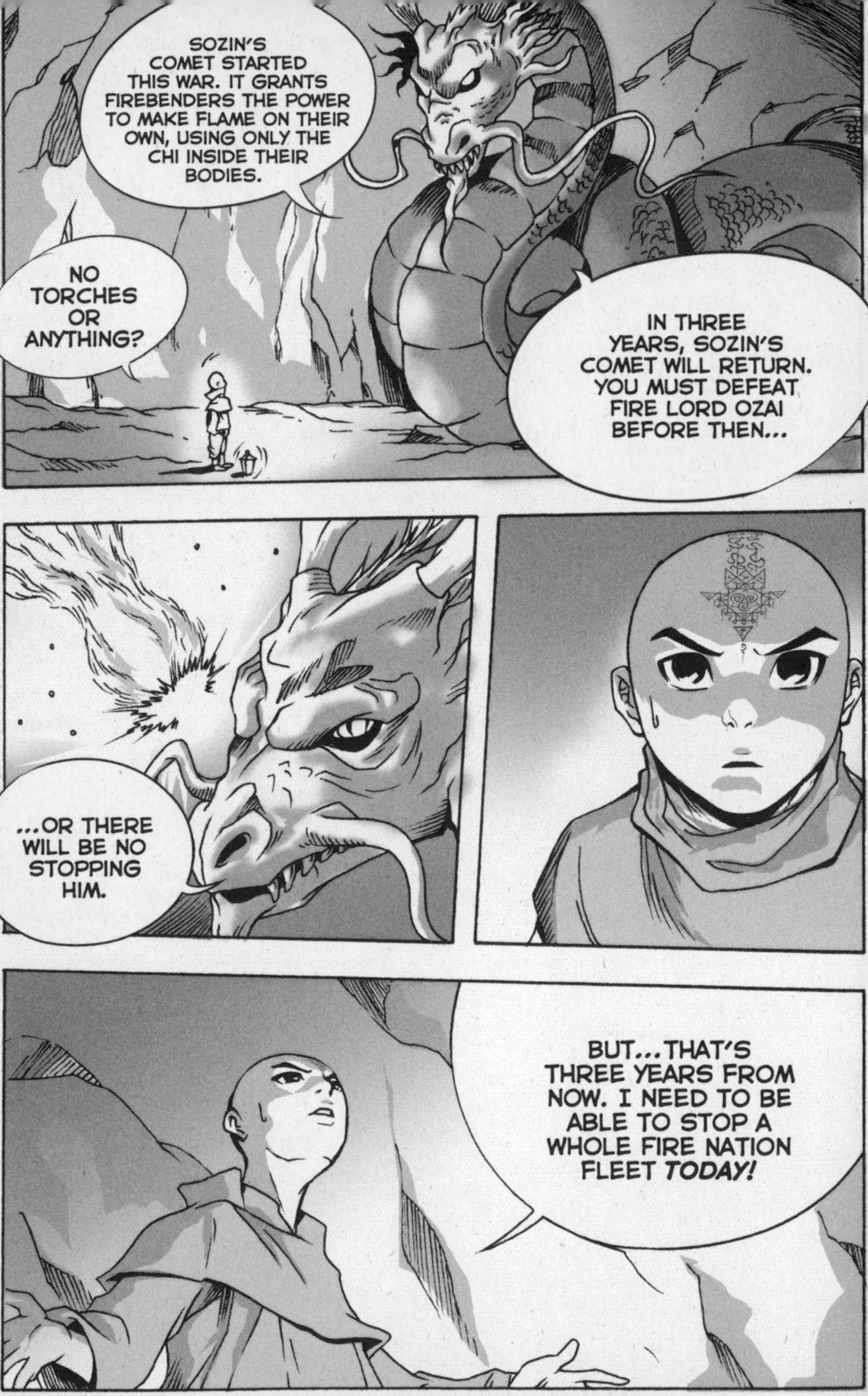
SOZIN'S COMET STARTED THIS WAR. IT GRANTS FIREBENDERS THE POWER TO MAKE FLAME ON THEIR OWN, USING ONLY THE CHI INSIDE THEIR BODIES.
NO TORCHES OR ANYTHING?
IN THREE YEARS, SOZIN'S COMET WILL RETURN. YOU MUST DEFEAT FIRE LORD OZAI BEFORE THEN...
...OR THERE WILL BE NO STOPPING HIM.
BUT...THAT'S THREE YEARS FROM NOW. I NEED TO BE ABLE TO STOP A WHOLE FIRE NATION FLEET *TODAY!*

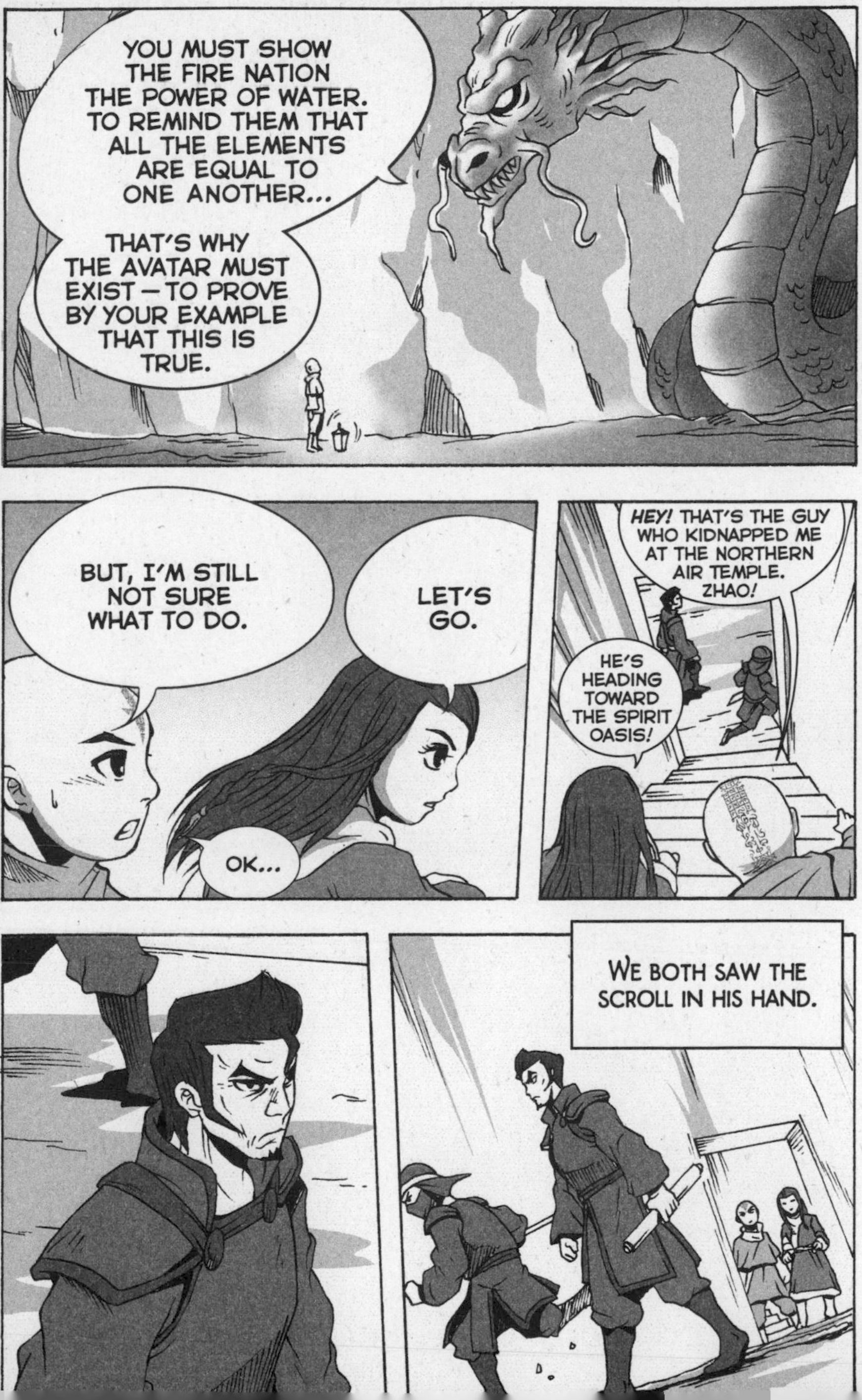
YOU MUST SHOW THE FIRE NATION THE POWER OF WATER. TO REMIND THEM THAT ALL THE ELEMENTS ARE EQUAL TO ONE ANOTHER...
THAT'S WHY THE AVATAR MUST EXIST — TO PROVE BY YOUR EXAMPLE THAT THIS IS TRUE.
BUT, I'M STILL NOT SURE WHAT TO DO.
LET'S GO.
OK...
*HEY!* THAT'S THE GUY WHO KIDNAPPED ME AT THE NORTHERN AIR TEMPLE. ZHAO!
HE'S HEADING TOWARD THE SPIRIT OASIS!
WE BOTH SAW THE SCROLL IN HIS HAND.

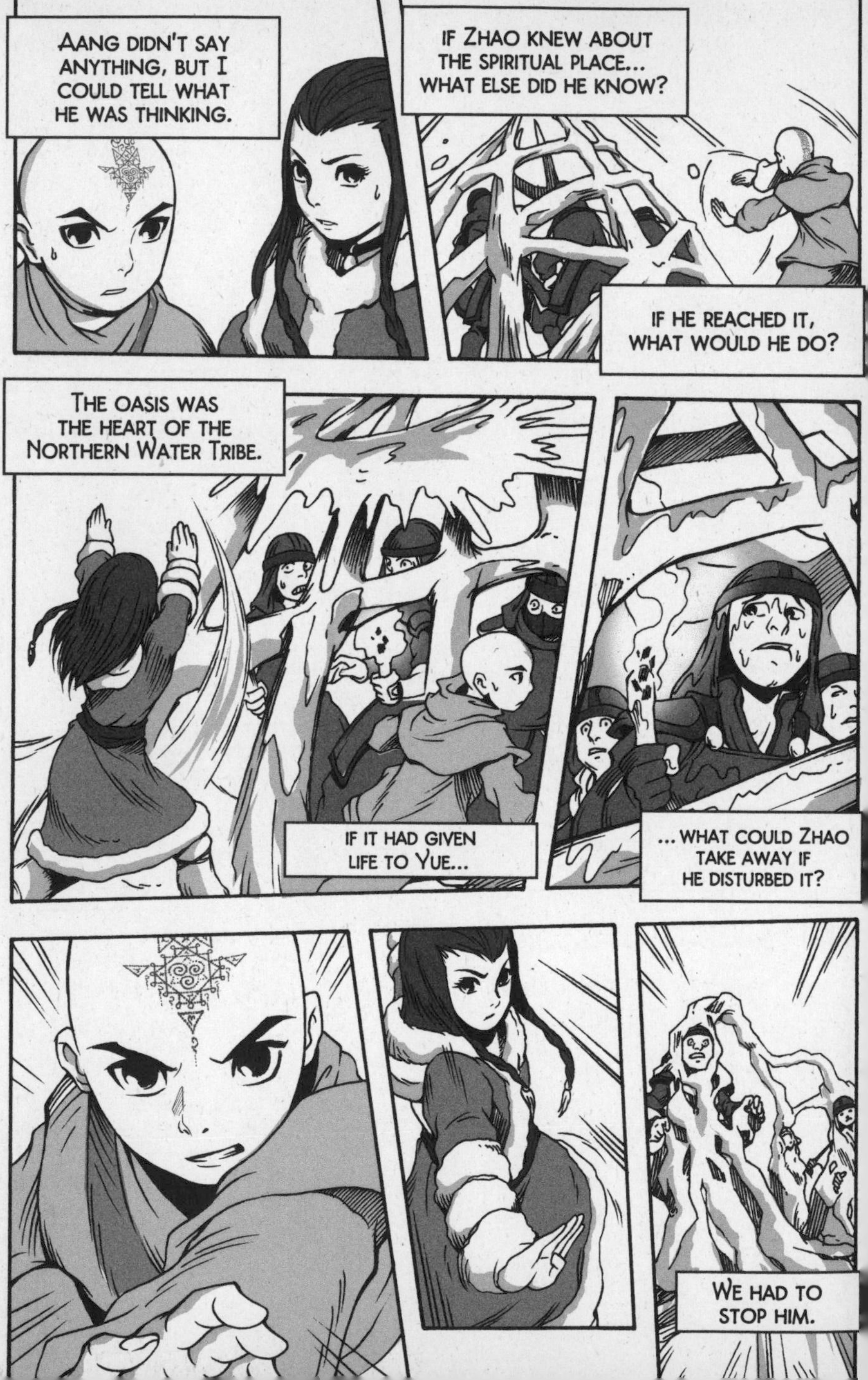
AANG DIDN'T SAY ANYTHING, BUT I COULD TELL WHAT HE WAS THINKING.
IF ZHAO KNEW ABOUT THE SPIRITUAL PLACE... WHAT ELSE DID HE KNOW?
IF HE REACHED IT, WHAT WOULD HE DO?
THE OASIS WAS THE HEART OF THE NORTHERN WATER TRIBE.
IF IT HAD GIVEN LIFE TO YUE...
...WHAT COULD ZHAO TAKE AWAY IF HE DISTURBED IT?
WE HAD TO STOP HIM.

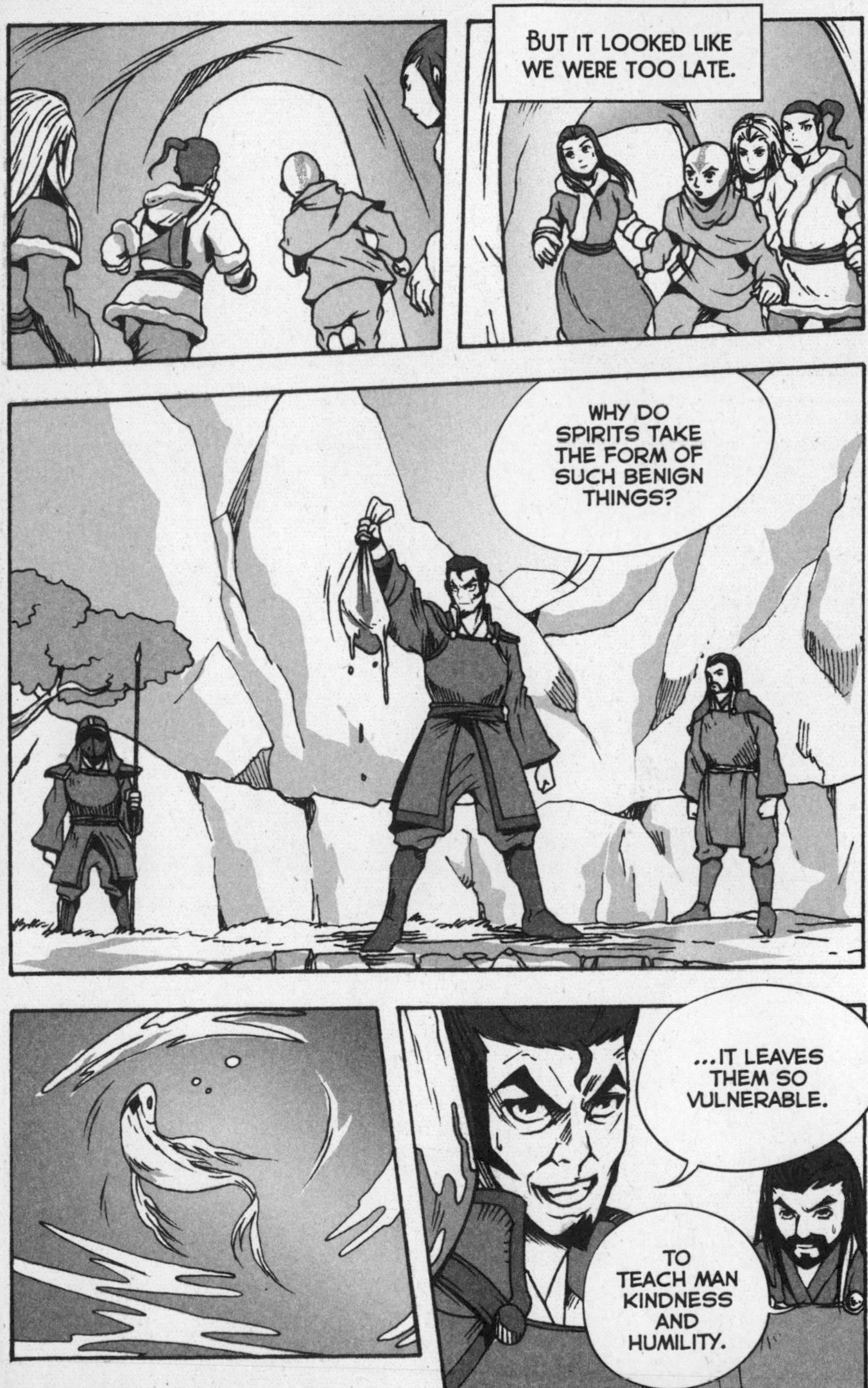
BUT IT LOOKED LIKE WE WERE TOO LATE.
WHY DO SPIRITS TAKE THE FORM OF SUCH BENIGN THINGS?
...IT LEAVES THEM SO VULNERABLE.
TO TEACH MAN KINDNESS AND HUMILITY.

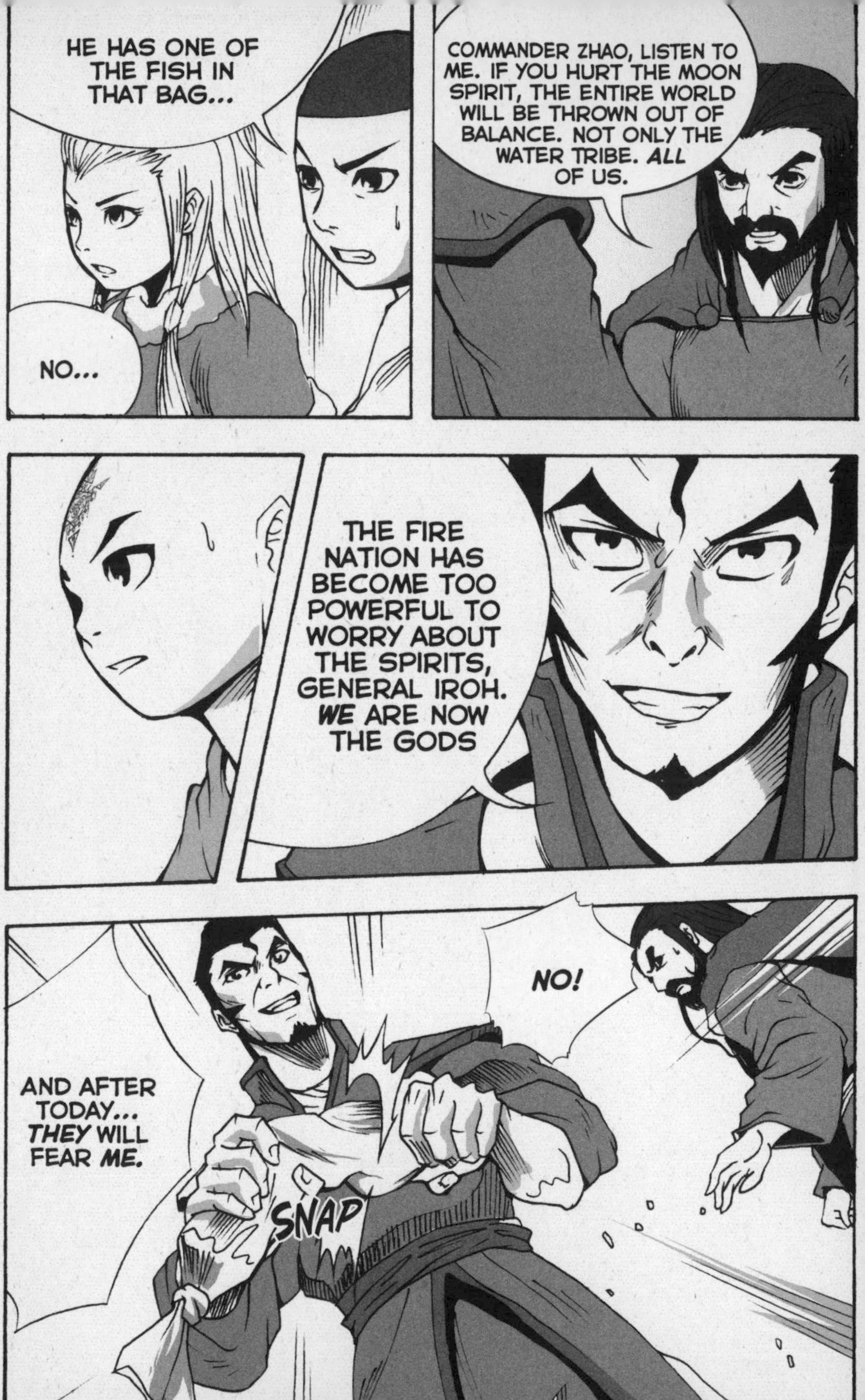
HE HAS ONE OF THE FISH IN THAT BAG...
NO...
COMMANDER ZHAO, LISTEN TO ME. IF YOU HURT THE MOON SPIRIT, THE ENTIRE WORLD WILL BE THROWN OUT OF BALANCE. NOT ONLY THE WATER TRIBE. *ALL* OF US.
THE FIRE NATION HAS BECOME TOO POWERFUL TO WORRY ABOUT THE SPIRITS, GENERAL IROH. ***WE*** ARE NOW THE GODS
AND AFTER TODAY... ***THEY*** WILL FEAR ***ME.***
SNAP
***NO!***

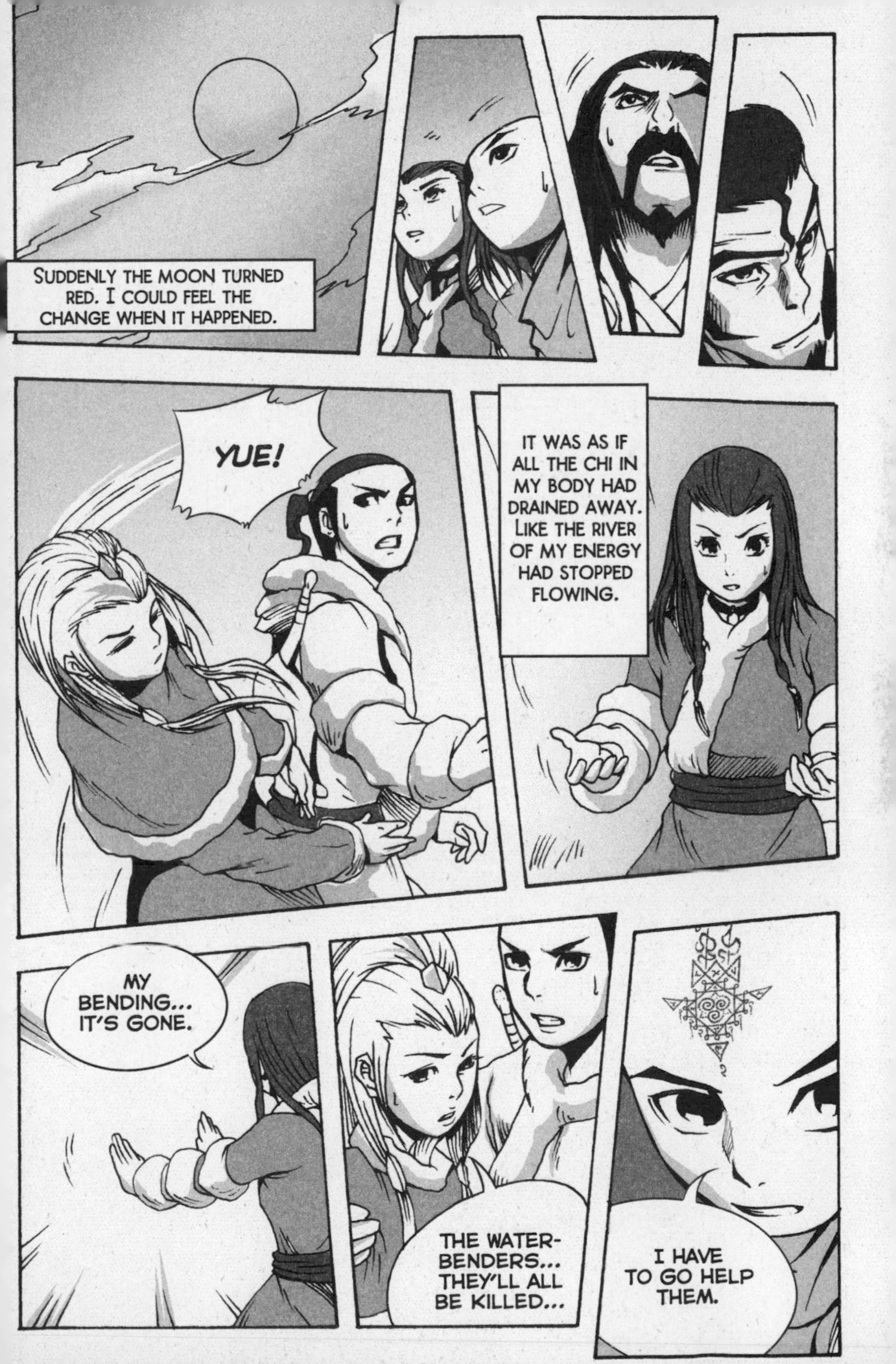

SUDDENLY THE MOON TURNED RED. I COULD FEEL THE CHANGE WHEN IT HAPPENED.
YUE!
IT WAS AS IF ALL THE CHI IN MY BODY HAD DRAINED AWAY. LIKE THE RIVER OF MY ENERGY HAD STOPPED FLOWING.
MY BENDING... IT'S GONE.
THE WATER-BENDERS... THEY'LL ALL BE KILLED...
I HAVE TO GO HELP THEM.

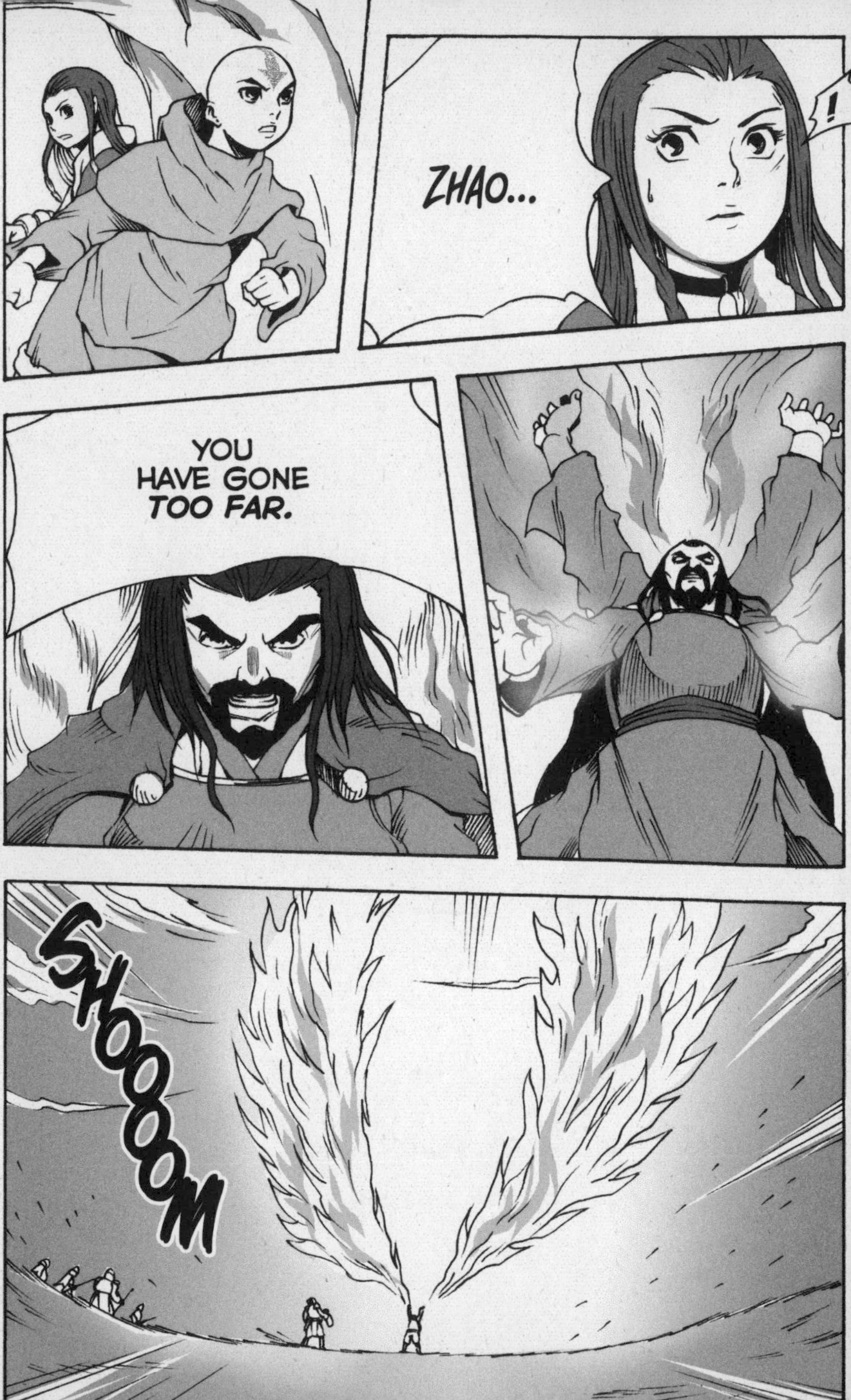

ZHAO...
!
YOU HAVE GONE *TOO FAR.*
SHOOOOM

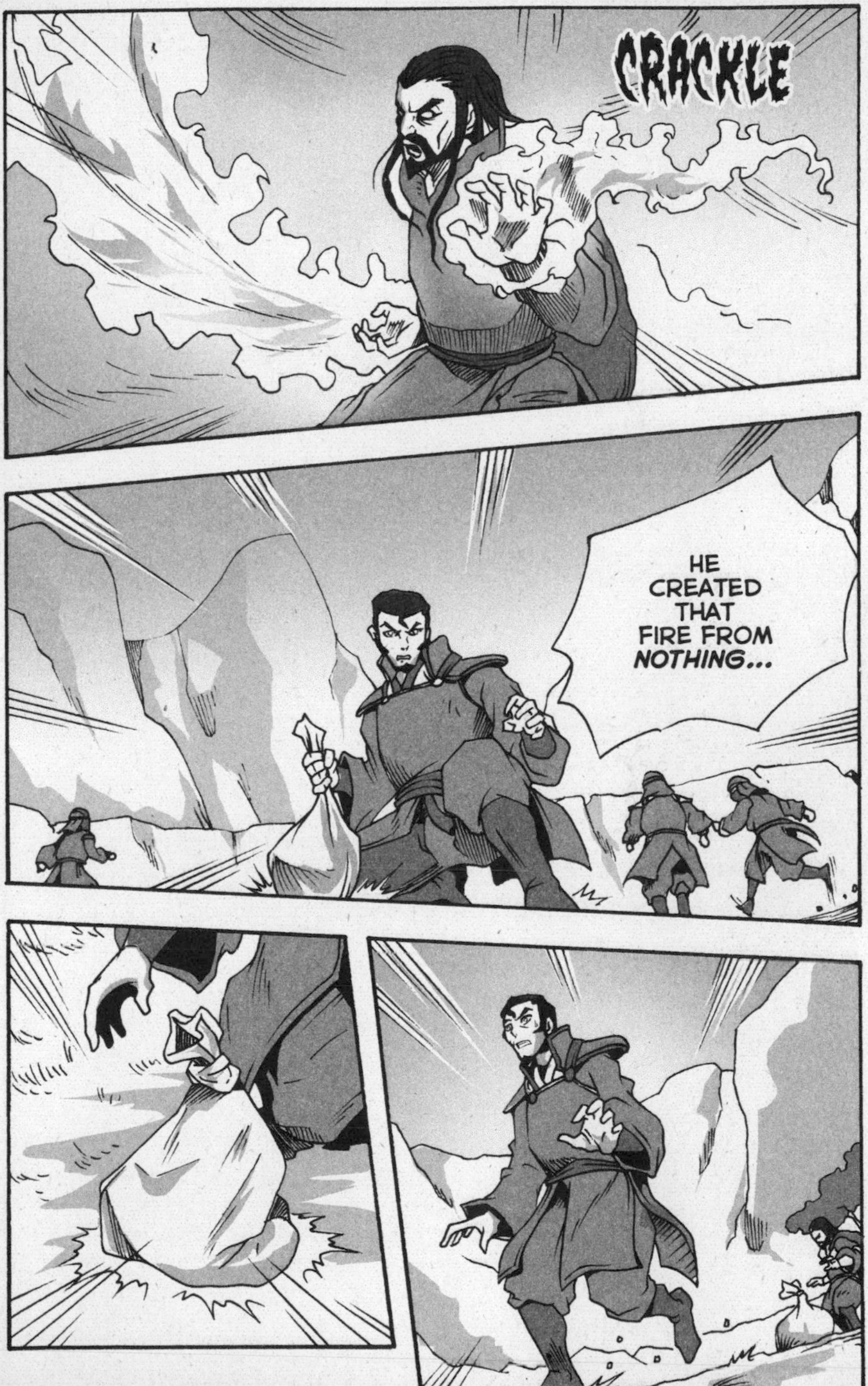
CRACKLE
HE CREATED THAT FIRE FROM NOTHING...

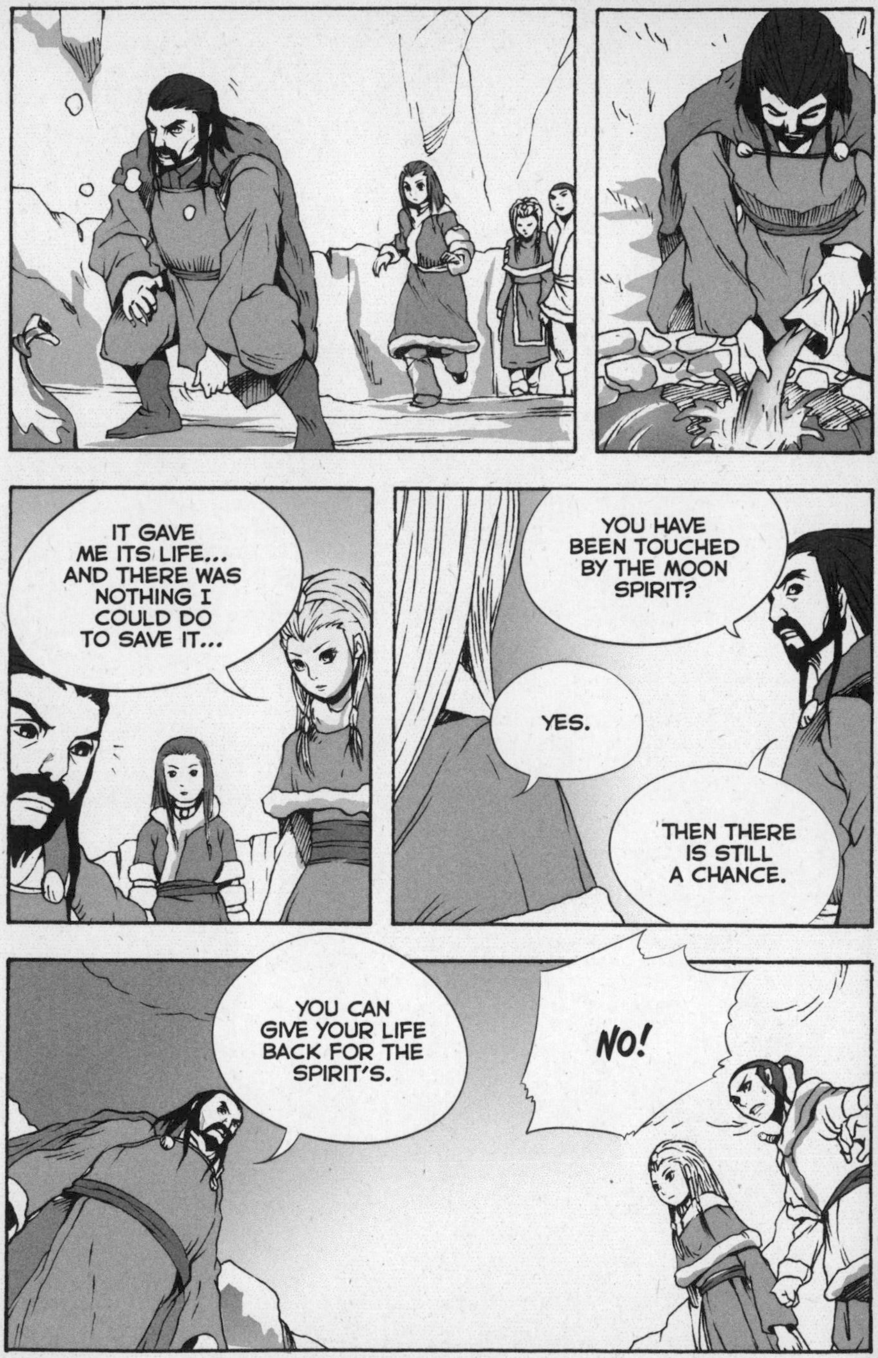
IT GAVE ME ITS LIFE... AND THERE WAS NOTHING I COULD DO TO SAVE IT...
YOU HAVE BEEN TOUCHED BY THE MOON SPIRIT?
YES.
THEN THERE IS STILL A CHANCE.
YOU CAN GIVE YOUR LIFE BACK FOR THE SPIRIT'S.
NO!

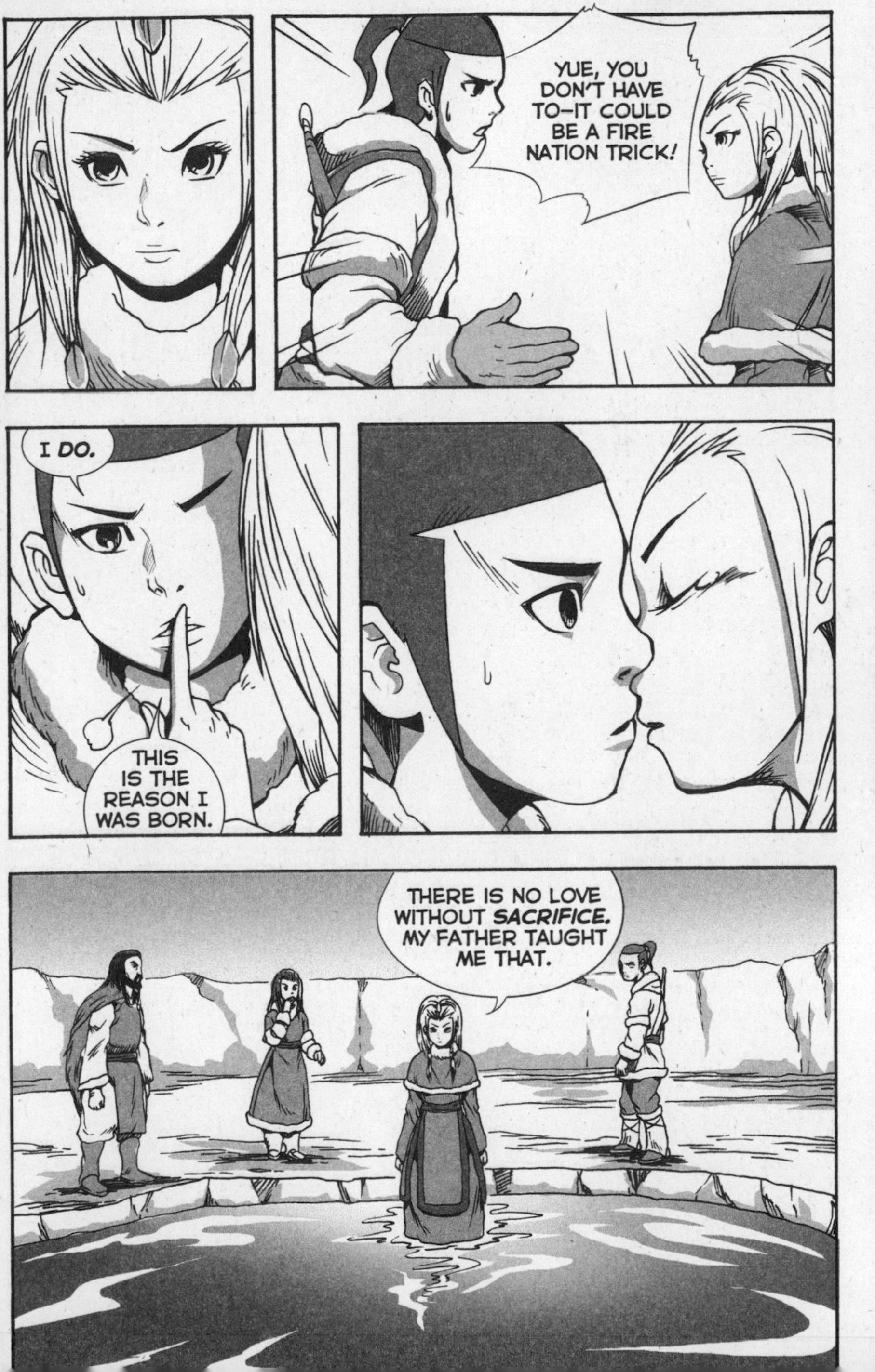
YUE, YOU DON'T HAVE TO—IT COULD BE A FIRE NATION TRICK!
I DO.
THIS IS THE REASON I WAS BORN.
THERE IS NO LOVE WITHOUT SACRIFICE. MY FATHER TAUGHT ME THAT.

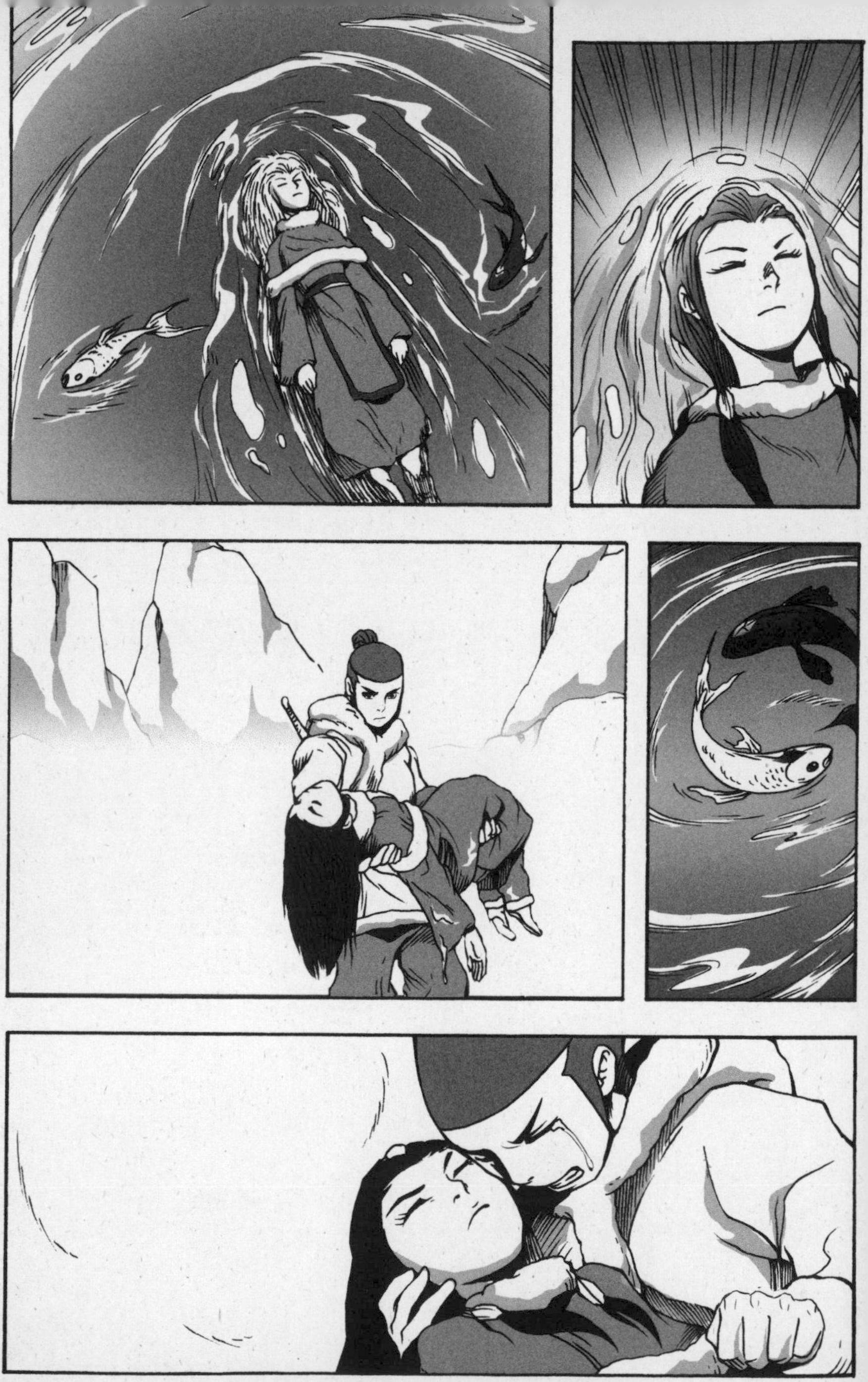

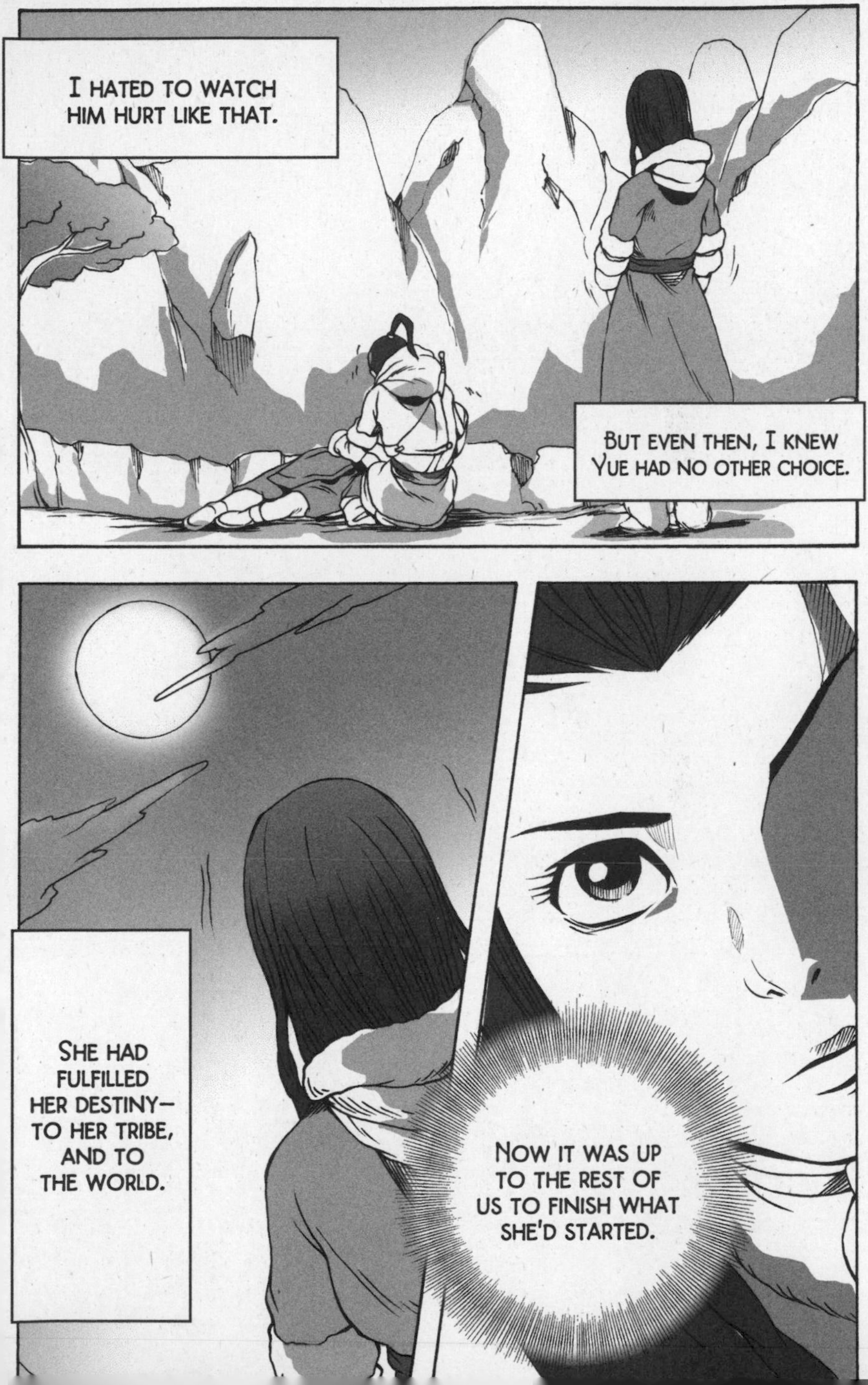
I HATED TO WATCH HIM HURT LIKE THAT.
BUT EVEN THEN, I KNEW YUE HAD NO OTHER CHOICE.
SHE HAD FULFILLED HER DESTINY— TO HER TRIBE, AND TO THE WORLD.
NOW IT WAS UP TO THE REST OF US TO FINISH WHAT SHE'D STARTED.

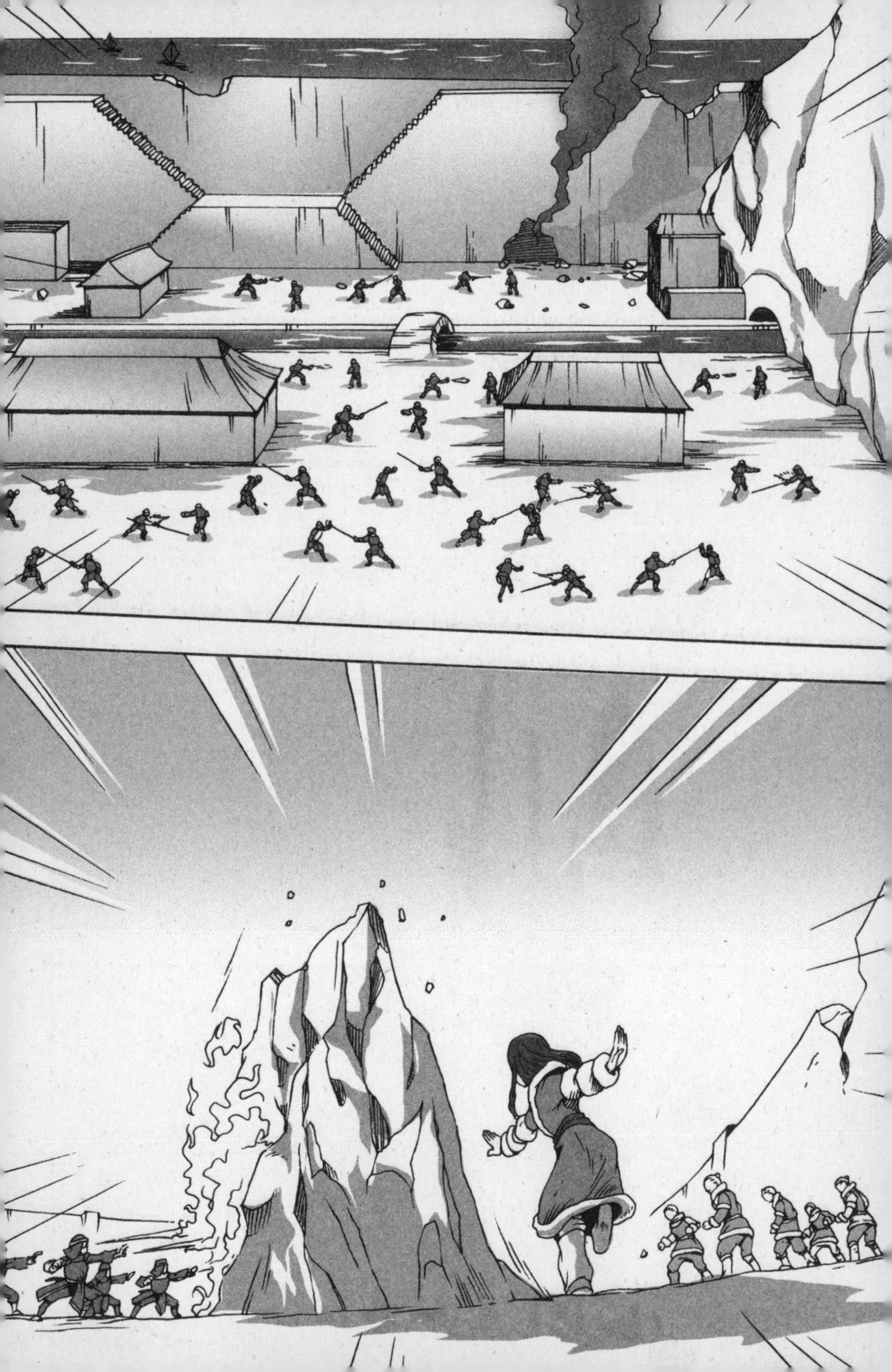

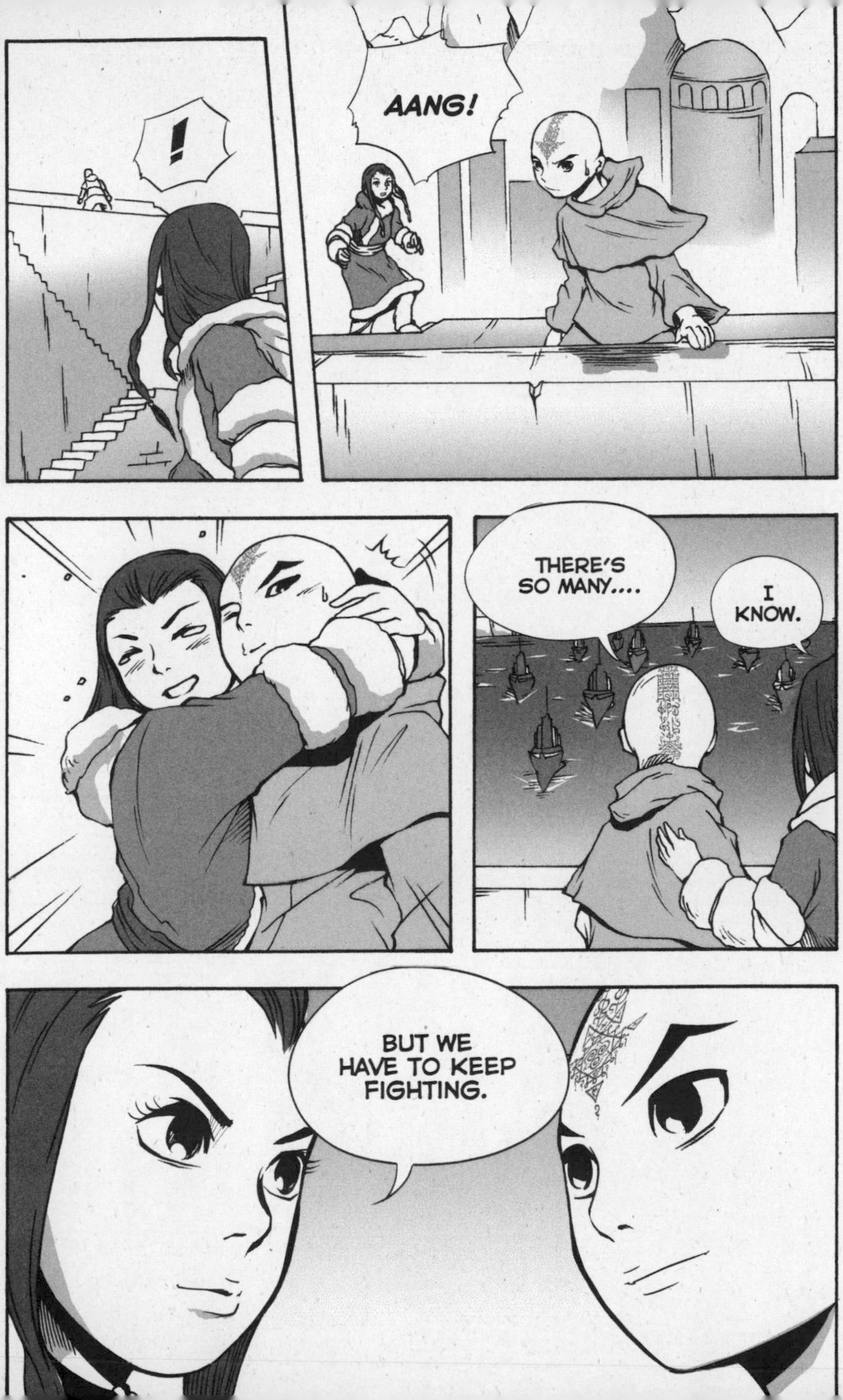
!
AANG!
THERE'S SO MANY....
I KNOW.
BUT WE HAVE TO KEEP FIGHTING.

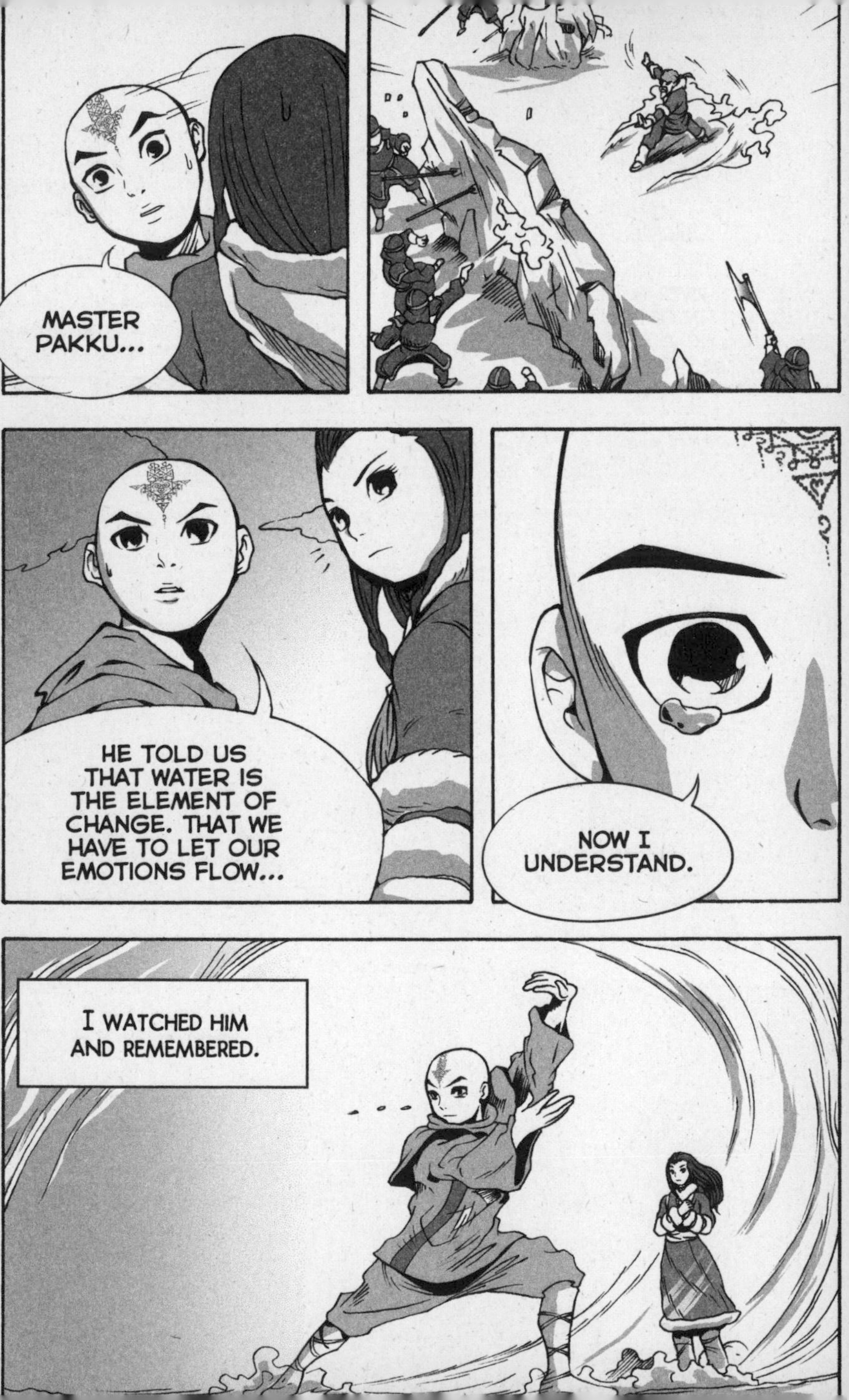
MASTER PAKKU...
HE TOLD US THAT WATER IS THE ELEMENT OF CHANGE. THAT WE HAVE TO LET OUR EMOTIONS FLOW...
NOW I UNDERSTAND.
I WATCHED HIM AND REMEMBERED.

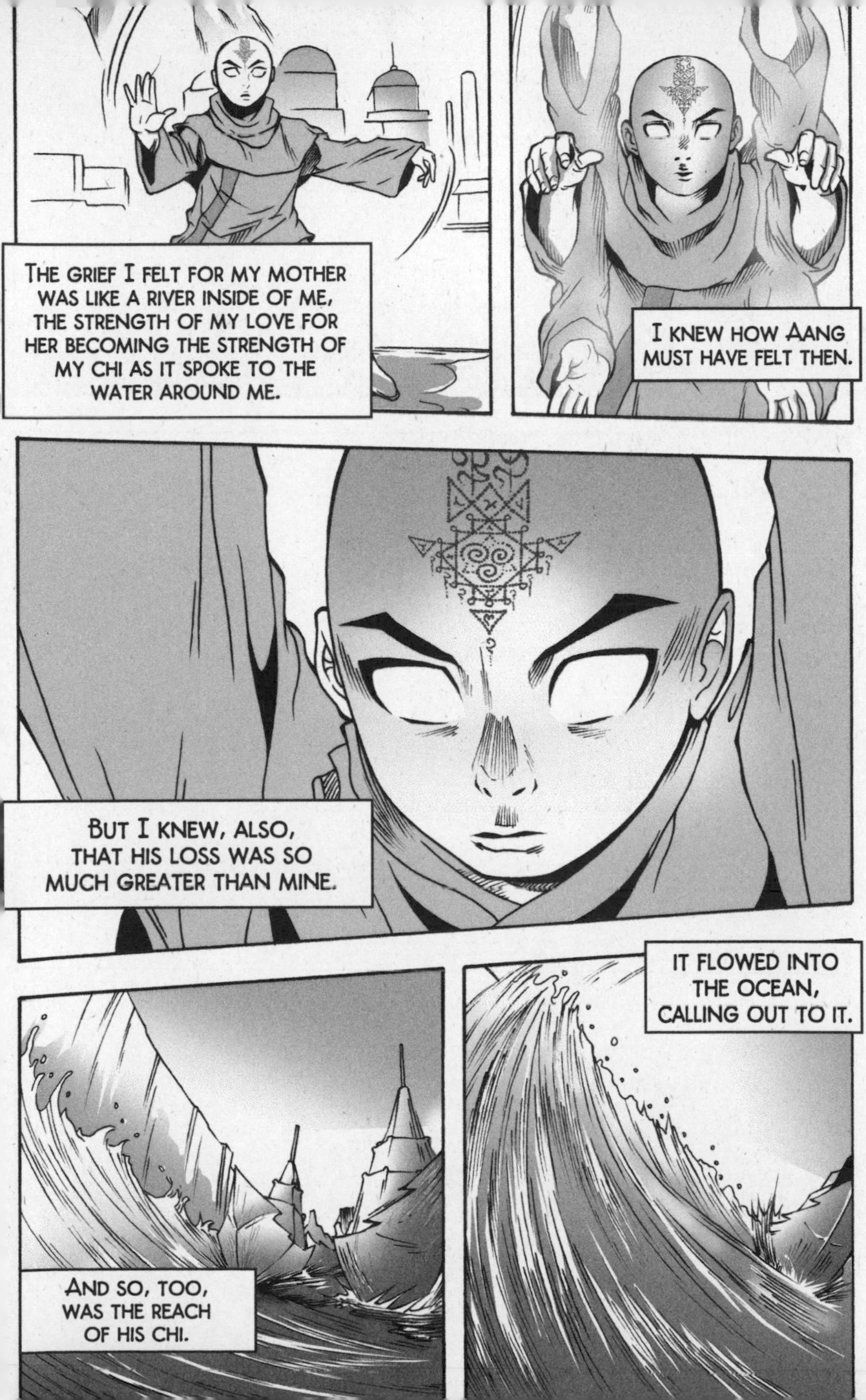
THE GRIEF I FELT FOR MY MOTHER WAS LIKE A RIVER INSIDE OF ME, THE STRENGTH OF MY LOVE FOR HER BECOMING THE STRENGTH OF MY CHI AS IT SPOKE TO THE WATER AROUND ME.
I KNEW HOW AANG MUST HAVE FELT THEN.
BUT I KNEW, ALSO, THAT HIS LOSS WAS SO MUCH GREATER THAN MINE.
AND SO, TOO, WAS THE REACH OF HIS CHI.
IT FLOWED INTO THE OCEAN, CALLING OUT TO IT.

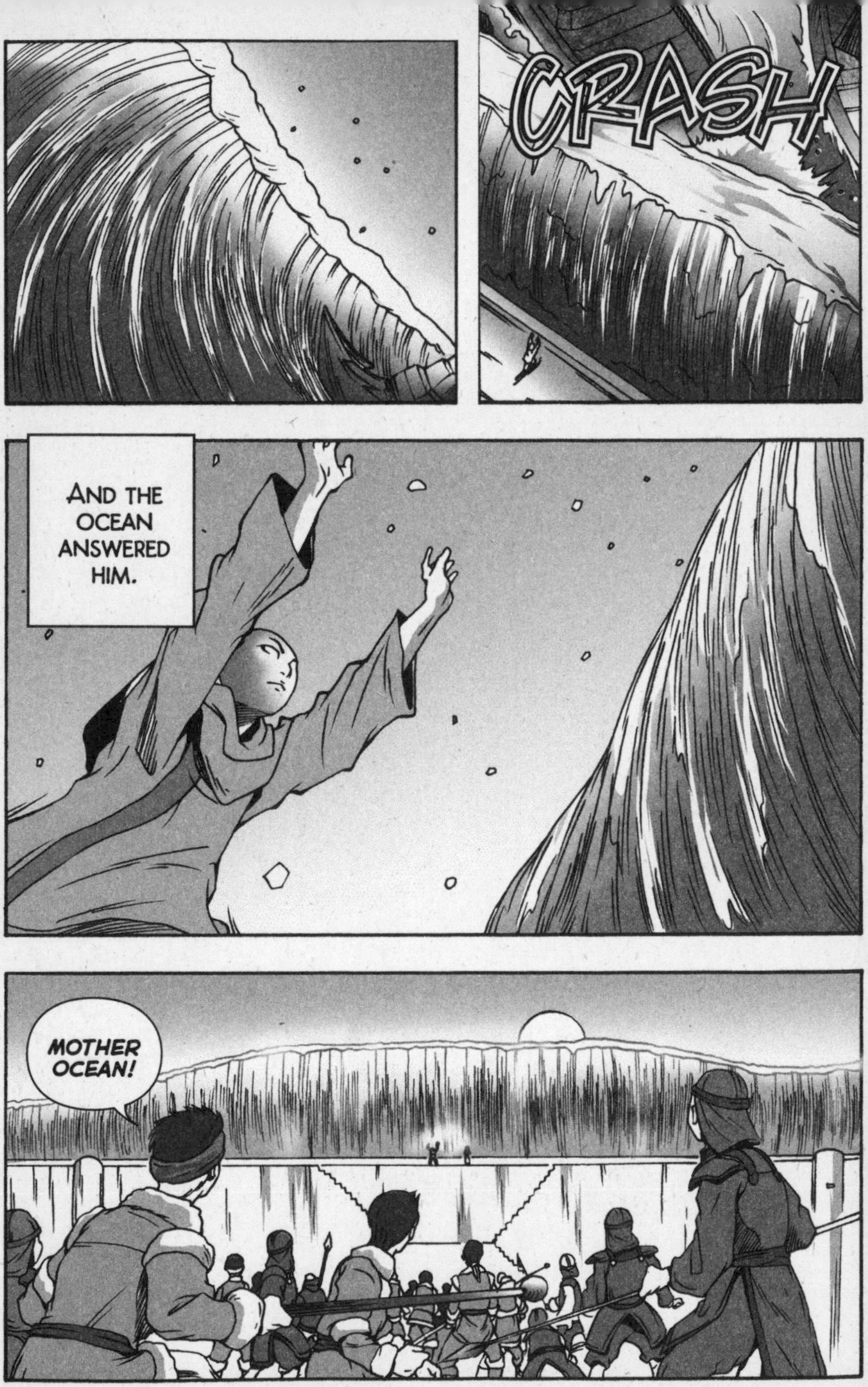
CRASH
AND THE OCEAN ANSWERED HIM.
MOTHER OCEAN!

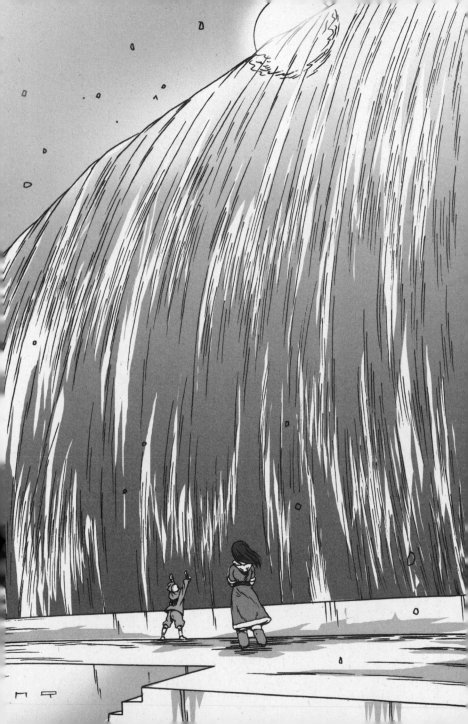

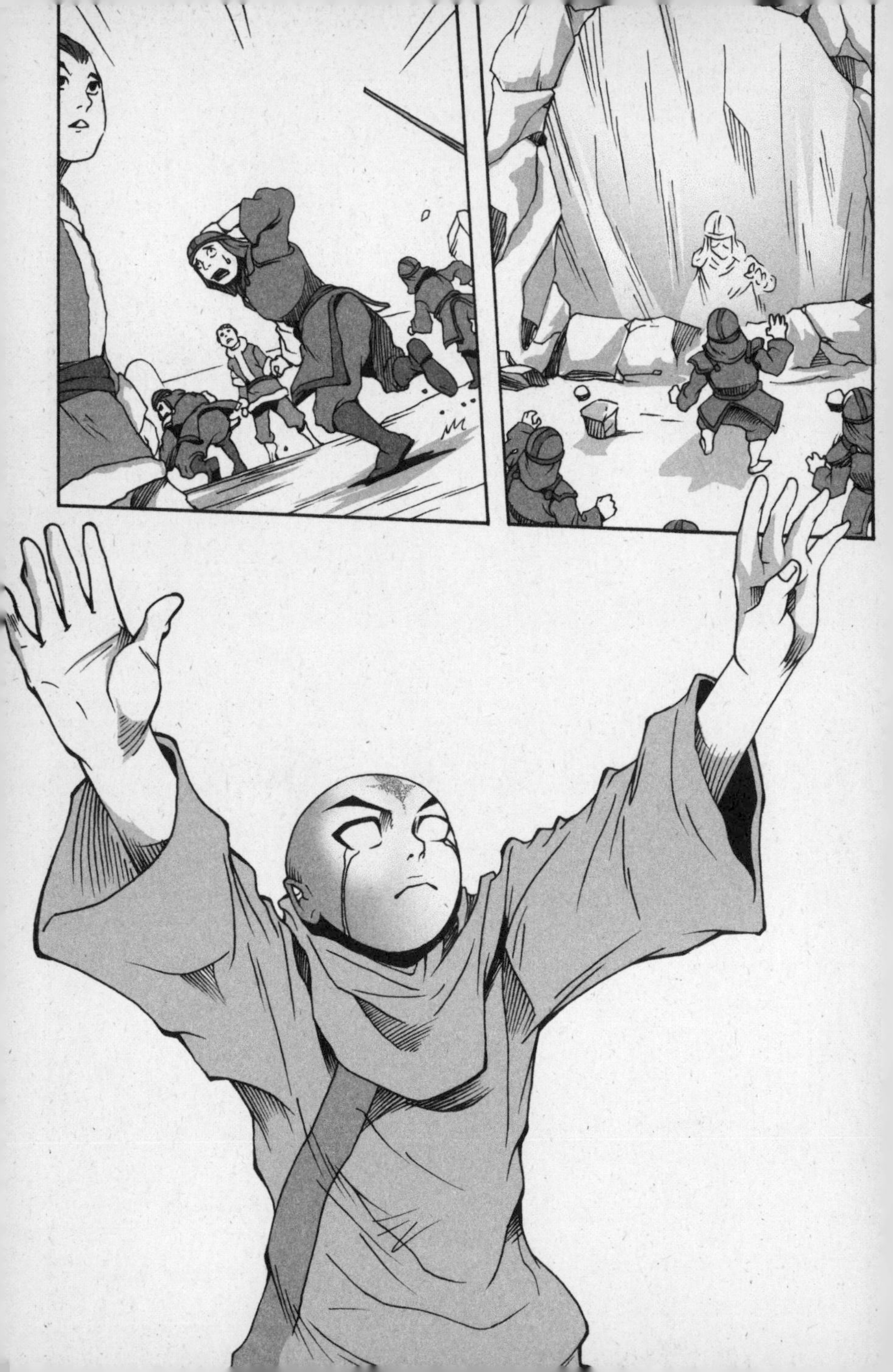

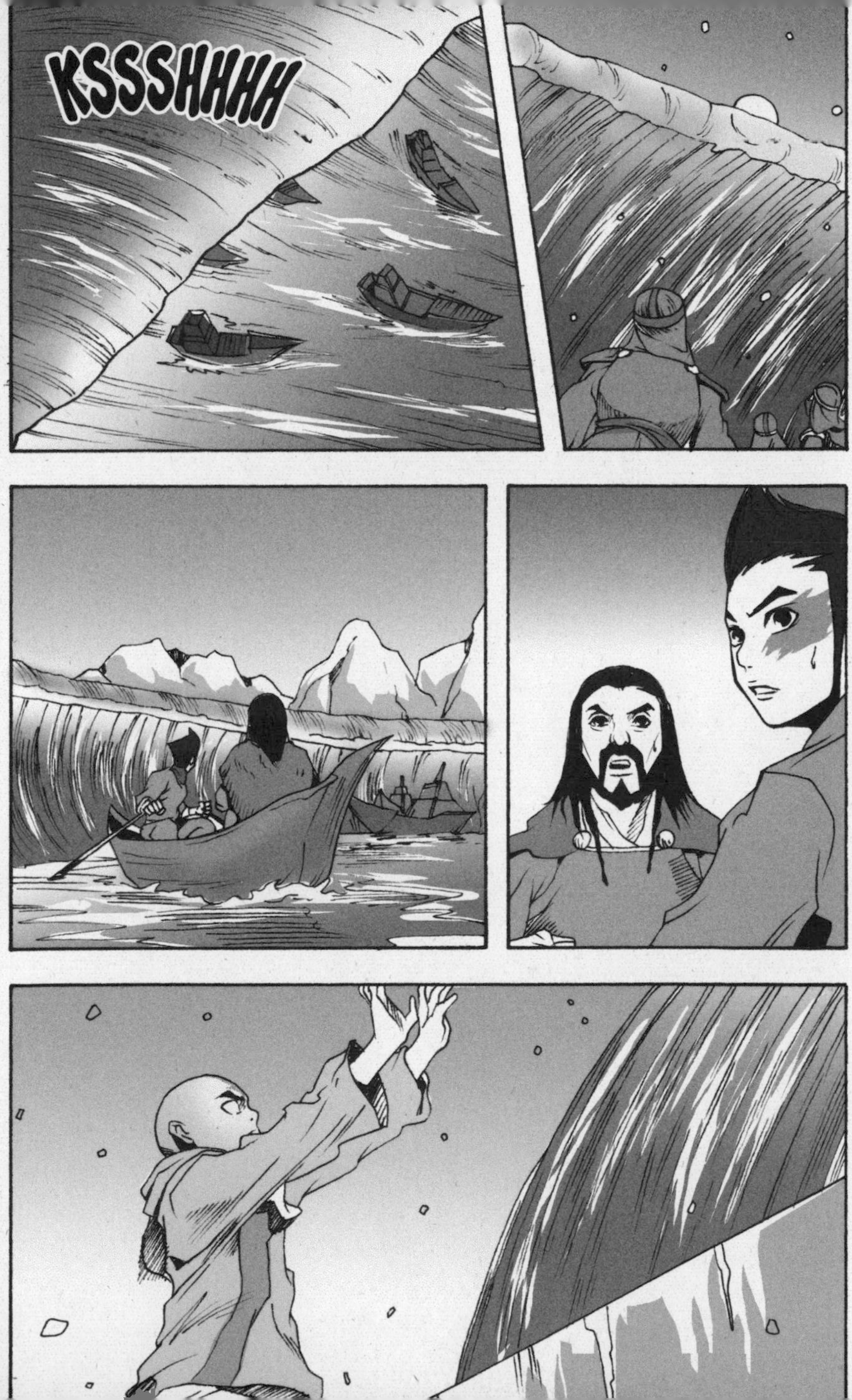
KSSSHHHH

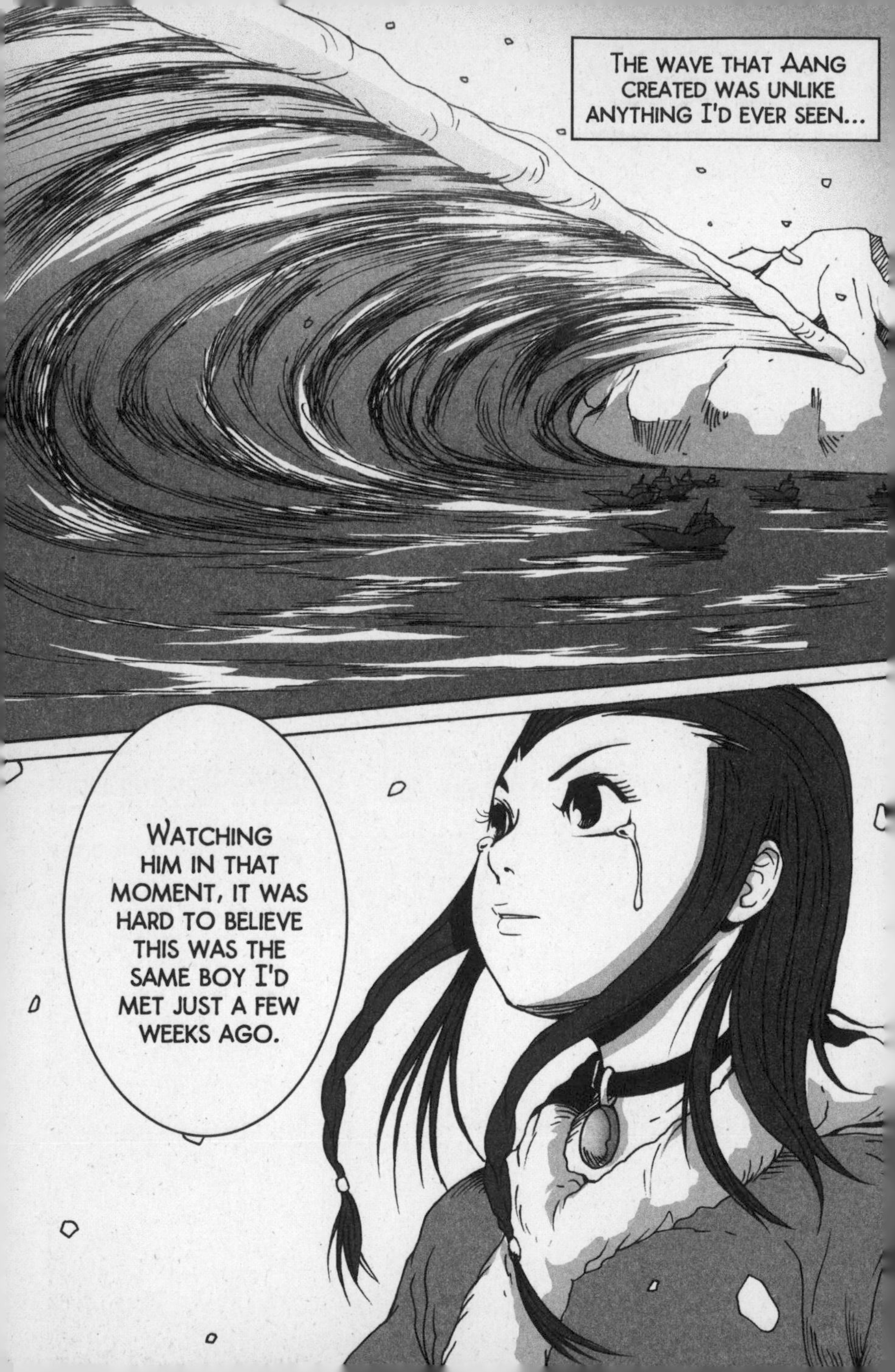
The wave that Aang created was unlike anything I'd ever seen...
Watching him in that moment, it was hard to believe this was the same boy I'd met just a few weeks ago.

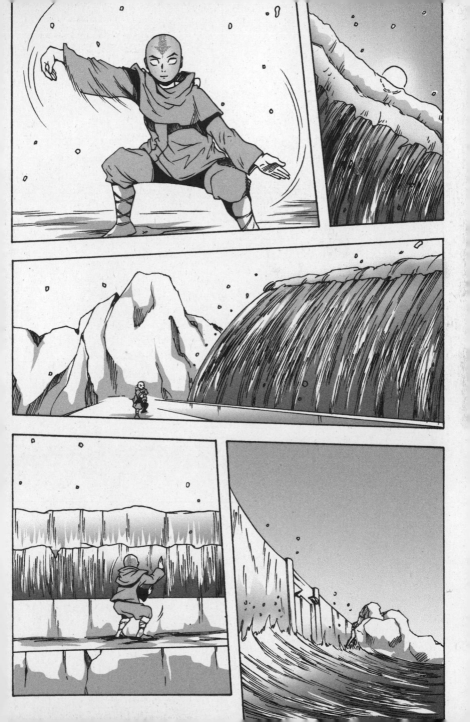

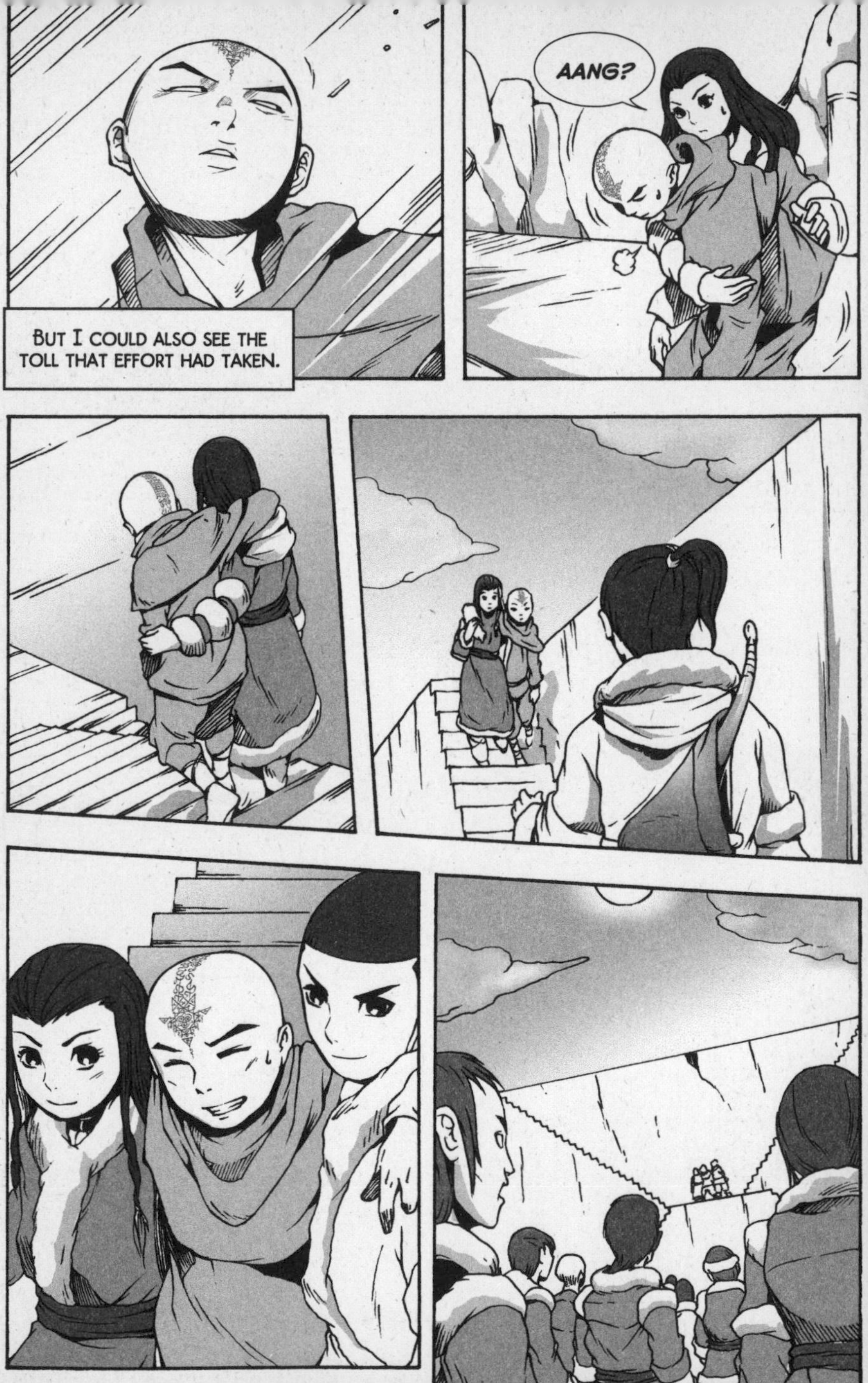
BUT I COULD ALSO SEE THE TOLL THAT EFFORT HAD TAKEN.
AANG?

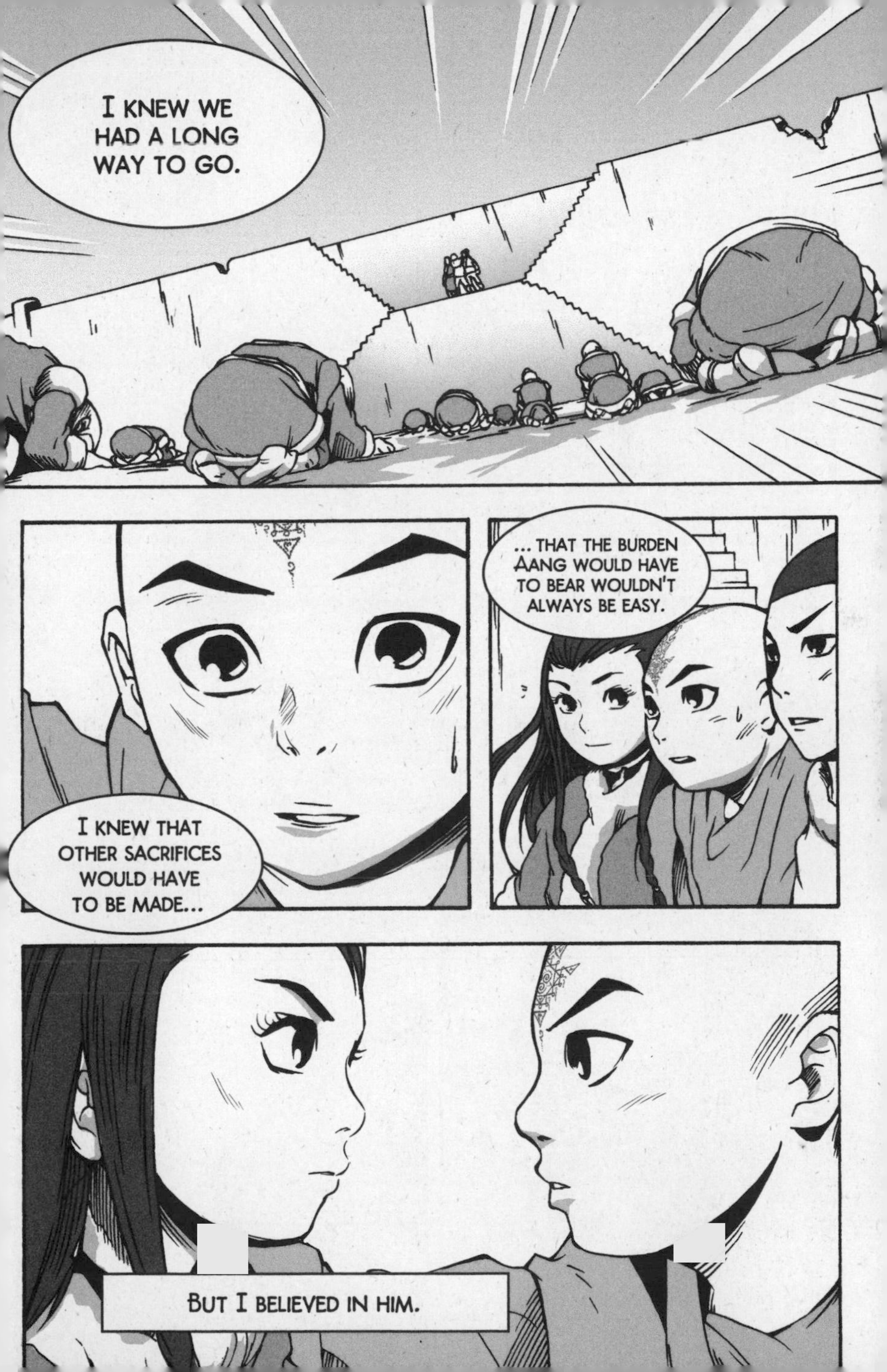
I KNEW WE HAD A LONG WAY TO GO.
I KNEW THAT OTHER SACRIFICES WOULD HAVE TO BE MADE...
...THAT THE BURDEN AANG WOULD HAVE TO BEAR WOULDN'T ALWAYS BE EASY.
BUT I BELIEVED IN HIM.

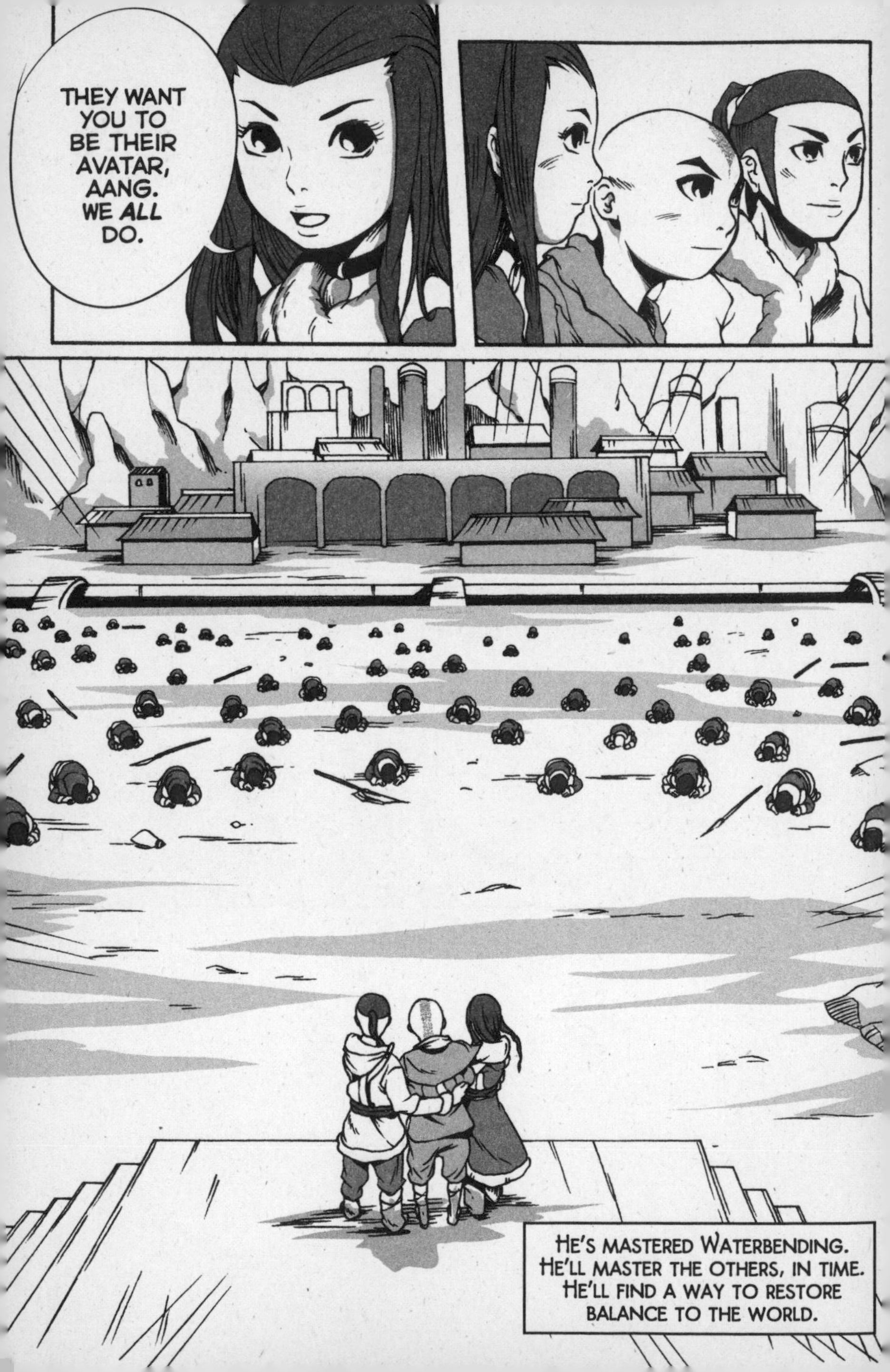
THEY WANT YOU TO BE THEIR AVATAR, AANG. WE ALL DO.
HE'S MASTERED WATERBENDING. HE'LL MASTER THE OTHERS, IN TIME. HE'LL FIND A WAY TO RESTORE BALANCE TO THE WORLD.